Cold War Mandarin

VIETNAM
America in the War Years

Series Editor
DAVID L. ANDERSON
California State University, Monterey Bay

The Vietnam War and the tumultuous internal upheavals in America that coincided with it marked a watershed era in U.S. history. These events profoundly challenged America's heroic self-image. During the 1950s the United States defined Southeast Asia as an area of vital strategic importance. In the 1960s this view produced a costly American military campaign that continued into the early 1970s. The Vietnam War was the nation's longest war and ended with an unprecedented U.S. failure to achieve its stated objectives. Simultaneous with this frustrating military intervention and the domestic debate that it produced were other tensions created by student activism on campuses, the black struggle for civil rights, and the women's liberation movement. The books in this series explore the complex and controversial issues of the period from the mid-1950s to the mid-1970s in brief and engaging volumes. To facilitate continued and informed debate on these contested subjects, each book examines a military, political, or diplomatic issue; the role of a key individual; or one of the domestic changes in America during the war.

Volumes Published

Melvin Small. *Antiwarriors: The Vietnam War and the Battle for America's Hearts and Minds.*

Edward K. Spann. *Democracy's Children: The Young Rebels of the 1960s and the Power of Ideals.*

Ronald B. Frankum Jr. *Like Rolling Thunder: The Air War in Vietnam, 1964–1975.*

Walter LaFeber. *The Deadly Bet: LBJ, Vietnam, and the 1968 Election.*

Mitchell K. Hall. *Crossroads: American Popular Culture and the Vietnam Generation.*

David F. Schmitz. *The Tet Offensive: Politics, War, and Public Opinion.*

Seth Jacobs. *Cold War Mandarin: Ngo Dinh Diem and the Origins of America's War in Vietnam, 1950–1963.*

Cold War Mandarin

Ngo Dinh Diem and
the Origins of America's War in Vietnam, 1950–1963

Seth Jacobs

ROWMAN & LITTLEFIELD PUBLISHERS, INC.
Lanham • Boulder • New York • Toronto • Oxford

ROWMAN & LITTLEFIELD PUBLISHERS, INC.

Published in the United States of America
by Rowman & Littlefield Publishers, Inc.
A wholly owned subsidiary of The Rowman & Littlefield Publishing Group, Inc.
4501 Forbes Boulevard, Suite 200, Lanham, Maryland 20706
www.rowmanlittlefield.com

PO Box 317
Oxford
OX2 9RU, UK

British Library Cataloguing in Publication Information Available

Library of Congress Cataloging-in-Publication Data

Jacobs, Seth, 1964–
  Cold war mandarin : Ngo Dinh Diem and the origins of America's war in Vietnam,
1950–1963 / Seth Jacobs.
    p. cm.— (Vietnam—America in the war years)
  Includes bibliographical references and index.
  ISBN-13: 978-0-7425-4447-5 (cloth : alk. paper)
  ISBN-10: 0-7425-4447-8 (cloth : alk. paper)
  ISBN-13: 978-0-7425-4448-2 (pbk. : alk. paper)
  ISBN-10: 0-7425-4448-6 (pbk. : alk. paper)
1. Vietnam (Republic)—Politics and government.   2. Ngô, Đình Diêm, 1901–1963.
3. United States—Foreign relations—Vietnam (Republic).   4. Vietnam (Republic)—
Foreign relations—United States.   5. Vietnamese Conflict, 1961–1975—United
States.   I. Title.   II. Series: Vietnam—America in the war years (Unnumbered)

DS556.9.J34   2006
959.704'31—dc22   2006003240

Printed in the United States of America

∞ ™ The paper used in this publication meets the minimum requirements of American
National Standard for Information Sciences—Permanence of Paper for Printed Library
Materials, ANSI/NISO Z39.48-1992.

For Miranda and Sophie

Contents

Abbreviations Used in Notes

American Friends of Vietnam Papers, Vietnam Archive, Texas Tech University, Lubbock, Texas	AFV Papers
Douglas Pike Collection, Vietnam Archive, Texas Tech University, Lubbock, Texas	Pike Collection
Dwight D. Eisenhower Library, Abilene, Kansas	EL
Foreign Relations of the United States	*FRUS, 1947*
	FRUS, 1950
	FRUS, 1951
	FRUS, 1952–1954
	FRUS, 1955–1957
	FRUS, 1958–1960
	FRUS, 1961–1963
John F. Kennedy Library, Boston, Massachusetts	JFKL
John Foster Dulles Papers, Seeley Mudd Library, Princeton University, Princeton, New Jersey	Dulles Papers
Joseph Buttinger Papers, Harvard-Yenching Library, Harvard University, Cambridge, Massachusetts	Buttinger Papers
Leo Cherne Papers, Mugar Library, Boston University, Boston Massachusetts	Cherne Papers
Record Group 59, National Archives II, College Park, MD	RG 59
Thomas A. Dooley Collection, Pius XII Library, St. Louis University	Dooley Collection
United States—Vietnam Relations, 1945–1971	*U.S.-VN Relations*

Acknowledgments

I am indebted to David Anderson for inviting me to contribute to this series and for his subsequent guidance, support, and boundless good cheer, even when the first draft of the manuscript landed on his desk with a discomfiting thud. (It has since been cut by over 50 percent, to the benefit of all involved, especially me.) Rowman & Littlefield's editorial team was a pleasure to work with. Laura Roberts Gottlieb, Andrew Boney, and Lynn Weber in particular proved unfailingly patient and professional as they steered this project through its various stages toward completion. My colleagues at Boston College helped make the junior professor's dreaded task of juggling scholarship and teaching not only feasible but downright enjoyable. Record keepers at several houses of research—notably Thomas Branigar and Herbert Pankratz of the Dwight D. Eisenhower Library and John Waide of the Thomas A. Dooley Collection at St. Louis University—contributed their wisdom and experience and reminded me yet again why a single good archivist is worth a dozen historians. My greatest debt, as always, is to the women in my life: Devora, Miranda, and Sophie Jacobs, who gamely put up with endless work-related distractions and whose radiance provided the perfect tonic for what Sophie calls "borin' grownup book stuff."

Introduction

About sixteen hours before he was murdered, South Vietnamese president Ngo Dinh Diem had his final dispute with an American policymaker. At 4:30 P.M. on 1 November 1963, Diem phoned U.S. ambassador Henry Cabot Lodge from the cellar of Gia Long Palace in Saigon. Although he had too much dignity to beg for American aid, he was clearly worried, and with good cause: the palace and its adjoining guards' barracks were surrounded by mutinous units of the South Vietnamese Army, Saigon's radio station was broadcasting tapes proclaiming the overthrow of the Diem regime and its replacement by a military revolutionary council, and coup leaders were threatening to shell the palace if Diem did not surrender unconditionally. With his government collapsing around him, Diem reached out to Lodge. The transcript of their exchange, as published by the *New York Times*, is painful to read:

Diem: Some units have made a rebellion, and I want to know what is the attitude of the U.S.

Lodge: I do not feel well enough informed to be able to tell you. I have heard the shooting, but I am not acquainted with all the facts. Also, it is four-thirty A.M. in Washington, and the U.S. government cannot possibly have a view.

Diem: But you must have some general ideas. After all, I am a chief of state. I have tried to do my duty. I want to do now what duty and good sense require. I believe in duty above all.

Lodge: You have certainly done your duty. As I told you only this morning, I admire your courage and your great contribution to your country. No one can take away

1

from you the credit for all you have done. Now I am worried about your personal safety. I have a report that those in charge of the current activity offer you and your brother safe-conduct out of the country if you resign. Had you heard this?

Diem: No. [Pause] You have my telephone number.

Lodge: Yes. If I can do anything for your physical safety, please contact me.

Diem: I am trying to reestablish order.

Diem's bodyguard recalls a longer and more heated conversation that concluded with Diem shouting:

> Mr. Ambassador, do you realize who you are talking to? I would like you to know that you are talking to the president of an independent and sovereign nation. I will only leave this country if it is the wish of my people. I will never leave according to the request of a group of rebellious generals or of an American ambassador. The U.S. government must take full responsibility before the world for this miserable matter.

Diem then slammed down the receiver.[1]

That wrenching colloquy spotlights both the defects and strengths of what had come to be known as America's "Diem experiment." Diem's apparent unawareness of the role Lodge himself played in the coup—at least until the ambassador gave the game away by revealing details of the rebels' terms for surrender—was typical of his ignorance of Vietnamese political and social realities. As Lodge complained in a cable to Washington five days before the insurgency, Diem was "cut off from the present." This was not a recent development. American observers in Saigon had noted Diem's indifference to the needs and problems of his people ever since the Diem experiment was launched in 1954. Fully three years prior to Diem's assumption of the South Vietnamese premiership, a State Department official warned his superiors that Diem was "out of touch with developments in [his] own country." Diem made little effort to remedy this deficiency after becoming America's hand-picked choice to man the ramparts of the "free world" in Southeast Asia. He never cultivated any rapport with the peasants or the bourgeoisie of South Vietnam; indeed, he seemed uncomfortable dealing with anyone outside his family. "Diem would have been a fascinating subject for a psychiatrist or a psychologist, and I am neither," notes former CIA operative Chester Cooper. "What comes through even to the layman, however, is a man who was almost totally disengaged from the world." Washington could scarcely have chosen a Cold War surrogate more intellectually unsuited to the task confronting him.[2]

Yet Diem did not lack courage. Throughout the nine years that he struggled to build a cohesive anticommunist state in South Vietnam, he faced hazards that would have broken the spirit of a less resolute leader. In 1955, when his actual authority did not extend beyond his palace walls and he could not even count on the loyalty of his own chief of staff, he triumphed in the epic "Battle for Saigon," putting down a citywide revolt by the gangster Binh Xuyen sect and destroying much of South Vietnam's capital in the process. Two years later, an attempt on Diem's life at a dedication ceremony in Ban Me Thuot did not unnerve him; he made no changes in the day's itinerary and rarely referred to the affair thereafter. In 1960 paratrooper battalions trapped Diem and his family in the palace for thirty-six nerve-shredding hours, while Diem simultaneously soothed them with promises of reform and sent pleas for help over his private radio net to loyal units in the countryside; the standoff ended with the palace grounds strewn with rebel corpses and Diem still in command. Another attempted putsch in 1962 involved two renegade air force pilots who dropped napalm and bombs on the palace and strafed their target with machine-gun fire; Diem, safe in his fortified cellar, waited for the storm to pass and emerged unruffled. Whatever his faults, Diem was not a coward.

Nor was he a puppet. None of America's Cold War allies worked harder than Diem to demonstrate that acceptance of American aid did not entail submission to American demands. Despite the efforts of its most powerful diplomats and military men, Washington could never impose its agenda on South Vietnam during the Diem era. Diem defied General J. Lawton Collins's commands to bring opposition figures into his cabinet and promote a more active role for the South Vietnamese legislature; he persisted in a nationwide program of relocating villagers in fortified "strategic hamlets" despite the warnings of Senator Mike Mansfield that this effort, rather than neutralizing the communists, was driving thousands of disgruntled South Vietnamese into their ranks; and he adamantly refused to comply with President John F. Kennedy's orders to conciliate Saigon's refractory Buddhist population, even when JFK threatened to cut off U.S. aid. Ultimately, Washington colluded in Diem's overthrow in the hope that his successor would prove more responsive to American direction.

Diem did not deviate from the path of stubborn nationalism during his final hours. By refusing to accept American offers of safe passage out of Vietnam and a comfortable life in exile, he made himself unique among the crew of Saigon politicos and generals whose dictatorships the United States underwrote. Nguyen Khanh, who overthrew the officers who overthrew Diem, fled Vietnam after only a year as president to begin managing a restaurant in Florida. Nguyen Cao Ky, South Vietnamese prime minister from 1965 to 1967, relocated to California and opened a liquor store. Nguyen Van Thieu, South Vietnam's longest-serving chief executive after Diem, ended his days in an affluent suburb of Boston. However great these men's love of country, it did not prevent them from pulling up stakes once American support for their respective regimes was withdrawn. Diem alone made the fatal—and characteristic—decision to remain among his people.

After rebuffing Lodge and cutting his last tie with the United States, Diem lingered in the palace cellar for about three hours. Only his brother Ngo Dinh Nhu and a few servants and military aides remained at his side; most members of the government were either in hiding or had gone over to the rebel camp. Nhu, Diem's chief political counselor, was not surprised to learn of Lodge's complicity in the coup; he had never trusted the Americans, and this final proof of U.S. treachery only confirmed his suspicions that Washington intended to turn South Vietnam into an imperial appendage of the United States. Nhu told Diem to ignore Lodge's feigned concern for his safety and none-too-oblique suggestion that he resign. The appropriate response to the present crisis was boldness, if only to show these overbearing Americans that the president could not be pushed around. Diem needed little convincing. When the rebels telephoned the palace around 7:00 P.M. and threatened to "blast [Diem] off the face of the earth" if he did not surrender, Diem hurled defiance at them.[3]

Diem and Nhu made several attempts to rally support via radio transmitter. They called on provincial commanders, South Vietnam's Republican Youth Corps, and even a paramilitary women's committee chaired by Nhu's wife. No one responded. Recognizing that the palace might soon be overrun, Diem resolved to give his adversaries the slip. Accounts of how he accomplished this vary, but he and Nhu escaped either via a secret tunnel constructed for just such an occasion or through a gate the rebels had forgotten to seal off. Once outside the palace grounds, Nhu advised Diem that it would be best for the two of them to split up; that way, even if one brother were caught, the rebels would not risk killing him as long as the other was still at large. Diem rejected the plan. "We have always been together during these last years," he insisted. "How could we separate in this critical hour?" Nhu reluctantly agreed to remain at Diem's side, come what may.[4]

An officer loyal to Diem picked up the brothers in a British Land Rover and drove them to Cholon, Saigon's Chinese suburb, where they took refuge in the villa of a wealthy Chinese merchant. There, they tried to contact one of Diem's most trusted officers, General Ton That Dinh, who had been invested with military control of Saigon months before. They finally reached him by telephone around midnight. Dinh's response to his commander-in-chief's plea for help must have made clear to Diem that his reign as president was over. Unlike past crises, there would be no last-minute reprieve. Dinh, who was at the moment surrounded by other coup leaders in the headquarters of the Army Joint General Staff, relished the opportunity to display his contempt for Diem to his fellow conspirators. When Diem demanded that Dinh order his troops into battle against rebel units, the general shot back: "I've saved you motherfuckers many times, but not now, you bastards. You shits are finished."[5]

Thunderstruck, Diem and Nhu decided to seek sanctuary in a Catholic church. They managed to elude rebel troop patrols and make their way to Saint Francis Xavier, a French church in Cholon, where they prayed and took communion. It was here that Diem apparently bowed to the inevitable. He phoned staff headquarters at 7:00 A.M. with an offer to surrender. But, he insisted, he wanted to receive the "military honors" due a resigning chief executive. Rebel leader General Duong Van Minh refused. The surrender had to be unconditional. The most Minh could guarantee was that Diem and his family would not be harmed. Diem hung up.[6]

He called back half an hour later to accept the rebels' terms. He really had no choice. The Americans were not going to rescue him; indeed, Ambassador Lodge had gone to bed a few hours after speaking to Diem and was fast asleep as the coup unfolded. Most army unit commanders had defected to the rebels. Even if there were a few loyal officers left, Diem could not reach them. He was, for all practical purposes, alone. While he might conceivably have survived for a few months on the run in Cholon's labyrinthine streets, his pride would not permit him to become a fugitive. Besides, he had to think of his family: he had siblings, cousins, and other blood relations installed in government posts throughout South Vietnam. What if his refusal to surrender were to prompt acts of reprisal against them? The most drastic option—suicide—was out of the question; Diem's Catholic faith would not permit it. There was nothing to do but admit defeat, a gesture which, for Diem, was all but unendurable.

After Diem revealed his whereabouts to Minh, he and Nhu waited for what they assumed would be a limousine sent to pick them up. An armored personnel carrier arrived instead, accompanied by several jeeps filled with rebel soldiers. The first man to exit the carrier was Colonel Duong Ngoc Lam, head of the Civil Guard and a friend of Diem's. General Mai Huu Xuan, who headed the convoy, had arranged for Lam to lure Diem and Nhu out of the church. The stratagem worked: despite their dismay at seeing the armored car, the Ngo brothers emerged when they saw Lam. They even shook Xuan's hand, although Nhu could not resist snarling: "You use such a vehicle to drive the *president?*" Xuan responded that the personnel carrier had been chosen to protect its distinguished passengers against "extremists." Diem seemed to accept this explanation, and asked if they could make a stop at the palace to collect personal items. Xuan politely replied that this was impossible, that his orders were to proceed directly to headquarters. Soldiers then tied the brothers' hands behind their backs with wire. Diem and Nhu were shoved into the carrier, which sped off for Saigon.[7]

There are numerous accounts of what happened next, but journalist Stanley Karnow probably obtained the most reliable report when he interviewed an eyewitness, Major Duong Huu Nghia, several days later. Nghia had been among the officers under General Xuan's command when the general was sent to fetch Diem. For some reason, Xuan did not ride with Diem and Nhu back to headquarters, choosing instead to lead the motorcade in a jeep and leaving Nghia in charge of the vehicle carrying the Ngo brothers. Nghia was assisted by Captain Nguyen Van Nhung, whose close friend had recently been executed on Nhu's orders. Nhung sat alongside Diem and Nhu, while Nghia climbed into a gun turret overlooking them. According to Nghia, Diem "sat silently" during the drive to Saigon, but Nhung and Nhu began to argue. "The name-calling grew passionate. [Nhung] had hated Nhu before. Now he was charged with emotion." After a particularly nasty exchange of insults, Nhung leapt at Nhu and stabbed him with his bayonet. The sight of blood only enraged Nhung further. He plunged the bayonet into Nhu over and over—"maybe fifteen or twenty times," Nghia told Karnow. Nhung then turned to Diem, took out his revolver, and shot the president in the head. Observing that Nhu was still alive and "twitching," Nhung put a bullet in his head as well. "Neither Diem nor Nhu ever defended themselves," Nghia recalled. "Their hands were tied."[8]

The coup leaders were appalled when the armored car reached staff headquarters and disclosed its grisly contents. Almost immediately, they began disseminating "official" reports that the brothers had killed themselves. "Due to an inadvertence," one rebel general told Lodge, "there was a gun inside the vehicle. It was with this gun . . . that they committed suicide." Another general claimed that Diem and Nhu "took poison" while waiting in the church. Within days, photographs of the brothers' corpses became available, clearly showing their hands tied behind their backs, and the government in Saigon was forced to admit that they had been murdered—although the issue of who was responsible has yet to be resolved. Some blamed Nhung for losing his head; others claimed he was acting on General Xuan's instructions; still others insisted that the real culprit was South Vietnam's new president, Duong Van Minh, who employed Nhung as a bodyguard and who had ample motive to order a "hit." Since neither the South Vietnamese nor the American government ever conducted a public inquiry into Diem's assassination, it is unlikely that all of the pieces of this jigsaw puzzle will ever come together.[9]

Still, a large measure of the guilt for Diem's death unquestionably rested with his superpower sponsor. Ngo Dinh Nhu's wife, Madame Nhu, was more insightful than she could have known when she called the assassinations an "indelible stigma against the United States." The Kennedy administration had in fact sanctioned and even encouraged the coup. The generals who overthrew and murdered Diem would not have acted without American approval; they waited until they received a green light from Washington before launching their insurrection. Furthermore, they had been in more or less constant contact with Lodge and various CIA officers in the months leading up to the revolt. Lodge had lobbied Washington for a change in South Vietnamese leadership since the day he arrived in Saigon. Although Kennedy appears to have been stunned by the news of Diem's death, the coup had been executed with his full knowledge. For Kennedy and his fellow policymakers to claim after the fact that they were unaware of the possibility of a violent outcome strains credibility. Madame Nhu was justified in her charge that "my family has been treacherously killed with either official or unofficial blessing of the American government."[10]

More important than the Kennedy administration's involvement in the coup was the fact that Diem never would have become South Vietnam's leader in the first place without U.S. patronage. From the beginning, the Diem regime was an American creation. It was Americans who determined that the southern half of Vietnam had to be prevented from falling to communism, Americans who chose Diem as the Vietnamese best suited to preserve an anticommunist outpost in the Far East, and Americans whose money, weaponry, and expertise kept Diem's government afloat for nearly a decade. As a CIA officer stationed in Saigon in the mid-1950s recalled, Diem was "so wholly dependent on American support that he would have fallen in a day without it." Like a terminally ill patient on life support, Diem required progressively larger infusions of U.S. aid to stay in power. When Washington reduced its aid, Diem's government collapsed.[11]

The nine-year "experiment" that ended when Diem died was America's crossover point from advice and support to active cobelligerency in a Vietnamese civil war. Washington's commitment to Diem may have been the most ruinous foreign policy decision of the postwar era. President Dwight Eisenhower's entire Southeast Asian policy came to rest, to a large extent, on the shoulders of South Vietnam's first president, and after Diem fell from power in the Kennedy years, his country was in even greater need of U.S. economic and military assistance than before. Some of the consequences of Washington's effort to construct a viable state around Diem were:

A far greater U.S. military presence in the former French Indochina. When Diem first visited the United States in late 1950 to seek American backing, Washington's stake in Vietnam, as represented by Americans "in country," was roughly sixty men. That was the staff of the Military Assistance and Advisory Group (MAAG), a team set up by Washington to channel military aid to the French, who were fighting to retain their colonial empire in Asia against the communist Viet Minh. The MAAG had no responsibility for training or advising the anticommunist Vietnamese National Army (VNA), and the French proved extremely reluctant to listen to American counsel. The Americans in Vietnam did not play a meaningful role in the ongoing conflict. This changed in June 1954, the month that Diem became prime minister of South Vietnam. The French, reeling from their defeat in the Battle of Dien Bien Phu, requested that the United States join them in training and organizing the VNA. France's withdrawal from Vietnam by mid-1955 created an even greater demand for American advisers, and Washington employed a variety of legal devices to increase their number to roughly seven hundred. When Diem still proved incapable of subduing his nation's communist insurgency, the incoming Kennedy administration sent more men and increased the scope of their activities. By the time of Diem's assassination in 1963, there were over sixteen thousand U.S. military personnel on duty in South Vietnam. Their ranks would continue to swell until they exceeded half a million.

The conversion of Vietnam from a French to an American "problem." For almost a decade after the close of World War II, Washington deferred to Paris when crafting U.S. policy toward Indochina. Because America needed French support for its Cold War policies in Europe, and because no U.S. president wanted to replace French troops with American ones in the war against the Viet Minh, France exerted considerable control over the "free world's" approach to containing Vietnamese communism. But the French could not abide Diem. Without exception, French political and military leaders objected to Diem's installation as South Vietnamese premier, citing his Francophobia, inexperience, incompetence, and lack of popular support. "Diem is not only incapable but mad," declared French prime minister Edgar Faure in 1955. When the Eisenhower administration made plain that it would not accept anyone other than Diem, Faure's government interpreted this as an abrogation of shared Franco-American responsibility for Vietnam. France pulled its forces out of its former colony and liquidated its political and economic interests there within a year of Diem's assumption of office. From that point on, the stability and security of South Vietnam depended on the United States.[12]

Postponement of Vietnam's unification for two decades. The 1954 Geneva Conference, which ended the eight-year Franco–Viet Minh War, drafted a number of political arrangements for Vietnam. Along with imposing a ceasefire throughout the country and temporarily dividing it into North and South Vietnam, the Geneva Accords provided for nationwide elections in 1956, with the goal of reunification and elimination of the artificial barrier at the 17th parallel. America's adoption of Diem as a client made the United States a sponsor in Diem's fateful refusal to participate in these elections. Diem recognized that he had no chance to garner more votes than the communist leader Ho Chi Minh, even assuming elections were administered fairly, and that by submitting to such a popularity contest he would doom all of Vietnam to red domination; consequently, he denied that South Vietnam was bound by any of the decisions taken at Geneva. By backing Diem in his noncompliance with the accords, America shared in a suppression of the people's will, leaving those Vietnamese who dreamed of unifying their country no alternative but war.

A legacy of anti-American sentiment among the Vietnamese. Hard as it is to believe, the United States enjoyed a positive reputation in Vietnam at the close of World War II. Ho Chi Minh quoted from the Declaration of Independence in announcing his nation's freedom from colonialism, Americans took part in the ceremonies celebrating Vietnamese independence in Hanoi, and a Vietnamese band played the "Star Spangled Banner." Ho wrote to President Harry Truman no fewer than eight times, begging for U.S. support, and even volunteered to place Vietnam on the same footing as the Philippines—that is, to make it an American colony—in return for formal diplomatic recognition and aid. But America squandered its immense prestige in Vietnam through fruitless attempts to strengthen and stabilize Diem at the expense of his people. By the time Washington's Diem experiment reached its bloody climax, most Vietnamese had concluded that the United States was no different from France or any other selfish Western power.

The commitment to Diem was the most fundamental decision of America's lengthy involvement in Vietnam, the prerequisite to the subsequent incremental steps that culminated in defeat and disgrace. Any attempt to understand the origins of the Vietnam War must therefore begin with a detailed knowledge of the Diem experiment. How did Diem win backing among Americans for his views on the direction South Vietnam should take and his role as the nation's leader? Why were so many prominent Americans convinced that Diem could guide Vietnam to independence from colonial or communist rule? And why did America stick by Diem for so long?

To answer these questions, this book orients the Diem experiment within the context of the early Cold War. Three separate sets of environing conditions were crucial to Diem's seizure of power and his retention of that power for so many years. First was the international setting, where communist and anticommunist superpowers shifted their focus from deadlock in Europe to seemingly more malleable arenas in the so-called third world of Africa, the Middle East, Latin America, and Asia. Among the newly emergent nations where the United States, Soviet Union, and People's Republic of China jockeyed for influence was Vietnam, because of the country's material and strategic value and, more importantly, because of its symbolic significance as a "domino" whose fall to the enemy could not be permitted lest it trigger a chain reaction. Since none of the superpowers wanted to be tarred with the brush of colonialism, all preferred to exercise military, political, and economic control over their third-world satellites through a native strongman, either communist or noncommunist. The degree of indigenous support on which those strongmen could call varied greatly; sometimes, as in the case of Ho Chi Minh, it was considerable, while in Diem's situation it had to be cultivated by outsiders. Rarely did the local viceroy's agenda mesh perfectly with that of his bankroller; indeed, American journalists tagged Diem as a "puppet who pulled his own strings." But both communist and anticommunist superpowers waged their Cold War, to a large extent, by proxy in nations like Vietnam. This enabled them to minimize their own casualties and preserve the illusion that they had no imperialistic intent. Few South Vietnamese were deceived by this artifice, and the Diem regime earned the detested nickname *"My-Diem"*—"American Diem"—before Diem completed his first year in office.[13]

Also vital to Diem's ascent and durability was the domestic environment in the United States, where anticommunist hysteria, commonly dubbed McCarthyism, made Diem uniquely appealing to Americans endeavoring to prevent South Vietnam's absorption by the red empire. Diem's fervent anticommunism rendered him almost immune to criticism in the American media. Crusading press lords like Henry Luce portrayed Diem as the "Miracle Man" who single-handedly saved twelve million Vietnamese from communist slavery, and Washington cold warriors of conservative and liberal dispositions embraced this myth, either out of genuine conviction or because they recognized that to do otherwise would be political suicide. It was not until the early 1960s, when fissures within the communist "monolith" started to discredit the Manichaean worldview of the Truman and Eisenhower years, that Washington cast a more disapproving eye on the regime it had created in South Vietnam.

Finally, conditions within Diem's own country facilitated the emergence and persistence of his dictatorship. The trauma of two wars, one against the Japanese and the other between the French and Viet Minh, created an extremely volatile situation in Vietnam by the mid-1950s in which numerous groups contended for dominance. Diem's capacity to draw on the United States as an ally proved sufficient to elevate him above his rivals and establish a shaky bastion, after which he took the revolutionary step of deposing Vietnam's emperor and proclaiming a "republic." His subsequent reign of terror, subsidized by the United States, succeeded in killing, jailing, or frightening into submission most opposition, with the exception of a communist guerrilla movement that gained increasing force and popularity as the 1950s gave way to the 1960s. The decision of the North Vietnamese Politburo to concentrate on domestic problems in its half of Vietnam during the first five years of Diem's rule helped Diem solidify his position as absolute master in the south and preside over a regime of apparent order and prosperity. Not until 1960 did Ho Chi Minh authorize the formation of the National Liberation Front (NLF) to foment a general uprising against the Saigon government. By that point, American policymakers had invested so much money and prestige in their Diem experiment that they could not detach themselves from it without suffering an unacceptable diplomatic loss of face. Their only option, as they perceived it, was to invest more.

Also important, of course, was Diem himself, a complex, tragic figure who continues to inspire strong reactions among students of the Vietnam War. One historian noted in 1963 that treatments of Diem consisted "either of totally uncritical eulogy or of equally partisan condemnation." For the most part, that observation still holds true today, although some scholars have begun to move beyond the hero-villain dichotomy to present a more nuanced portrait of the man whose strengths and defects so profoundly shaped a major phase in Vietnamese and American history. Ironically, Diem's most fitting epitaph may have been written by the American policymaker with most cause to hate him. General J. Lawton Collins, who served as President Eisenhower's special representative to South Vietnam for six months at the start of Diem's reign, campaigned more strenuously than anyone for abandonment of the Diem experiment. As we will see in chapter 3, Collins sent numerous cables from Saigon to Washington pleading with Eisenhower to jettison Diem and replace him with another South Vietnamese. For his efforts, Collins was slandered in the halls of Congress, ignored by his commander-in-chief, and ultimately relieved of his duties when Eisenhower determined that Diem would be better served by a more pliable U.S. ambassador. Collins had ample justification for "I told you so" gloating when the Diem experiment crashed and burned in 1963. Yet his reaction was anything but smug. "Unfortunately," Collins notes in his memoirs, "my forecast of Diem's inability to overcome the vast obstacles that beset him proved to be largely correct. Despite his, and our, failures in Vietnam, he was a dedicated Vietnamese patriot whose brutal murder was despicable and wholly unwarranted. He deserved a better fate at the hands of his countrymen."[14]

And, Collins might have added, at the hands of the United States.

Notes

1. Diem and Lodge cited in Lodge's Last Talk with Diem, *The Pentagon Papers: New York Times Version* (New York: Quadrangle Books, 1971), 238; Anne E. Blair, *Lodge in Vietnam: A Patriot Abroad* (New Haven, Conn.: Yale University Press, 1995), 69.

2. The Embassy in Vietnam to the Department of State, 28 October 1963, *Foreign Relations of the United States* [hereafter *FRUS*], *1961–1963* (Washington, D.C.: Government Printing Office, 1991), 4:442; Cory, Memorandum of Conversation with Mr. Ngo Dinh Diem, 21 July 1951, file 751G.00/7-2651, Record Group 59, National Archives II, College Park, Maryland [hereafter RG 59]; Chester L. Cooper, *The Lost Crusade: America in Vietnam* (New York: Dodd, Meade, 1970), 155.

3. Rebel generals cited in National Security Files, Countries—Vietnam: CIA Memorandum: The Coup in South Vietnam, 1 November 1963: Box 201, John F. Kennedy Library, Boston, Massachusetts [hereafter JFKL].

4. Diem cited in Ellen J. Hammer, *A Death in November: America in Vietnam, 1963* (New York: Dutton, 1987), 293.

5. Dinh cited in Stanley Karnow, *Vietnam: A History* (New York: Viking, 1983), 308.

6. Diem cited in Hammer, *Death in November*, 294.

7. Nhu and Xuan cited in Howard Jones, *Death of a Generation: How the Assassinations of Diem and JFK Prolonged the Vietnam War* (New York: Oxford University Press, 2003), 429.

8. Nghia cited in Stanley Karnow, "The Fall of the House of Ngo Dinh," reprinted in *Reporting Vietnam, Part I: American Journalism, 1959–1969* (New York: Library of America, 1998), 104–105; Jones, *Death of a Generation*, 529.

9. Rebel generals cited in National Security Files, Countries—Vietnam: Lodge to Rusk, 2 November 1963: Box 201, JFKL.

10. Madame Nhu cited in Jones, *Death of a Generation*, 433.

11. CIA officer cited in Denis Warner, *The Last Confucian* (Baltimore, Md.: Penguin, 1964), 98–99.

12. Faure cited in the Secretary of State to the Department of State, 8 May 1955, *FRUS, 1955–1957* (Washington, D.C.: Government Printing Office, 1985), 1:372–378.

13. Correspondents cited in Harry Maurer, *Strange Ground: Americans in Vietnam, 1945–1975: An Oral History* (New York: Henry Holt, 1989), 80.

14. Bernard B. Fall, *The Two Viet-Nams: A Political and Military Analysis*, 2nd rev. ed. (New York: Praeger, 1967), 235; J. Lawton Collins, *Lightning Joe: An Autobiography* (Baton Rouge: Louisiana State University Press, 1979), 411.

CHAPTER ONE

~

"The Kind of Asian
We Can Live With"

Diem Wins American Support

Ngo Dinh Diem could not have picked a more propitious time to make his first visit to the United States. America's red scare was at its zenith in 1950. Just seven months before Diem deplaned in Washington in late August of that year, former State Department official Alger Hiss was convicted of perjury in a high-profile trial. Hiss, a New Deal establishment figure and adviser at numerous international conferences, had been accused by a repentant former communist of transmitting government documents to the Soviet Union. Since the statute of limitations for espionage had expired, the government prosecuted Hiss for lying before a grand jury about his past communist ties. Hiss's conviction seemed to confirm charges from the Republican Right that communists had infiltrated the government and were working to sabotage America's foreign policy. Secretary of State Dean Acheson lent persuasiveness to those charges when, upon learning of the guilty verdict, he declared to a reporter, "I do not intend to turn my back on Alger Hiss." Acheson defended his pledge of loyalty to his former associate by directing journalists to "the 25th chapter of the Gospel according to St. Matthew beginning with verse 34."[1]

Two weeks after the jury convicted Hiss, a senator named Joe McCarthy cited Acheson's comment as evidence of the secretary's "apathy to evil." "Today we are engaged in a final, all-out battle between communistic atheism and Christianity," McCarthy blared to the Ohio County Women's Republican Club in Wheeling, West Virginia. "The secretary of state, in attempting to justify his continued devotion to the man who sold out the Christian world to the atheistic world, referred to Christ's Sermon on the Mount as justification." Such "blasphemy" could be overcome, McCarthy claimed, "only when the whole sorry mess of twisted, warped thinkers are swept from the national scene." It was in this soon-to-be-notorious speech that McCarthy first claimed to have "in my hand" a list of State Department employees who were members of the Communist Party. How many names were on that list was never clear—McCarthy initially said 208, then 57, then 4—but it did not matter. He had tapped into America's postwar anxieties brilliantly. While American anticommunism predated the senator's Wheeling speech, the strain known as McCarthyism came into existence on 9 February 1950.[2]

National Security Paper no. 68, which a leading diplomatic historian calls "the American blueprint for waging the cold war during the next twenty years," was approved by President Harry Truman two months after McCarthy made his charges. Better known as NSC-68, the paper identified external forces rather than domestic subversion as the principal threat to American security; nonetheless, it echoed McCarthy's warnings of an "all-out battle" between good and evil. Truman had ordered the National Security Council to reevaluate U.S. policy toward the communist bloc in light of Moscow's explosion of a nuclear device and the fall of China to Mao Zedong's followers. The NSC responded with a manifesto that accused the Soviet Union of "seek[ing] to impose its absolute authority over the rest of the world." The challenge facing America, NSC-68 contended, was "momentous, involving the fulfillment or destruction not only of this Republic but of civilization itself." NSC-68 recommended that the United States undertake a "rapid and sustained build-up" of its "political, economic, and military strength": conventional and nuclear forces needed to be enlarged, public opinion mobilized and focused, and taxes raised to unheard-of levels to pay for this rearmament program. "[T]he cold war is in fact a real war in which the survival of the free world is at stake," advised NSC-68. Truman accepted this analysis but doubted whether he could persuade a budget-minded Congress to vote the necessary increases in defense spending. Then, as one proponent of NSC-68 recalled, "Korea came along and saved us."[3]

Most significant in preparing the ground for Diem's arrival in America was the outbreak of the Korean War in late June 1950. The communist government of North Korea sent troops in Soviet-made tanks thundering across the 38th parallel in an invasion of America's client state in the south. Washington's response was immediate: Acheson rammed a resolution through the

United Nations Security Council designating the North Koreans as the aggressors and calling for a cessation of hostilities; when this failed to halt the communist advance, Truman ordered U.S. air and naval units into action; three days later, he committed ground forces. Still, the war went badly. By early August, the communists had overrun most of South Korea.

For millions of Americans, the ominous scenario laid out in NSC-68 now seemed credible. Truman had little difficulty convincing Congress to quadruple U.S. defense spending, reintroduce selective service, and speed up development of the hydrogen bomb. Significantly, in his first address to the nation after North Korea's attack, Truman announced, "I have . . . directed acceleration in the furnishing of military assistance to the forces of France . . . in Indochina." The president assumed a connection between the struggles in Korea and Vietnam; he considered them both manifestations of the Kremlin's drive to dominate Asia. Whereas previously Washington had been loath to support France's attempt to reclaim its Indochinese colonies, the summer of 1950 saw anticommunism trump anticolonialism in U.S. foreign policy.[4]

It was against this backdrop of onrushing events that Diem arrived in the United States. Under different circumstances, his visit would have excited little notice; if Washington's elite had paid any attention to him, they would have regarded him as a curiosity. He hardly cut a commanding figure. As the journalist Robert Shaplen recalls, Diem was "a short, broadly built fellow, with a round face and a shock of black hair, who walked and moved jerkily, as if on strings." Diem did not compensate for these idiosyncrasies with a dynamic personality. Quite the contrary: almost every characterization of him stresses his lack of what may be termed "political" skills. Notoriously longwinded, he turned every social encounter into an occasion for one of his marathon monologues, which, one acquaintance remembers, had the effect of "inducing a state of profound, indeed vertiginous, boredom in almost everyone." Other Americans who dealt with Diem found him "utterly without warmth," "humorless, egotistical, . . . neurotically suspicious," "stubborn, self-righteous, and a complete stranger to compromise."[5]

None of this augured well for Diem's political future, either in the United States or his native country. Yet four years after Diem first set foot on American soil the administration of Dwight Eisenhower would compel Vietnamese emperor Bao Dai to install this man as prime minister of the "State of Vietnam," with "full civil and military powers"—more authority than Bao Dai had ever granted to any of his premiers. Diem's rise derived in equal parts from the exigencies of the moment in Washington and strengths within his own character that more than offset his defects. While Diem was fortunate to come to the United States at a time when Americans were receptive to the message he bore, his ascent to dictatorship was in great measure his own accomplishment.[6]

Reporter Bernard Fall noted in the 1960s that "[i]t is, to say the least, remarkable that Ngo Dinh Diem has thus far escaped the attentions of a biographer." A few authors have attempted book-length accounts of Diem's life since Fall made that observation, but these mostly fit into the categories of hagiography and hatchet job. No "definitive" treatment has emerged, possibly because it is difficult to separate fact from myth when dealing with Diem's early years. Still, it seems clear that his pre-1950 résumé indicated an odd blend of cunning, piety, and nerve.[7]

Diem often boasted that he descended from one of the great families of Vietnam, a clan of mandarins so revered that people believed it brought good luck if they buried their dead near the Ngo family tombs. Most historians reject such stories, insisting that Diem's forebears were of lowly birth and that no one before his father ever attained mandarinal rank. Less controversial was Diem's claim that the Ngos were among the first Vietnamese to embrace Catholicism. Portuguese missionaries converted Diem's ancestors a century before the French colonial presence, thereby conferring on them both a symbolic and a literal cross, since the Catholic Church was pointedly unwelcome in Vietnam. Emperor Minh Mang inaugurated a policy of persecution of Catholics in the 1830s. In 1848 and 1851, Emperor Tu Duc issued edicts impelling Catholics to convert or face execution. As France tightened its hold over Vietnam in the 1880s, anti-Catholic violence grew worse; Catholicism was identified with the foreign oppressor, and Catholic Vietnamese held to their faith at a ghastly price. The Ngo clan was almost wiped out when a Buddhist mob raided their village, herded over one hundred of them into a church, and burned it down.

One of the few family members to survive was Ngo Dinh Kha, who was studying in Malaya when the massacre occurred. Kha returned to Vietnam upon learning that his parents, brothers, and sisters had been murdered. He was so devastated by the tragedy that he gave up plans of becoming a priest and vowed to raise a family of his own. His first wife died childless, but the second bore him nine children—six boys and three girls. Diem, the third boy, was born on 3 January 1901 near the imperial capital of Hue. Kha joined the court of Emperor Than Thai and rose quickly in the ranks of the mandarinate, becoming minister of the rites, grand chamberlain, and keeper of the eunuchs. Formal portraits show that Kha adopted the attributes of traditional mandarins: black turban, two-inch fingernails, nine-button silken robes. Yet his devotion to the Catholic Church remained unshaken. Every morning he took his family to mass, and he encouraged his sons to study for the priesthood.

The family fell on hard times in 1907 when the French, irritated by Than Thai's complaints about their exploitation of his country, deposed him on pretext of insanity and replaced him with a more tractable sovereign. Kha resigned in protest, retiring to the countryside to farm a few acres of riceland. He managed to provide Diem and his brothers with an education, despite having little money. At age fifteen, Diem followed in the footsteps of his older brother Ngo Dinh Thuc and entered a monastery, but he left after a few months. According to Thuc, who ultimately rose to the rank of archbishop, "the Church was too worldly for him." Diem then took competitive examinations for the equivalent of a high school diploma at the French lycée at Hue and achieved such a high score that the French offered him a scholarship in Paris. He rejected the offer, enrolling instead at Hanoi's School of Public Administration and Law, where he compiled a stellar record. He also experienced the only romantic relationship of his life when he fell in love with the daughter of one of his teachers. She broke off the affair to join a convent. He remained celibate from then on.[8]

After graduating at the top of his class in 1921, Diem went into government service. Although he entered the imperial bureaucracy as a mandarin of the lowliest grade, promotion came swiftly. His first appointment was at the royal library at Hue. Within a year, he had become administrative supervisor of a district of seventy villages. At age twenty-five, he ascended from district to province chief, and the number of villages under his supervision grew to three hundred.

Diem's advance was facilitated by Nguyen Huu Bai, the Catholic head of the council of ministers in Hue, whose daughter married Diem's brother Ngo Dinh Khoi before Diem began working in the imperial administration. Family ties and shared religious affiliation caused Bai to take an interest in Diem, and he became the young man's patron. This was a piece of good luck, for Bai was one of the top Vietnamese power brokers, having served his colonial masters loyally for years and earned a measure of backstairs influence in Paris. He managed to get Khoi promoted to provincial governor, but devoted more attention to Diem, whose patriotism appealed to him. Bai was a late-blooming nationalist; in the 1920s and early 1930s, he had become critical of French reluctance to grant Vietnam true autonomy, and he worked with Diem to loosen colonial restrictions on many aspects of Vietnamese life.

The French found Diem industrious but were irritated by his repeated requests that villages be given more self-government. Diem, for his part, resented the colonialists' inattention to his demands. He contemplated resigning but, as he remembered years later, village elders persuaded him to stay on. "They told me of their confidence in me," Diem recalled, "and predicted that I would someday lead my country." Diem found another cause for remaining at his post. While riding around the countryside near Hue, he became one of the first Vietnamese officials to recognize how widespread the communist resistance movement was. In 1925 he exposed some of the earliest communist cells in Quang Tri, a province sixty miles north of Hue. Four years later, when the communists staged demonstrations throughout Vietnam, Diem rounded up the leaders of the movement in his administrative area and filed a report with the colonial government detailing communist maneuvers. The French rewarded Diem, promoting him to governor of the province of Phan-Thiet, where he continued to root out communists. In 1930 and 1931 the Communist Party fomented the first peasant revolts in central Vietnam, and Diem helped the French put them down.[9]

Eventually, Emperor Bao Dai learned of this talented and seemingly inexhaustible public servant. Bao Dai, still in his teens, was not yet the dissolute caricature he would become in the 1940s; he fancied himself a liberal reformer and had dreams of establishing a modern constitutional monarchy. Diem struck him as the perfect candidate for minister of the interior. Nguyen Huu Bai concurred with the emperor's judgment, and pressed the French to give Diem another promotion. The French agreed. In May 1933 Diem—only thirty-two years old—assumed control of the most important ministry in Bao Dai's cabinet. He seemed on the cusp of an extraordinary political career.

Yet that career quickly self-destructed. One of Diem's first assignments was to head a commission examining possible administrative reforms. He submitted a list of suggestions, none of which the French would consider. Disgusted, Diem resigned, having served less than three months at his post. The French stripped him of decorations, kept him under surveillance, and even threatened him with arrest. Diem was not intimidated. As he told a reporter three decades later, "I was convinced that the people must be alerted to the need for wholesale reforms and . . . must strive for them energetically—even violently."[10]

These Jacobinic statements notwithstanding, Diem did not plunge into anticolonial activism after leaving the imperial court. Instead, he withdrew to his family home in Hue. He held no public office—or, in fact, any job whatever—for the next twenty-one years. While Ho Chi Minh lobbied for Vietnamese independence in Thailand, the Soviet Union, and China, Diem adopted a less aggressive posture: reading, meditating, going to mass, and receiving communion every morning. For recreation, he tended his rose garden, developed photographs in a homemade darkroom, and hunted. He also occasionally traveled south to Saigon and conferred with nationalist leaders—among them Phan Boi Chau, Vietnam's most famous anticolonial activist—and he kept up a correspondence with Prince Cuong De, who had once led a resistance movement against the French and now lived in Japan. But Diem had no organization or any popular support. Indeed, while his refusal to take part in a figurehead government would be cited by his American admirers as evidence of patriotism, his hostility toward the foreign occupiers of his country rarely expressed itself in positive action to expel them.

This did not signify lack of courage, but, rather, a conviction that reform ought to be effected through traditional Vietnamese authorities instead of mass uprisings. Diem was a conservative man, despite his habitual use of the word "revolution" to describe his political program. Although he yearned to free Vietnam from the yoke of French colonialism, he did not believe that this required abandonment of institutions like the monarchy and the mandarinate. Rather, he thought such cultural uprooting was a recipe for chaos. From Diem's perspective, the problems plaguing his country derived from the fact that Bao Dai was a bad king, not from any defects in the system of monarchy itself; they neither justified turning the social structure upside down nor freed Vietnamese nationalists from their obligation to observe the Confucian principles of respect for authority, acceptance of one's station in life, and reliance on the past as a guide for the future. Ellen Hammer notes that "Diem had never been a revolutionary. He chose to act according to a Confucian tradition that a scholar during a difficult period of history should retire to a tranquil spot and wait for better times in which he might be useful."[11]

Diem believed those times had arrived with the onset of World War II. Like Ho Chi Minh, he understood that Japan's victories over European forces signaled the beginning of the end of colonialism in Asia. When the Japanese completed their occupation of French Indochina, Diem tried to convince Japanese officials to grant Vietnam its independence. His pleas struck a chord with some occupiers, who took literally Japan's wartime propaganda about liberating fellow Asians from European colonialism, but Tokyo decided to leave the outward form of French administration in place. Undeterred, Diem founded a secret political party, the Association for the Restoration of Great Vietnam, near Hue. When the French learned of this party in the summer of 1944, they declared Diem a subversive and ordered his arrest. Diem escaped capture, fleeing from Hue to Saigon in the disguise of a Japanese officer and hiding out in the houses of friends.

After the Japanese dispensed with the façade of French rule and took over Vietnam in March 1945, they offered Diem the premiership of a puppet regime under his old sovereign, Bao Dai. Diem turned down this request, probably because he recognized that the new Vietnamese government would lack any real independence. Tellingly, however, he regretted his decision and tried to get Bao Dai to make the offer again. He may have concluded that Japanese neocolonialism was preferable to French colonialism, or that he could persuade Tokyo to give Vietnam greater autonomy. In any event, it was too late: Bao Dai had already chosen another premier. Although this was a disappointment for Diem, it proved fortuitous, for it ensured that he would not be branded a collaborationist once the Allies liberated Vietnam.

Diem was scandalized when, shortly after Japan's surrender, the communist Viet Minh marched into Hanoi and proclaimed the Democratic Republic of Vietnam with Ho Chi Minh as its leader. Suspecting that Bao Dai might be willing to share power with Ho, Diem set out from Saigon to Hue to warn the emperor against any such arrangement. He never made it to the imperial capital. Viet Minh soldiers apprehended him and took him under custody to a communist camp near the Chinese border. Unaccustomed to the jungle climate, Diem contracted malaria, dysentery, and influenza; he later claimed that he would have died if local tribesmen had not ministered to him. Still, he fared better than his brother Khoi. When the Viet Minh seized power in September 1945, they arrested Khoi and his son, convicted them of counterrevolutionary acts, and buried them alive. Diem learned of his brother's murder while recuperating in prison. The news reinforced his hatred of the Viet Minh.

Yet if Diem saw nothing good in the government Ho had established, Ho recognized some virtues in Diem. Eager to extend the base of his support, Ho reached out to anticommunist nationalists; he especially wanted to attract Vietnam's Catholic minority, and understood that the presence of a prominent Catholic in his first coalition cabinet would go a long way toward accomplishing this goal. Therefore, in February 1946, Ho ordered Diem brought to Hanoi for medical treatment. When Diem had been restored to health, Ho summoned him to his office in Viet Minh headquarters. The conversation between the two men was explosive. Ho offered Diem the post of minister of the interior, the same job he had held under Bao Dai. Diem refused. "You are a criminal who has burned and destroyed the country, and you have held me prisoner," Diem declared. "Why did you kill my brother?" Ho protested that he "had nothing to do with your brother's death," that it had been a random killing in the "confused" postliberation environment. "When people who have been oppressed revolt, mistakes are inevitable," the Viet Minh leader noted. He suggested that Diem forget past "grievances" and "take a position of high importance in our government." Diem was not moved. "My brother and his son are only two of the hundreds who have died," he said. "How can you dare to invite me to work with you? . . . Look me in the face. Am I a man who fears?" "No," Ho replied. "You are not such a man." Diem asked if he were free to go. Ho said yes, but warned that the countryside would be hostile. "I am not a child, and will take the risks," Diem retorted. Then he walked out.[12]

In the months after Ho released him, Diem tried to organize an anti–Viet Minh movement in the north. He did not meet with much success, but proved sufficiently bothersome that Ho ordered him seized again. Diem barely eluded capture by communist soldiers until French infantry and armored divisions devastated the port of Haiphong in November 1946, thereby inaugurating the Franco–Viet Minh War and diverting Ho's attention from Diem and every other thing not directly connected with the war's outcome. As fighting spread throughout the north, Diem made the journey south to live with his brother Thuc outside of Saigon.

Safe for the moment, Diem joined with the conservative Catholic politician Nguyen Ton Hoan to found a political party, the Vietnam National Alliance, which called for Paris to accord Vietnam dominion status within the French Union, a relationship resembling the bond between Great Britain and its Commonwealth. The alliance attracted enough support to enable Diem to publish newspapers in Saigon and Hanoi, but this venture was short-lived. The French, who controlled Hanoi after driving out the Viet Minh, shut down both papers, arrested the Hanoi editor for subversion, and hired thugs to kill the editor in Saigon. Still, these efforts earned Diem public notice as a patriot who was both anticommunist and anticolonialist. That reputation made him attractive to the French as their war with the Viet Minh ground on and it became apparent that they would have to make concessions to Vietnamese nationalists if they wanted to preserve their empire in Indochina. When the French sought to establish a specious "Republic of Vietnam" with Bao Dai as its leader, they asked Diem to go to Hong Kong and convey their proposal to the emperor.

Given his prior experiences with Bao Dai and the French, Diem cannot have been enthusiastic about this mission. Nonetheless, he traveled to Hong Kong three times and tried to broker an agreement that would confer domin-ion status on Vietnam. During one visit, he met with the American consul general and asked for Washington's help in freeing his country from "French domination." The consul general was unimpressed, describing Diem to Sec-retary of State Acheson as "a nervous young man" who was "suffering from a bad cold." Diem proved even less effective at swaying Bao Dai, who told him that he was inclined to accept the terms proffered by Paris, terms under which Vietnam would enjoy only limited independence. In an effort to stiffen his former boss's spine, Diem invited several leading Vietnamese nationalists to Saigon, where they formed a "Congress of Notables" and insisted on being included in any negotiations between Bao Dai and the French. Paris rejected such demands. When Bao Dai signed an agreement that gave France control of the Republic of Vietnam's finances, military forces, and foreign policy, Diem washed his hands of the entire business and returned to his brother's house.[13]

The government established by Bao Dai and the French lacked credibility and ran into trouble at once. Bao Dai was so ashamed of what he had agreed to that he ran away to Europe to avoid being held to his commitment. The French managed to entice him back to Vietnam long enough to witness the signing of an accord between French high commissioner Emile Bollaert and the new South Vietnamese premier, Nguyen Van Xuan, a French citizen who barely spoke Vietnamese. This duty completed, Bao Dai fled again for the nightclubs of Europe, aware of how odious he had become in the eyes of Vietnamese patriots. Xuan admitted to his French sponsors that he did not believe the government he headed would succeed. When Xuan's forecast appeared to be coming true, with the Viet Minh attracting thousands of fresh recruits and anticommunist nationalists refusing to support the new regime in the south, the French took another step toward granting Vietnam self-rule in their "Bao Dai solution" of 1949.

The emperor signed another treaty, this time with French president Vin-cent Auriol at the Elysée Palace in Paris, in which the French agreed to "independence" for a "State of Vietnam" that Bao Dai would lead. Accord-ing to the Elysée Agreement, France pledged to recognize Vietnam as an associated state within the French Union and support its application for membership in the United Nations. This looked impressive on paper, but France never carried out its promised concessions, and even if it had Vietnam would have enjoyed nothing approaching independence. According to the terms of the Elysée Agreement, Paris retained control of Vietnam's military, financial, and diplomatic affairs. The Elysée Agreement proved less effective in attracting support in Vietnam than in persuading the Truman administration to subsidize France's war against the Viet Minh. Washington could now pretend that the conflict in Indochina was no longer a colonial struggle, and that the United States was not betraying its anticolonial principles by siding with the French.

Diem was not fooled by such logic-chopping. He knew the State of Vietnam was a sham and that French economic and political primacy remained unchanged. When Bao Dai, in an effort to lend his new regime a degree of legitimacy, renounced the title "emperor" in favor of "chief of state" and invited Diem to be his premier, Diem declined. Indeed, while Nguyen Ton Hoan and other nationalists decided to serve in the Bao Dai regime, reasoning that it might evolve into a more independent government, Diem made one of the most daring gestures of his career. He published a manifesto in two Saigon newspapers that argued for the creation of a new movement, aligned neither with the French nor the Viet Minh, that would force Paris to make greater concessions on the extent of Vietnamese self-government. He called for a "social revolution," for "reforms that are sweeping" to enable all Vietnamese "to live in a manner befitting the dignity of a man who is truly free." But the manifesto failed to provoke any widespread demand for reform, and Diem again joined the ranks of the *attentistes*, or "fence-sitters," waiting for a government of real sovereignty that he could serve with a clear conscience.[14]

Diem had made himself so obnoxious to the French by 1950 that it is hardly surprising that Paris was disinclined to help him when, in the spring of that year, Ho Chi Minh sentenced him to death in absentia. Diem's application to the French for protection was rejected on the grounds that no police were available. Unwilling to martyrize himself, Diem applied for permission to travel to Rome for the Holy Year celebrations at the Vatican. The French granted this request, and he set sail in August, accompanied by his brother Ngo Dinh Thuc. He was at this point forty-nine years old. With the communists poised to overrun Vietnam, he seemed destined to end his days in exile, a politically irrelevant figure fading into obscurity.

And then the Americans intervened. The first American to take an interest in Diem was Wesley Fishel, a professor of political science who met Diem during the latter's stopover in Japan. Fishel, whose professional career combined academic work in America with service for the U.S. government in Asia, was an advocate of the fashionable "third force" theory, a postwar school of thought that shaped most American discussion about third-world nationalism. Briefly, this theory called for Washington to support a third force, neither communist nor colonialist, in former colonies undergoing struggles for independence. From the perspective of Fishel and other third-force enthusiasts, colonialism was dying out; for the West to retain any influence in the developing world, it would have to ally itself with anticommunist movements of national liberation.

Diem did not go to Japan to meet Fishel. He intended to pay his respects to Cuong De and enlist him in a plot to seize control of the State of Vietnam's government. This enterprise never got off the ground, and Diem turned his attention to General Douglas MacArthur, supreme commander in postwar Japan. But MacArthur could not be bothered by a Vietnamese politician; the Korean War had broken out two months earlier and was absorbing all of the general's attention. After being rebuffed by MacArthur's staff, Diem visited with the journalist Koyashi Komatsu, whom he had befriended years earlier during Japan's occupation of Indochina. Komatsu introduced Diem to Fishel, and the two men hit it off. The professor concluded that Diem represented the third force America required in Vietnam. Diem's anticommunist and anticolonialist credentials were impeccable, and he had displayed élan in his dealings with the French, Bao Dai, and the Viet Minh. Moreover, he portrayed conditions in Vietnam as auspicious for the "free world." Diem told Fishel that the Vietnamese were "resolutely hostile to communism," but that Viet Minh propaganda profited from France's refusal to "consent to true independence." Consequently, if someone like Diem were able to present a genuinely nationalist alternative to Ho Chi Minh and the current gang of Paris's hirelings, the appeal of communism would evaporate. Fishel urged Diem to seek support for his cause in the United States.[15]

Other Americans were similarly impressed by Diem, who could hardly have timed his departure from Vietnam more perfectly to coincide with America's burgeoning interest in that country. The eruption of the Korean War shifted the focus of Washington's attention from Europe to Asia, impelling the Truman administration not only to step up its assistance to French forces battling the Viet Minh but also to recognize France's puppet Bao Dai regime as the government of Vietnam. Yet Truman and his advisers were aware of Bao Dai's lack of popular support, and were therefore responsive to information relayed by American diplomats regarding prominent Vietnamese who might assist or even replace the emperor. Diem's name appeared several times in reports sent to Washington from the embassies in Saigon and Tokyo. One cable informed Acheson that Diem had "achieved a strong reputation for nationalist views while eschewing association either with the Viet Minh or with the Viet-Nam government of Bao Dai." When word filtered back to Washington that Diem, having decided to take Fishel's advice, was on his way to America accompanied by Thuc, the State Department's Bureau of Far Eastern Affairs made arrangements for a reception for the Ngo brothers at the capital.[16]

Despite these advance notices, Diem's Washington debut was a flop. Possibly intimidated by Acting Secretary of State James Webb, Diem uncharacteristically allowed Thuc to do much of the talking in his first encounter with State Department representatives. As a consequence, Webb found Thuc the more substantial of the two men, informing the Saigon embassy that Thuc "might be [an] important figure in [the] present IC [Indochina] complex." Diem, however, struck Webb as "less precise, realistic, and authoritative. . . . He fits more into [the] mold of [a] present-day Vietnamese politician, steeped in Oriental intrigue."[17]

Diem had made a poor first impression. He and Thuc hung about Washington for a few weeks, meeting with lower-level officers in the Truman administration, but no one with real authority seemed eager to talk to them. They did, however, manage to make one invaluable contact in their subsequent travels through the United States: Cardinal Francis Spellman of New York, the most politically active prelate of his time. Spellman had a remarkable number of connections in international, national, state, and local politics. From his Manhattan chancery, known as "the Powerhouse," he communicated with presidents, congressmen, governors, and mayors, as well as officials in the Federal Bureau of Investigation (FBI) and the Central Intelligence Agency (CIA). He had studied with Thuc in Rome during the 1930s and had long been interested in Vietnam, first visiting Saigon in 1948 to organize a demonstration against the massacre of priests by the Viet Minh. Thuc introduced Diem to Spellman, and the two became friends. Spellman would later prove one of Diem's most important American advocates, but he made no immediate moves to promote Diem's cause, and the Ngo brothers, sensing that there was little hope of laying the groundwork for a Diem-led Vietnam in the United States, left America for Italy in mid-October.

They scored some political points in their European tour. Diem was able to obtain an audience with Pope Pius XII in Rome. He and Thuc continued on to Switzerland, Belgium, and France, establishing contacts with Vietnamese exile groups. Diem even arranged for a message to be delivered to Bao Dai at Cannes in which he offered to serve as the State of Vietnam's premier but insisted that he could only accept the office if it came with a broad grant of power. Bao Dai had a lackey inform Diem that the matter was "under consideration." It was a polite thumbs-down.[18]

After this latest stillborn attempt to fulfill Vietnam's nationalist aspirations, Thuc returned to Saigon. Diem, however, made the momentous decision to try his luck with the U.S. State Department again. The reasons for his choice are unclear. Perhaps he felt the Americans could pressure Bao Dai into offering him a cabinet post. Perhaps he recognized that America would soon surpass France as the chief Western power in Vietnam, and that any anticommunist Vietnamese hoping to compete with Ho would need American backing. Or he may have concluded that he had nothing to lose. He was marked for death in his native land and reviled in Paris. What could it hurt to give the Americans another try? In any event, Diem was back in the United States before the year was out. This time, he enjoyed greater success.

Robert Hoey, the State Department's officer in charge of Vietnam-Cambodia-Laos affairs, consented to give Diem an interview in mid-January 1951, and Diem seized the opportunity masterfully, portraying the Indochina conflict in a fashion calculated to impress an American policymaker striving to cope with the seemingly unmanageable torrent of events in Asia. First, he portrayed Ho Chi Minh and Mao Zedong as working cheek by jowl to communize Indochina, thereby confirming American views that communism was monolithic and that the centuries of antagonism between Vietnamese and Chinese did not matter in the context of the present East-West struggle. Such reductive notions would later give rise to the "domino theory," which held that if one nation fell to communism, surrounding countries would inevitably topple, performing with the uniformity of dominoes. According to this theory, U.S. intervention in Vietnam was justified not so much because of Vietnam's strategic or economic importance but because failure to intervene would produce a domino effect in neighboring nations. Second, Diem insisted that France's "Bao Dai solution" was all but handing Indochina to the Viet Minh. Only a Vietnamese leader who had not collaborated with either the French or the communists could succeed in forming a government to rival that of Ho.

Diem's persistence paid off. He was able to arrange a meeting with Acheson, who came armed with Webb's earlier evaluation and was prepared to dismiss Diem as readily as had his subordinate. Diem, however, surprised Acheson. The secretary noted in a postmeeting memorandum that Diem "spoke with much more balance than heretofore." While not a ringing endorsement from Truman's top cabinet officer, this indicated that Diem had begun to catch the attention of elite policymakers. He settled in for a lengthy stay in the United States.[19]

Several Americans were willing to furnish Diem with living quarters while he lobbied for support, notably Cardinal Spellman, who offered Diem lodging at the Maryknoll seminary in Lakewood, New Jersey. Diem accepted. For three years, he lived as Spellman's guest in Lakewood and at another seminary in Ossining, New York. Spellman saw to it that Diem was introduced to figures in Catholic and right-wing circles, among them Edmund Walsh, head of Georgetown University's foreign service program, and the millionaire Joseph Kennedy. It is unclear whether Diem met Joe McCarthy, but Spellman, Walsh, and Kennedy were all friends of the Wisconsin Republican and definitely would have informed McCarthy about Diem's efforts to enlist U.S. patronage. Apart from his rabid anticommunism and repeated insistence that the Cold War would be decided in its Asian theater rather than in Europe, McCarthy's Catholicism would have predisposed him in Diem's favor.

Diem's Catholic connections were vital to his support in the United States. American Catholics provided him with his most loyal constituency. One historian concludes that "Diem's Catholic faith was his most positive political attribute in this country, for it was the only thing about him that did not seem irredeemably foreign to America's parochial leaders." Certainly, U.S. policymakers understood little about the political situation in postwar Vietnam: there were no authorities on Vietnam at the State Department; no classes on Vietnamese culture or history were offered at any American university; no published works on Vietnam in English were still in print. Most Americans could not begin to sort out the multitude of factions jockeying for power in Diem's country, but they could appreciate that his religion made him incapable of harboring communist sympathies, and Diem made considerable capital of his Catholicism as evidence of his commitment to America's cause in the Cold War.[20]

But Diem did not restrict his networking to conservative Catholics on what was already becoming known as the "lunatic fringe." Like a good lobbyist, he sought to broaden the base of his support, reaching out to figures ordinarily at odds with the likes of Spellman and McCarthy. Diem recognized that his proposals had wide appeal, that America's red scare touched every shade of the political spectrum, and that progressives—and even socialists—would give him a respectful hearing. While Diem lived as a ward of Spellman's diocese in the Maryknoll seminaries, he engaged in a speaking tour at eastern and midwestern universities, arguing that Vietnam could only be saved for the "free world" if America sponsored a government of Vietnamese nationalists like himself who were neither aligned with the Viet Minh nor compromised by collaboration with the French.

Wesley Fishel, who joined the faculty of Michigan State University (MSU) in 1951, got Diem appointed as a consultant to the school's Governmental Research Bureau, thereby providing a forum from which to promulgate Diem's vision of an independent, noncommunist Vietnam. There was no university in America more dedicated than Michigan State to working with the federal government to wage the Cold War. John Hannah, the university's president, pioneered the use of university assistance abroad, cooperating with the Truman and Eisenhower administrations to promote economic development in third-world countries threatened by communism. When Diem arrived on campus in 1951, MSU was administering government-sponsored technical assistance programs in Colombia and the Ryukyuan Islands and preparing a similar venture for Brazil. Diem's appeals for American aid in modernizing Vietnam's agriculture, public administration, business management, and other concerns were enthusiastically received. Shortly after Diem's recruitment as consultant, he and Fishel began collaborating on a proposal for a technical assistance project for Vietnam, a project that would become the most ambitious of all of Michigan State's nation-building efforts.

Diem befriended many American academics. In addition to his relationship with Fishel, he forged ties to I. Milton Sacks, a political scientist at Brandeis University who had worked for the State Department, and Raymond de Jaegher, regent of Seton Hall University's Far East Institute. Diem's capacity to present himself as representative of Vietnam's third force—neither communist nor colonialist, favoring national self-sufficiency through social reform rather than violent class struggle—helped him win a following in the predominantly liberal academic community. He was also fortunate that the early Cold War years were the era of the "action intellectual," when political scientists, economists, and other scholars strove to translate their ideas into policy rather than generating knowledge for knowledge's sake in an ivory tower. Professors like Fishel, Sacks, and de Jaegher seized on Diem as the vehicle through which they could steer a decolonizing Vietnam away from communism toward a liberal, democratic, and capitalist future.

Left-wing American political activists and journalists also found themselves drawn to this Vietnamese statesman who seemed such a perfect mix of anticommunism and anticolonialism. One of the first to commit himself to Diem was Peter White, a liberal Catholic reporter and public-relations expert who met Diem in 1950. White introduced Diem to his cousin Chris-

topher Emmet, who had been at the vanguard of antifascist and anticommunist work for two decades and who, like White, saw Diem as an ideal
candidate to galvanize the latent third force in Vietnam. Emmet's position
as secretary of the American Friends of Captive Nations lent his words rare
authority when he wrote on Diem's behalf to the House Foreign Affairs
Committee. Diem, Emmet affirmed, was "one of the greatest of the Indo-
Chinese anti-communist leaders." Other Cold War liberals impressed by
Diem were the journalists Gouverneur Paulding, Gary MacEoin, and Sol
Sanders; these and other newsmen struck up friendships with Diem in 1950
and 1951 and later published articles lauding his accomplishments in such
left-of-center magazines as the *Reporter* and the *New Leader*.[21]

It was not until Diem's final months in the United States that he secured
the support of some of Washington's most influential figures. First was
Supreme Court Justice William O. Douglas, who heard of Diem while travel-
ing through Asia in the summer of 1952 and made arrangements to meet
with him after returning to America in the fall. Diem and Douglas talked
over lunch at New York's Yale Club, and the justice found Diem's views on
independent nationalism, anticommunism, and social reform consistent with
American foreign policy goals in Asia. When Douglas published *North from
Malaya*, an account of his reconnaissance of the Far Eastern front lines of the
Cold War, he informed readers that Diem was "a hero, . . . revered by the
Vietnamese." Douglas introduced Diem to John McCormack, then Demo-
cratic whip and later majority leader and speaker of the House. He also
brought Diem to the attention of the Central Intelligence Agency; at an
April 1953 Washington cocktail party, Douglas took aside Robert Amory,
deputy director at the CIA, and told him, "You know who's going to fix you
up in Vietnam? He's here in this country now—that's Ngo Dinh Diem."
Most important, Douglas orchestrated the first meeting between Diem and
Senator Mike Mansfield, Democrat of Montana.[22]

Mansfield proved a valuable ally for Diem because he had been a professor
of Asian history before his election to Congress. Journalists and government
officials therefore tended to accord Mansfield's views on Indochina greater
weight than they did those of other legislators. On 7 May 1953 Douglas
invited Mansfield to a luncheon at the Supreme Court building, where Diem
was to be guest of honor. Douglas informed Mansfield beforehand that Diem
was "the kind of Asian we can live with." The luncheon was also attended by
Senator John F. Kennedy, Cardinal Spellman, and Representative Clement
Zablocki, soon to become chairman of the House Foreign Affairs Committee.[23]

Diem gave a compelling performance before his audience, regaling them with an account of the 1946 meeting in which he called Ho Chi Minh a criminal to his face. He also played the third-force card to great effect. "The trouble in Vietnam," he declared, was that there was "no rallying point between the communists and the French." He maintained that he could be that rallying point, that an independent Vietnam under his leadership would "satisfy the Vietnamese population that they have something to fight for." But he needed American help to create that third way. Kennedy, who had toured Indochina and delivered speeches critical of French policy, asked Diem a few questions, while Mansfield took notes. At the end of the meeting, Diem announced his intention to leave for Paris, where, he claimed, he hoped to "find understanding among . . . groups who had begun to be . . . resentful of France's failure in Indochina." Mansfield told the journalist Don Oberdorfer years later that, after the luncheon in Douglas's chambers, he was "left with the feeling that if anyone could hold . . . Vietnam, it was somebody like Ngo Dinh Diem."[24]

As he had promised the guests at Douglas's luncheon, Diem left for France in late May 1953. His lobbying efforts there, however, were unsuccessful. Members of the Vietnamese community in Paris told CIA operative Chester Cooper that Diem made "a very bad impression," that he was "obscure" and "murky," and that his ideas were "obsolete." One Vietnamese intellectual found Diem "stupid." Americans responded more enthusiastically to Diem's appeals than his own countrymen did.[25]

Yet this turned out to be all the advantage Diem would need to win power, for events in Vietnam soon increased America's participation in the war wracking that nation. By mid-1953, the Viet Minh dominated two-thirds of Vietnam, while French control had been reduced to enclaves around Hanoi, Haiphong, and Saigon. Over 74,000 French troops had been killed or wounded since the onset of hostilities, and another 190,000 were bogged down in defensive positions that restricted their ability to seek out the enemy. Lacking the airplanes, tanks, and artillery of the French, the Viet Minh, led by a self-taught military genius named Vo Nguyen Giap, learned to conserve their forces and attack only when the French were vulnerable, preferably in ambushes that caught the colonial overlords with their guard down.

There seemed to be a ray of hope for the "free world" when General Henri Navarre took command of France's army in Indochina. The Eisenhower administration invested $300 million in the so-called Navarre plan, a strategy for luring Giap into a set-piece battle that would allow the French to employ their superior weaponry. Navarre sent several French battalions to an outpost on the Laotian border called Dien Bien Phu, and Giap rose to the bait; instead of ordering mass assaults, however, he had his troops build a series of trenches to choke off the outer French strongholds one by one. In addition, the Viet Minh were able to emplace over twenty 105-millimeter cannon overlooking the French defenses, escaping allied aerial detection through camouflage. Navarre underestimated the Viet Minh's capacity to transport heavy artillery up the hills surrounding Dien Bien Phu and overestimated the ability of French air interdiction to shut off the flow of supplies to Giap's front-line troops. The result was that Giap managed to assemble an attacking force that approximated the three-to-one ratio considered necessary for a successful attack against a fortified position. Rather than affording Navarre an opportunity to trick the Viet Minh into standing and fighting, Dien Bien Phu became a deathtrap. Within weeks, the defensive perimeter of the French, originally fifteen miles around, shrank to the size of Yankee Stadium.

Clearly, France was on its way out of Vietnam. Just as clearly, the Eisenhower administration had no intention of allowing Ho Chi Minh to seize the country. If France could no longer continue in its role of principal Western combatant in Indochina, the United States would assume that role, and Americans would decide who among the crop of anticommunist Vietnamese would lead the opposition to the Viet Minh. It was unlikely to be Bao Dai, long an object of ridicule among U.S. policymakers. Anticommunist politicians like Phan Huy Quat, Tran Van Huu, and Nguyen Van Tam were hardly the toast of the town in Washington, having conducted their campaigns for high office either in their native land or with Bao Dai on the French Riviera. Diem, however, had courted American political, academic, and religious leaders. He had been clever or lucky enough to devote his time to building a power base in the nation that would prove to matter most. Joseph Buttinger, America's leading authority on Vietnam for decades, recalls that "Washington never considered supporting another man. The explanation is simple: Diem was the only Vietnamese leader who had made himself known in the United States." And Americans liked what they saw. Diem was as anticommunist as Joe McCarthy, as pious as Cardinal Spellman, and untainted by collaboration with colonialism. In short, as Douglas remarked, Diem was "the kind of Asian we can live with." Whether he was the kind the Vietnamese could live with was another matter.[26]

Notes

1. Dean Acheson, *Present at the Creation: My Years in the State Department* (New York: Norton, 1967), 360.

2. Joseph R. McCarthy, "The Internal Communist Menace," in *A History of Our Time: Readings on Postwar America*, 4th ed., ed. William H. Chafe and Harvard Sitkoff (New York: Oxford University Press, 1995), 62–64.

3. Walter LaFeber, *America, Russia, and the Cold War, 1945–1992*, 7th ed. (New York, McGraw-Hill, 1993), 96; National Security Council Paper No. 68 (NSC-68), 1950, in *Major Problems in the History of American Foreign Relations*, vol. 2, *Since 1914*, 5th ed., ed. Dennis Merrill and Thomas G. Paterson (Boston: Houghton Mifflin, 2000), 223–226; NSC-68 advocate cited in LaFeber, *America, Russia, and the Cold War*, 98.

4. Truman cited in Loren Baritz, *Backfire* (New York: Ballantine, 1985), 55.

5. Robert Shaplen, *The Lost Revolution* (New York: Harper & Row, 1965), 104; Frances FitzGerald, *Fire in the Lake: The Vietnamese and the Americans in Vietnam* (New York: Vintage, 1972), 122–123; Hilaire du Berrier, *Background to Betrayal: The Tragedy of Vietnam* (Belmont, Mass.: Western Islands Press, 1965), 29; John Mecklin, *Mission in Torment: An Intimate Account of the U.S. Role in Vietnam* (Garden City, N.Y.: Doubleday, 1965), 31; Neil L. Jamieson, *Understanding Vietnam* (Berkeley: University of California Press, 1993), 234.

6. Bao Dai cited in McClintock to Dulles, 27 June 1954, file 751G.00/6-2754, RG 59.

7. Bernard B. Fall, *The Two Viet-Nams: A Political and Military Analysis*, 2nd rev. ed. (New York: Praeger, 1967), 231.

8. Thuc cited in Anthony Bouscaren, *The Last of the Mandarins: Diem of Vietnam* (Pittsburgh: Duquesne University Press, 1965), 3.

9. Diem cited in Shaplen, *Lost Revolution*, 107.

10. Diem cited in Robert Shaplen, "A Reporter in Vietnam," *New Yorker*, 22 September 1962, 106.

11. Ellen J. Hammer, *A Death in November: America in Vietnam, 1963* (New York: Dutton, 1987), 51.

12. Diem and Ho cited in Marguerite Higgins, *Our Vietnam Nightmare* (New York: McGraw-Hill, 1965), 157–158; Stanley Karnow, *Vietnam: A History* (New York: Viking, 1983), 232–233.

13. The Consul General at Hong Kong to the Secretary of State, 30 December 1947, *FRUS, 1947* (Washington, D.C.: Government Printing Office, 1972), 6:152–155.

14. Diem cited in Edward Miller, "Vision, Power, and Agency: The Ascent of Ngo Dinh Diem, 1945–54," *Journal of Southeast Asian Studies* 35 (October 2004): 440.

15. Diem cited in John Ernst, *Forging a Fateful Alliance: Michigan State University and the Vietnam War* (East Lansing: Michigan State University Press, 1998), 9.

16. The Chargé at Saigon to the Secretary of State, 23 June 1950, *FRUS, 1950* (Washington, D.C.: Government Printing Office, 1979), 6:829.

17. The Acting Secretary of State to the Legation at Saigon, 28 September 1950, *FRUS, 1950*, 6:885–886.

18. Bao Dai cited in "Conversation with Ngo Dinh Diem," 15 January 1951, Records of the Philippine and Southeast Asian Division, Country Files, 1923–1953, Box 7, file 751G.00/1-1551, RG 59.

19. The Secretary of State to the Legation in Saigon, 16 January 1951, *FRUS, 1951* (Washington, D.C.: Government Printing Office, 1977), 7:348.

20. Thomas D. Boettcher, *Vietnam: The Valor and the Sorrow* (Boston: Little, Brown, 1985), 107.

21. Emmet cited in Joseph G. Morgan, *Vietnam Lobby: The American Friends of Vietnam, 1955–1975* (Chapel Hill: University of North Carolina Press, 1997), 4–5.

22. William O. Douglas, *North from Malaya* (Garden City, N.Y.: Doubleday, 1953), 180–181; Douglas cited in Dana B. Larsen, "In Search of the Third Force: The American Lobby for Ngo Dinh Diem" (master's thesis, University of Arizona, 1985), 62.

23. Douglas cited in David Halberstam, *The Best and the Brightest* (New York: Random House, 1969), 147.

24. Memorandum of Conversation by Edmund A. Gullion of the Policy Planning Staff, 7 May 1953, *FRUS, 1952–1954* (Washington, D.C.: Government Printing Office, 1982), 8:553–554; Mansfield cited in Don Oberdorfer, *Senator Mansfield* (Washington D.C.: Smithsonian Books, 2003), 117.

25. Vietnamese exiles cited in Chester L. Cooper, *The Lost Crusade: America in Vietnam* (New York: Dodd, Meade, 1970), 122–124.

26. Joseph Buttinger, *Vietnam: A Dragon Embattled*, vol. 2 (London: Pall Mall, 1967), 850.

CHAPTER TWO

~

"Let Our People Go!"
The Geneva Accords and Passage to Freedom

On 7 May 1954 the last defenders of "Strongpoint Isabelle" in the valley of Dien Bien Phu gave way under the human-wave assaults of the Viet Minh. The siege of the supposedly impregnable French garrison had lasted fifty-five days and was distinguished by ruthlessness uncommon even by the standards of what citizens of the Fourth Republic had come to call "the dirty war." Over two thousand French soldiers were killed and over six thousand wounded. As one historian notes, "It was the end, indeed. The end of the Indochina War. The end of France as a colonial power." It was also a beginning. On 8 May, less than twenty-four hours after Dien Bien Phu fell, the "Indochina Phase" of an international conference meeting in Geneva, Switzerland, began. The near simultaneity of these two events—one occurring on a battlefield in northeast Vietnam and the other around a table at the old League of Nations building—confirmed President Dwight Eisenhower's retrospective judgment that "the Geneva Conference could not have begun or been conducted under worse circumstances."[1]

If the United States had had its way, there would not even have been an "Indochina Phase" to the Geneva Conference. America had suffered a diplomatic defeat in this regard at the Berlin Conference held earlier in the year. In this, the first meeting of the World War II "Big Four" allies since 1949, representatives from France, Great Britain, the Soviet Union, and the United States had gathered in an attempt to secure Germany's reunification and the "liberation" of Austria. No progress toward either objective was made, which hardly came as a surprise to Eisenhower and his fellow cold warriors, most of whom accepted the division of Europe as permanent. More

37

distressing, from Washington's perspective, was the fact that French foreign minister Georges Bidault succumbed to Soviet pressure and agreed to put Indochina on the agenda for the Korean Political Conference, scheduled for the upcoming April in Geneva. Secretary of State John Foster Dulles, who represented the United States at Berlin, protested this capitulation, insisting that "any *suggestion* of Indochina negotiations" would give the Viet Minh an incentive to intensify their military efforts.[2]

Bidault countered that if France refused to negotiate, the government of Joseph Laniel would topple, and its replacement would probably reject French membership in the European Defense Community (EDC). The EDC was a subject of overriding importance in America's foreign policy, a means of rearming West Germany so as to provide the North Atlantic Treaty Organization (NATO) with troops to resist a potential Soviet attack on Western Europe. The French executive had indicated that France would join the EDC as early as 1952, but Parliament had yet to ratify membership, and Dulles did not want to do anything to jeopardize this common European military force. Consequently, Dulles had no choice but to join other members of the "Big Four" in announcing the Geneva itinerary in a joint communiqué, although he warned Washington that "[t]he prospect of a conference on Indo-China will increase the communist effort for [a] knock-out this season."[3]

Dulles's prediction proved accurate. As the Viet Minh artillery barrages and infantry assaults on Dien Bien Phu ground down the French defenses, it became apparent that General Vo Nguyen Giap was indeed looking for a knockout during the "Korea phase" of the Geneva Conference, before the delegates moved on to Indochina. French officials tried to avert defeat by asking for American air strikes against Viet Minh positions surrounding the garrison, but Eisenhower turned down these requests after objections by the Joint Chiefs of Staff, congressional representatives, and the British government. Without U.S. intervention, the paratroops and foreign legionnaires defending Dien Bien Phu were doomed. One day short of the ninth anniversary of V-E Day, they surrendered. The following morning, Bidault was expected to represent French interests as the "Indochina Phase" of the Geneva Conference began. Understandably, Washington had little faith in its ally's determination to withstand communist pressure for concessions.

French burnout, however, played into Ngo Dinh Diem's hands. Contrary to the claims of some historians, Diem was *not* the only candidate for premier in Bao Dai's tottering Republic of Vietnam. Numerous Vietnamese politicians, some with excellent credentials, were in France angling for the job. Among these aspirants, Phan Huy Quat seemed especially qualified. In 1939 he had been one of the founders of the Dai Viet Quoc Dan Dang, or Nationalist Party of Greater Vietnam. This organization, along with being virulently anti-French, was no less virulently anticommunist, which was why Ho Chi Minh outlawed the Dai Viet and forced its followers into exile in South Vietnam. The Dai Viet declined in the south, but still attracted the loyalties of many civil servants, among whom Quat was most venerated. Unlike Diem, Quat had considerable experience in government; in the early 1950s, he held several cabinet posts, including minister of defense. Had Bao Dai been free to choose, there is little doubt that he would have selected Quat over Diem.

But the emperor was no fool. He knew that Diem was popular among many in the American political, intelligence, and diplomatic communities, and that by appointing Diem he was likely to obtain U.S. aid. The fall of Dien Bien Phu signaled the end of French predominance in Indochina, meaning that Bao Dai had to find another great-power patron to finance his playboy lifestyle. As he recalls in his memoirs, Diem "had known some Americans who admired his intransigence. . . . Washington would not spare him its support." The fact that Bao Dai chose Diem's brother Ngo Dinh Luyen to be his personal representative in dealings with the U.S. delegation at Geneva made his intentions unmistakable. Taking the hint, Dulles cabled the Eisenhower administration's approval from Washington.[4]

Diem's induction as premier was as portentous as the event warranted. According to Bao Dai, Diem at first played hard to get, declining the post and indicating that he planned to enter a religious order. But the emperor's appeals to his patriotic duty overcame all qualms, and Diem agreed to serve. As a price for taking office, though, Diem demanded "full powers" over all aspects of the South Vietnamese government, military, and economy. Bao Dai conceded. He then produced a crucifix and had Diem swear before his God to defend Vietnam against the communists.[5]

To a man, French policymakers were appalled by Diem's appointment. Guy LaChambre, minister for the Associated States of Vietnam, Laos, and Cambodia, reacted with dismay to the news that the emperor favored a Diem-led government, noting Diem's "almost total lack of professional competence." Maurice DeJean, former French commissioner general in Indochina, characterized Diem as "too narrow, too rigid, [and] too unworldly . . . to have any chance of creating an effective government." Paul Ely, DeJean's successor, concurred. "Ngo Dinh Diem will probably prove ineffectual in rallying elements here," Ely remarked to the U.S. chargé in Saigon. Pierre Mendès-France, who replaced Joseph Laniel as French premier midway through the Geneva Conference, was even more opposed to Diem, informing

U.S. ambassador Douglas Dillon that he "expected to have considerable difficulty with the new Vietnam government." "Diem is a fanatic," Mendès-France declared. He considered Bao Dai's decision "most unfortunate." Diem's installation as premier made plain that French influence in Indochina was eroding and that South Vietnam, like South Korea and Nationalist China, was on the verge of becoming an American client state.[6]

Although Diem and his Washington backers faced a formidable task in trying to create some order out of the chaos prevailing in Diem's country, they obtained a surprisingly favorable outcome at the Geneva Conference. On 20 July 1954 a truce was signed by representatives of the French high command and the Viet Minh, bringing hostilities to a halt. The agreement fixed a demarcation line along the 17th parallel, dividing Vietnam into two temporary political entities. It moreover established provisions for elections to be held in both North and South Vietnam in 1956, with reunification to follow. Both signatories agreed that they would be bound by the results of these elections, whether they resulted in the formation of a socialist government or a capitalist democracy. In addition to the truce between France and the Viet Minh, a separate final declaration "took note" of the various elements of the agreement. This entire package came to be known as the Geneva Accords. The American delegate declined to sign the accords, but Washington agreed not to use force to violate them and to support the principle of self-determination throughout Indochina.

The accords did not reflect battlefield reality. Giap's forces were close to achieving the kind of military dominance that would render any negotiations over the future of the country superfluous. The Viet Minh were entitled, at least, to partition south of the 17th parallel, so that the ancient capital of Hue fell within their lines, and nationwide elections in six months rather than two years. The outcome of any such elections was a foregone conclusion. Eisenhower himself concedes in his memoirs that "had elections been held at the time, . . . eighty percent of the population would have voted for the communist Ho Chi Minh as their leader." Yet the Eisenhower administration and Diem secured advantageous terms because all of the great powers negotiating at Geneva had agendas to fulfill that meshed perfectly with American interests.[7]

The Korean War had ended just the year before. That conflict had cost China over a million casualties. Zhou Enlai, head of the Communist Chinese delegation at Geneva, had one all-absorbing objective: to keep the United

States from intervening again in a country on China's southern border. He was willing to accommodate France in its desire to retain part of Vietnam, reasoning that a few thousand exhausted French soldiers were better than another expeditionary force of gung-ho Americans. Moreover, it was in China's interests to keep Vietnam divided; the Chinese and the Vietnamese had a history of mutual hatred dating back to the third century BC. In addition, the People's Republic was only five years old in 1954, and Zhou was anxious for his nation to be taken seriously in international affairs. Stung by American propaganda that depicted the Chinese as incapable of understanding the finer points of diplomacy, Zhou intended to use the Geneva Conference as an opportunity to display China's moderation and maturity. Geneva was Communist China's debut on the world stage, and Zhou was not going to allow Viet Minh demands to spoil it for his country.

The Soviet Union was likewise in an accommodating mood at Geneva. Joseph Stalin had died in March 1953, and his successors, Georgi Malenkov and Nikita Khrushchev, were making every effort to distance themselves from the departed tyrant's foreign policies. It was during these first post-Stalin years that the word "détente" made its appearance in the speeches of Soviet policymakers, as Malenkov and Khrushchev urged a peaceful settlement of the Korean conflict and less rancorous negotiations over the future of Europe. The Geneva Conference presented an occasion for the USSR to demonstrate its good faith in pursuing what Khrushchev would later term "peaceful coexistence" with the United States. More important than concern for improved superpower relations was the Soviets' desire to keep France out of the EDC. French politicians were already ambivalent about joining, given the loss of French military sovereignty that would result, and the USSR wanted to encourage France in its belief that the EDC was unnecessary, that the Soviets posed no threat. Hence, Moscow was prepared to support Paris's efforts to retain part of its empire in Indochina; this would be a small price to pay for defeat of the EDC.

Given the positions of the two communist superpowers, what appeared to Western delegates at Geneva as a united front comprising the Soviet Union, China, and the Viet Minh was in fact an unstable alliance in which the Soviets and Chinese were willing to sell out their junior partner as soon as the opportunity presented itself. In accordance with their own national interests, China and the Soviet Union forced the Viet Minh to conclude an agreement that allowed France to cover its defeat with the fig leaf of a diplomatic "draw." The Viet Minh were not capable of carrying on the war without external sources of supply, and Zhou and Soviet foreign minister

Vyacheslav Molotov let Viet Minh delegate Pham Van Dong know that these sources would be cut off if the Viet Minh did not accede to France's terms. Under protest, Dong complied and left Geneva howling about having been "double crossed."[8]

Despite the felicitous outcome at Geneva, Diem ordered the South Vietnamese delegation not to sign the accords and denounced the French for having signed them without prior consultation with his government. "We cannot recognize the seizure by Soviet China . . . of over half of our national territory," Diem proclaimed the day after the conference concluded. "We can neither concur in the brutal enslavement of millions of compatriots." This was not the posture of a man aware that he had just been handed an unmerited diplomatic grand slam. Still, Diem's attitude was pleasing to Washington. The premier of South Vietnam clearly had no intention of making concessions to the communists. Dulles warned the U.S. embassy in Saigon not to "make it appear that Ngo Dinh Diem is in our pocket or that we are irrevocably committed to him." Nonetheless, Dulles noted, "we do believe the kind of thing he stands for is a necessary ingredient for success."[9]

Success in knitting together a unified state in South Vietnam would require more ingredients than rock-ribbed anticommunism. Diem's country was in disarray after eight years of war. The Viet Minh had paralyzed communications by blowing up railroad tracks and obstructing roads, canals, and rivers. Much of the arable land lay uncultivated. Numerous towns and villages were under Viet Minh control, and bandits roamed freely in the countryside. Thousands of peasants who had fled their farms because of the fighting found themselves without work in the cities. The government was bankrupt. Roughly one quarter of the Vietnamese National Army (VNA) had deserted.

The ceremony surrounding the new premier's arrival in Saigon did nothing to inspire confidence. Bao Dai wrote a check for one million piasters to pay for demonstrations of support for Diem when his plane touched down at Tan Son Nhut Airport on 26 June 1954, but only a meager crowd turned out, including a few hundred Catholics, some French officials, a handful of foreign diplomats, and some representatives of the American embassy who showed up out of pity. They probably wished they had stayed home when they saw Diem step out of the plane, glance at the acres of barbed wire the French had strung to protect their aircraft from Viet Minh attacks, and trot briskly across the runway to a waiting limousine. He gave a wave to the well-wishers, but could not manage a smile. After he ducked into the back of the car, a curtain was drawn across his window. The Saigonese who congregated alongside the Rue Général de Gaulle to get a peep at Diem as he rode to the Norodom Palace were disappointed.

Colonel Edward Lansdale, chief of the CIA's covert-action Saigon Military Mission, watched as the limousine sped past, surrounded by a police phalanx of motorcycles, and felt that Diem had blown an opportunity to generate enthusiasm about his arrival. "Diem should have ridden into the city slowly in an open car," Lansdale wrote years later, "or even have walked to provide a focus for the affection his people . . . had been waiting to bestow on him." In fact, Diem had deliberately set the tone of his regime from the outset. He was less concerned with commanding affection than respect. He had never been a man of the people and did not intend to become one now, after twenty-one years of refusal to compromise had finally borne fruit. Any American expectations that Diem would play the role of baby-kissing popular leader ought to have been dispelled by his swift, guarded entry into South Vietnam's capital. Any notions that he would serve either Washington or Paris as a figurehead should likewise have evaporated during his first public address after returning to Saigon. "In this critical situation, I will act decisively," Diem declared. "A total revolution will be implemented in every facet of the organization and life of the nation." Whatever else could be said of the Diem experiment at this early stage, it was not going to be business as usual.[10]

In addition to its other problems, the new Diem regime had to cope with an influx of refugees from North Vietnam that threatened to capsize the south's economy. Article 14(d) of the Geneva Accords stipulated that "any civilians residing in a district controlled by one party who wish to go and live in the zone assigned to the other party shall be permitted and helped to do so." Delegates at Geneva paid little attention to the logistics of population resettlement, assuming it would be a minor matter. Diem himself did not expect more than ten thousand refugees. General Ely believed that roughly thirty thousand landlords and businessmen would move south, and proclaimed that he would take responsibility for the transport of all Vietnamese who decided to rejoin territory controlled by the French Union. Mendès-France's government planned to provide for about fifty thousand displaced persons.[11]

These prognoses were woefully off the mark. As news about the possibility for relocation filtered throughout the north, thousands of mostly Catholic fugitives descended on Hanoi and the port of Haiphong, both of which were still in French hands. The refugees overloaded the services made available by

Refugees from North Vietnam, 16 November 1954.
Bettman/CORBIS.

the French and caused confusion as they fought over shelter, food, medicine, and places on the ships and planes that were leaving for Saigon. By early August 1954, over two hundred thousand refugees were awaiting evacuation from Hanoi and Haiphong. The French navy and air force, unprepared to deal with so many people, asked Washington for assistance, and the U.S. Defense Department ordered the navy to mobilize a task force for evacuation action. Task Force 90, under the command of Rear Admiral Lorenzo Sabin, was accordingly inaugurated. American servicemen renovated cargo vessels and tank carriers to accommodate the thousands of people who would be crowded onto them. Frequently, they made these adjustments at sea as ships steamed from Subic Bay in the Philippines toward Haiphong.

The first American ship to participate in the mass migration left Haiphong on 17 August with two thousand refugees for a one-thousand-mile, three-day journey south. Until the free movement period prescribed by the accords elapsed, French and U.S. ships departed as fast as the refugees could be loaded aboard, making over five hundred trips in three hundred days, and the United States provided emergency food, medical care, clothing, and shelter at reception centers in Saigon and elsewhere. In all, about one million Vietnamese moved from north to south in what the U.S. Navy called Operation Passage to Freedom.

The religious balance of Vietnam was drastically altered by the exodus. Before Passage to Freedom, most of Vietnam's Catholics lived north of the 17th parallel; afterward, the majority lived south of it. One of Diem's principal objections to the Geneva Accords had been that they denied him the Catholic districts of North Vietnam, which would have been a basic source of his support. Yet Passage to Freedom provided a solution to this problem. Entire northern Catholic provinces packed up en masse and relocated to the south. By 1956 the Diocese of Saigon had more Catholics than Paris or Rome. Of Vietnam's approximately 1,450,000 Catholics, over 1,000,000 lived in the south, fifty-five percent of them refugees from the north.

Many of America's most prestigious Catholic voluntary agencies worked with the U.S. and French governments to handle this upheaval in human geography. The National Catholic Welfare Conference (NCWC) and Catholic Relief Services (CRS) contributed over $35,000,000 and sent hundreds of workers to South Vietnam. American churchmen like New York's Monsignor Joseph Harnett spent over a year in Saigon and the surrounding countryside, supervising the establishment and maintenance of orphanages, hospitals, schools, and churches. CRS volunteers, under Harnett's direction, fed rice and warm milk to one hundred thousand refugees daily. Tens of thousands of blankets donated by American Catholic organizations served as beds for refugees sleeping on the ground, as temporary walls in mass housing facilities, or as roofs over refugees' heads when the monsoon rains lashed the reception camps.

Washington reaped propaganda benefits from the tidal wave of humanity flooding into South Vietnam. It seemed graphic confirmation of the allure of the "free world," especially since migration from south to north was, comparatively speaking, minimal. The list of American reporters who filed stories on Passage to Freedom read like an honor roll of 1950s journalism: Tillman Durdin and Peggy Durdin of the *New York Times*, Homer Bigart and Marguerite Higgins of the *New York Herald Tribune*, John Mecklin of *Time-Life*, and John Roderick of the Associated Press all did a tour of duty in Vietnam and sent back stirring accounts of the refugees' flight from oppression. In a representative piece, *Life* called the exodus "a tragedy of almost nightmarish proportions. . . . Many [refugees] went without food or water or medicine for days, sustained only by the faith in their hearts."[12]

Such hyperbole paled in comparison to the treatment accorded Passage to Freedom in the American Catholic press. The operation received front-page coverage in America's diocesan newspapers, and the coverage was invariably lurid. Many features included accounts of communist atrocities against refugees. The San Francisco *Monitor* told of a priest whom the Viet Minh "beat with guns until insensible and then buried alive in a ditch" before his own parishioners. The Milwaukee *Catholic Herald Citizen* described how two priests chained together by the Viet Minh "suffered atrocious and endless agony. . . . They were devoured by sores and swollen with beriberi and left without any care." *Our Sunday Visitor* called the "persecution" in Vietnam "the worst in history" and charged the Viet Minh with "child murder and cannibalism." The Newark *Advocate* ran an editorial cartoon titled "Let Our People Go!" that depicted hordes of Vietnamese struggling to break through a blood-drenched barbed-wire fence. Other Catholic papers published reports of the Viet Minh blowing up churches, torturing children, and machine-gunning elderly refugees. So grisly were the reports, and so obtrusive the religious significance of the atrocities, that a treatment of Passage to Freedom published forty years after the operation's conclusion proclaimed that "the people of Vietnam became a crucified people and their homeland a national Golgotha."[13]

While many American reporters filed stories on Passage to Freedom, the one whose account of the exodus really moved Vietnam to the forefront of public concern in the United States was a twenty-eight-year-old Catholic navy doctor named Tom Dooley who served with Task Force 90 from August 1954 to January 1955. After he returned to the United States, he published a narrative of his experiences, first in condensed form in *Reader's Digest* and then in a book titled *Deliver Us from Evil* that, in the words of one historian, "quite literally located Vietnam on the new world map for millions of Americans." *Deliver Us from Evil* became the great early best seller on Vietnam. It was one of the most influential works of propaganda produced during the Cold War, and the most significant in terms of cementing America's alliance with Diem.[14]

Dooley seemed an unlikely anticommunist crusader when he joined Task Force 90. Born into St. Louis high society, he had relied more on family connections than hard work to get through medical school, and his grades were so poor that one of the few options open to him upon graduating was service in the Navy Medical Corps. After performing a one-year internship at Fort Pendleton, California, he was granted an overseas transfer to the United States Naval Hospital in Yokosuka, Japan. It was there that he got the opportunity to volunteer for duty aboard the U.S.S. *Montague*, which was under orders to move Vietnamese refugees from Haiphong to Saigon.

The young lieutenant was initially directed to remain on board ship to supervise the construction of the *Montague*'s medical and sanitary equipment, but his fluency in French earned him a promotion. American officers were having difficulty communicating with the refugees at Haiphong, most of whom could not speak English, and Dooley offered to translate the officers' instructions into French. (A century of colonial domination had made French truly a "lingua franca" in Vietnam.) The officers accepted Dooley's help, which sped up the boarding process, and Dooley was soon reassigned to a special task force centered in Haiphong. There, while serving as interpreter, he became concerned about the lack of facilities with which to inocu-

North Vietnamese refugees boarding a landing craft bound for the south, 15 August 1954.
Bettman/CORBIS.

late the thousands of epidemically dangerous escapees being transported on U.S. navy ships. He convinced his superiors of the need for a processing station where the refugees could be screened and treated. Impressed by Dooley's initiative, Rear Admiral Sabin appointed him medical officer for the unit that would monitor the refugees' health conditions, and Dooley waged an energetic campaign to stamp out contagious diseases before the hordes of exiles boarded the navy's vessels. His efforts earned him not only the Legion of Merit but a personal decoration from Diem.

More important than medals was the relationship Dooley cultivated with William Lederer, a reporter for *Reader's Digest* and the future coauthor of the Cold War classic *The Ugly American*. Lederer visited Haiphong in early 1955 looking for human interest stories to drum up support for Passage to Freedom. After listening to Dooley describe his work to a gathering of sailors, Lederer took the doctor aside, informed him that he had the makings of a "helluva book," and offered to help him fashion his story into a best seller. Dooley accepted. He and Lederer spent weeks in Hawaii polishing the text, after which Lederer introduced Dooley to DeWitt Wallace, publisher of *Reader's Digest*. Wallace shared Lederer's enthusiasm for Dooley's tale and agreed to run it as a condensed book. The publishing firm of Farrar, Straus, and Giroux signed a contract with Dooley for the full-length manuscript shortly thereafter.[15]

Deliver Us from Evil made Dooley's name a household word in the United States. After the book filled twenty-seven pages of *Reader's Digest* in one of the longest "abridgments" in that magazine's history, its success was guaranteed. The hardcover version shot up the best-seller list and received ecstatic reviews. Even the *New Yorker* was bowled over, calling *Deliver Us from Evil* a "poem of the human spirit victorious." Other critics groped for superlatives: "This is a moving tale that is recommended to all who are proud to be Americans"; "His story strikes with an impact that will bring tears to the eyes of the sourest reader"; "This is an inspiring story. Despite the horror and tragedy that fill its pages, it rings with hope." *Publisher's Weekly* was more cynical than most, observing: "If authors' looks sell books, . . . the handsome young navy doctor who wrote *Deliver Us from Evil* should have a big seller."[16]

The navy capitalized on Dooley's matinee-idol looks and engaging personality by sending him on a book-promoting tour that took him to eighty-six engagements in seventy-four cities. The tour, cosponsored by the pharmaceutical giant Charles Pfizer & Co., helped keep *Deliver Us from Evil* on the best-seller charts for months, as Dooley proved an even more effective orator than writer. Response to his addresses frequently bordered on the delirious.

Many who heard him speak later testified that they were overcome by an urge to run off to Southeast Asia and continue the crusade he had begun. Ngo Dinh Diem, recognizing Dooley's value as a propagandist, cabled the doctor in the middle of his speaking tour to thank him for "the wonderful service you have rendered Vietnam. . . . [Y]ou have eloquently told the story . . . of hundreds of thousands of my countrymen seeking to assure the enjoyment of their God-given rights."[17]

What was the story that Dooley told? Read today, *Deliver Us from Evil* seems a crude Cold War tract, bereft of any awareness of the complexities of Vietnamese history, embarrassing in its sentimentality, offensive in its racism. Dooley depicted Vietnam as cut in half by a "Bamboo Curtain" no different from the Iron Curtain that divided Europe. North of the 17th parallel was a "communist hellhole" run by "red vultures" determined to keep their captives from fleeing south. Dooley portrayed the refugees as one-dimensional objects of pity, incapable of solving problems on their own. None of them ever came up with an original or constructive idea. While readers were encouraged to rejoice in their escape from godlessness, it was difficult to feel respect for such helpless figures or recognize them as equal to the American sailors or doctors who ministered to them. By contrast, Dooley's Viet Minh were evil incarnate, so lacking in conscience and individual volition that Dooley referred to them collectively as a "ghoulish thing." No sin was beneath them. They told peasants desiring to relocate below the 17th parallel that the American sailors "would throw the old people overboard, cut off the right hands of the newborn, and sell the comely girls as concubines to capitalists." When such lies proved ineffective, they resorted to bureaucratic foot-dragging: forms that took forever to process, passports that mysteriously "expired," suspicious-looking "breakdowns" in transportation on the way to Haiphong, and the like. If refugees persisted in trying to get to the American reception centers, the Viet Minh employed their most Satanic methods of discouragement: torture, mutilation, and murder.[18]

The most arresting feature of *Deliver Us from Evil*—the attraction that contributed most to making the book a publishing bonanza—was Dooley's description of communist atrocities. Dooley told of how the Viet Minh jammed chopsticks into the ears of children because they had attended a class on religion. "The children screamed and wrestled and suffered horribly," he recounted. "Since their hands were tied behind them, they could not pull the wood out of their ears." Their religious instructor received a more ghastly punishment: "A guard cut off the tip of the teacher's tongue with his bayonet. Blood spurted from the man's mouth and gushed from his nostrils onto the ground." Elsewhere, Dooley told of a refugee boy whose legs had been pounded by Viet Minh rifle butts before he managed to board an American ship departing Haiphong. "His feet and ankles felt like moist bags of marbles," Dooley remembered. "He was crippled for life, but at least he was free." Not so lucky was another boy whom the Viet Minh accused of being "the head of a Christian Youth movement." The boy "was tied to a tree and brutally beaten with short bamboo sticks. Then his blood-soaked body was splashed with gasoline, ignited, and he was burned to death."[19]

The Viet Minh reserved their most hideous cruelty for Catholic priests. Dooley claimed to have discovered one priest whom the communists had left "a mass of blackened flesh from the shoulders to the knees. The belly was hard and distended and the scrotum swollen to the size of a football." It was "a masterpiece of systematic torture," Dooley recalled, carried out because the priest refused to stop "preaching the word of God." Another priest paid even more dearly for this refusal. The communists pounded nails into his head—"a communist version of the crown of thorns, once forced on the Saviour of whom he preached"—and left him to die. These images retain their capacity to shock even today. In 1956 they were stupefying—and engrossing. Millions of Americans consumed Dooley's message about the devoutness of democratic South Vietnam and the treachery of the communist north. They developed a deep emotional attachment to a far-off country they had known nothing about before reading or hearing Dooley's words.[20]

A few critics accused Dooley of manufacturing his Vietnamese Grand Guignol out of whole cloth, but these charges only became public decades after his death. Six U.S. officials who were stationed in the Hanoi-Haiphong area during Dooley's tour of duty submitted a lengthy, albeit secret, exposé to the U.S. Information Agency (USIA) in 1956 in which they held that *Deliver Us from Evil* was "not the truth" and that the accounts of Viet Minh atrocities were "nonfactual and exaggerated." The report was declassified in the late 1980s. Lederer, the man who prevailed on *Reader's Digest* to publish Dooley's story, told journalist Diana Shaw in 1991 that the atrocities the doctor described "never took place." Even more persuasive were statements by Norman Baker, who served as a corpsman under Dooley's command in Vietnam and who told Shaw that he never saw anything like the gruesome spectacles Dooley detailed.[21]

In the mid-1950s, however, it was not difficult for Americans to believe that the Viet Minh had committed the diabolical acts detailed in *Deliver Us from Evil*. Dooley's horror stories only confirmed the widespread perception, memorably articulated by evangelist Billy Graham, that communism was "inspired, directed, and motivated by the devil himself, who has declared war on Almighty God." Young, silver-tongued, and (conveniently) very handsome, Dooley became a genuine superstar, commanding top-tier lecture fees and receiving thousands of fan letters a day. While other influential spokesmen pled the cause of Diem's South Vietnam in the mid-to-late 1950s, none reached so large an audience or connected with that audience on so heartfelt a level.[22]

Dooley's ascent to what his biographer terms "celebrity sainthood" coincided with a crucial juncture in the history of postwar Vietnam. *Reader's Digest* published the condensed version of *Deliver Us from Evil* in its April 1956 issue, just three months before the date stipulated by the Geneva Accords for reunification elections. The *Digest* was at this time the most popular magazine in the world, with a circulation of twenty million, and the simplistic portrayal of Vietnamese politics it conveyed to a mass audience through Dooley's piece reinforced the convictions of American policymakers who insisted that all-Vietnam elections not be held. Privately, men like Eisenhower and Dulles wished to avoid such elections because they knew Ho Chi Minh would win, but they were uncomfortable taking a public posture in opposition to an apparently democratic means of deciding Vietnam's fate. They—and Diem—therefore argued that nationwide elections would not be truly free because citizens in the north would be compelled to vote the communist party line. Furthermore, they insisted, Washington and Saigon had not signed the accords and were under no obligation to abide by them. Dooley provided a more compelling reason to reject the Geneva election provisions. The Viet Minh, he declared, had already broken the promises their representatives made at Geneva; by preventing hundreds of thousands of Vietnamese from moving south, they had rendered the accords null and void. "To say that the communists tried to stop the refugees . . . was to put it mildly," Dooley wrote. "Though under the Geneva agreement anyone had a right to leave the north who wanted to, the communists began to violate the agreement on this point from the day it was signed." They violated it, moreover, not only with red tape, but with the most hellish methods that "the fiendish imagination of godless men" could devise.[23]

Dooley may have fabricated the atrocities he claimed to have witnessed in Vietnam, and he certainly aggrandized his role in Passage to Freedom by portraying a multinational relief operation as a one-man show. Such embellishments notwithstanding, what the United States accomplished—in cooperation with French forces and voluntary agencies—was staggering. It is doubtful whether any other nation could have moved so many refugees such a great distance on a crash basis, and Americans took pride in their nation's titanic, seemingly selfless, achievement. Yet the American public received an incomplete picture of Passage to Freedom. Media coverage of the exodus tended to omit two features that reflected less favorably on the United States and the Diem regime. First was the fact that the refugees' flight was not in every instance spontaneous. Second, and more important, was what happened *after* the refugees debarked in South Vietnam: their resettlement, the extent to which they were assimilated—or, rather, not assimilated—into the South Vietnamese population.

To be sure, thousands of North Vietnamese would have fled communist domination no matter what the Americans did. Washington, however, was hardly reluctant to give a nudge to any northerner vacillating between Diem and Ho. In fact, the CIA initiated a propaganda campaign toward that end that ranked with the most audacious enterprises in the history of covert action. The campaign's originator and manager was Colonel Edward Lansdale, nominally the assistant U.S. air attaché in Saigon but actually head of a covert CIA group that specialized in psychological warfare. Lansdale advised Diem after the Geneva Conference that "when the plebiscite comes between north and south, we have to have more people to vote on our side." Diem authorized Lansdale to launch an effort to bestir northerners into relocating, but pointed out that his nation was not equipped to absorb many refugees. The colonel assured the premier that U.S. governmental and nongovernmental agencies could handle this burden.[24]

Lansdale's "psywar" team used a number of gimmicks to swell the ranks of the refugees. South Vietnamese soldiers, dressed in civilian clothes, were sent north to spread rumors that the Viet Minh had made a deal with Red China to permit two divisions of Chinese troops to circulate throughout North Vietnam; the Chinese, so the story went, were raping and pillaging and the authorities in Hanoi were doing nothing to stop them. Lansdale enlisted the services of a Vietnamese counterfeiter to produce a bogus Viet Minh leaflet instructing citizens of the north on how to behave when the communists took over; the leaflet told them to make a tally of their possessions so that the Viet Minh would know what to confiscate. Lansdale's forgery was so well done that even Viet Minh officials accepted it as genuine. Lansdale also used U.S. funds to hire soothsayers who predicted disaster under communist rule and prosperity in the south. Perhaps the most inflammatory rumor disseminated by Lansdale's agents was that Washington intended to launch an offensive to liberate the north as soon as all anticommunist Vietnamese had moved below the 17th parallel. When the United States did this, North Vietnamese were told, it would use atomic weapons, and the only way to be sure of avoiding death in a nuclear holocaust was to go south. Lansdale's team printed up and distributed thousands of copies of a handbill depicting Hanoi with three circles of nuclear devastation superimposed on it.

While American "dirty tricks" were aimed at all Vietnamese north of the parallel, Lansdale paid especial attention to North Vietnamese Catholics. As he recalled, Washington "wanted to make sure that as many persons as possible, particularly the strongly anti-communist Catholics, relocated in the south." CIA-owned mimeograph machines churned out tens of thousands of fliers advertising that "Christ Has Gone to the South" and "The Virgin Mary Has Departed from the North," and Lansdale's men distributed them throughout North Vietnam. Lansdale also saw to it that posters were pasted in Hanoi and Haiphong depicting communists closing a cathedral and forcing the congregation to pray under a picture of Ho Chi Minh; the caption read, "Make Your Choice." Diem himself went to Hanoi when the city was still garrisoned by the French to encourage the hierarchy and its adherents to move south. Most North Vietnamese priests were eager to comply. They preached that a communist government would mean an end to freedom of worship, that the sacraments would no longer be given, and that any Catholics who remained in the north would thereby endanger their souls; they exhorted their parishioners to seize the opportunity offered by the Geneva Accords and escape to South Vietnam, where a fellow Catholic, supported by American aid, ran a prosperous regime. Unsurprisingly, over 60 percent of North Vietnam's 1.5 million Catholics joined the throng of refugees.[25]

Passage to Freedom was a godsend to Diem politically. Along with enlarging the population of his zone of Vietnam and depleting that of the Viet Minh, the exodus provided him with hundreds of thousands of people who owed him everything, trusted him because of his religion, and could therefore be relied on to support his government. Yet the refugees also presented Diem with an enormous practical problem. Now that they had made the move south, what was to be done with them? How was Diem to care for such a massive influx of dependents? Obviously, long stays in refugee camps needed to be avoided; the cramped living conditions and idleness entailed by such confinement would sap the refugees' enthusiasm for their new leader and possibly foster procommunist sentiment. Diem and his American advisors had to devise some way to make these exiles into productive units of the

South Vietnamese economy. That meant finding industrial employment for artisans, tillable land for farmers, and fishing grounds for fishermen. Most important, the refugees needed to be resettled in permanent homes and integrated into South Vietnam's society.

Diem established the Commissariat for Refugees, commonly referred to by its French initials as COMIGAL, to direct the resettlement program. He appointed Bui Van Luong, a family friend and ardent Catholic, as its head. COMIGAL worked in cooperation with the United States Operations Mission (USOM), the agency that administered nonmilitary American aid, and the Military Assistance Advisory Group (MAAG). Also involved in resettling the displaced northerners were the French army, a contingent of advisors from Diem's old stomping ground at Michigan State University (the Michigan State University Group, or MSUG), and various American Catholic voluntary agencies. These officials faced a daunting challenge. The refugees began arriving in Saigon in August 1954 at the rate of four thousand to seven thousand a day. The first arrivals were housed in twenty-man tents at a hippodrome; when that structure filled up, other buildings became refugee quarters: schools, hospitals, warehouses, churches, and even the municipal theater in the center of the city. COMIGAL supervised the construction of numerous temporary villages, primarily in the greater Saigon area, and the procurement and disbursement of sufficient food, money, and medicine to keep this great mass of people alive. By the spring of 1955, almost all of the one million refugees were living in rows of impermanent houses extending for miles along the highways leading north and east from Saigon.

COMIGAL had met the test of providing temporary shelter, but the next phase—that of permanent resettlement and integration—proved more difficult. While there was no dearth of cultivable land in South Vietnam, much of the land was not secure when Passage to Freedom began in 1954. The Viet Minh still dominated about half of the territory south of Saigon, other regions of the Mekong lowlands were in the hands of the Cao Dai and Hoa Hao religious sects, and the bandit Binh Xuyen gang controlled the immediate approaches to the Saigon-Cholon urban area. It was not until mid-1955, after most Viet Minh forces moved north and Diem crushed the Binh Xuyen in the "Battle for Saigon" (see chapter 3), that COMIGAL could conduct surveys of the countryside. Its prospecting commissions, made up of specialists and refugee representatives, were dispatched in search of suitable resettlement sites. When they found areas capable of accommodating the refugees, the commissions drew up project plans and submitted them to the USOM for approval and allocation of necessary funds. If a project was approved, the

Aerial view of a refugee "tent city" on the outskirts of Saigon, 16 October 1954.
Bettman/CORBIS.

refugees—usually about three thousand—traveled by truck to the selected site and began the work of creating a village: digging wells, building roads and bridges, clearing brush, draining swamps. They lived in American aid tents or hangars until they had time to construct thatched-roof houses, and COMIGAL supplied them with farm implements, fertilizers, and plow animals paid for by the United States. In all, America provided 97 percent of the foreign-government monetary support of refugee relief.

By mid-1957, a total of 319 resettlement villages had been created. On 31 December Diem dissolved COMIGAL, declaring its purpose fulfilled: the refugees were, he said, self-sufficient and integrated into the national polity. This conclusion, however, was flawed. Many of the refugees had yet to find gainful employment and were living from government hand-outs. More important, as the journalist Robert Scheer noted in a critique of the Diem regime published in 1965, "the refugees were *not* integrated into South Vietnamese society." Rather they became a much resented special-interest group.[26]

The reasons for this were not complicated. First, COMIGAL officials decided not to split up refugees belonging to the same village; wherever possible, those refugees were relocated together. Since many of the Catholic villages of the north moved south as a body, it was easy for COMIGAL to assign the villagers to a common settlement site. This was less troublesome than creating a fresh community from elements originating from different villages or provinces, but it also all but ensured that these displaced persons would never assimilate into the native southern population. Their villages remained culturally self-contained, preserving their hierarchical structure and discipline, flying the yellow-and-white Vatican flag alongside the yellow-and-red nationalist one. Not only did the Catholic refugees have little contact with their more numerous Buddhist compatriots; they tended to hold them in contempt, believing that the southern Buddhists, who had never experienced the horror of communist rule, were unreliable soldiers in the anti–Viet Minh crusade.

More important was the fact that Diem favored his new Catholic constituents. He granted them a disproportionately high number of civil and military appointments in the government and continued the French practice of legally defining Catholicism as a "religion" while Buddhists were designated members of an "association." The preferential treatment given the Catholic refugees alienated many peasants and city dwellers from the Diem regime. Graham Greene, the British novelist and journalist, visited Saigon in early 1955 and reported, "Mr. Diem may well leave his tolerant country a legacy of anti-Catholicism." Diem did more than that. His insensitive treatment of the Buddhists during resettlement laid the foundation for the 1963 Buddhist demonstrations that brought his government, and his life, to a violent end.[27]

In the mid-1950s, however, few could foresee such developments. The Eisenhower administration was confident of its capacity to make the Diem experiment a success, and with good reason. After all, the United States and France had just worked a logistical miracle akin to uprooting a million New Hampshire residents, moving them one thousand miles south by ship, and resettling them in South Carolina. If the "free world" could do this, it could do anything. Moreover, Washington had no alternative but to "sink or swim" with Diem now. After the spectacle of Passage to Freedom was promulgated in American newspapers and periodicals and on movie and television screens, any abandonment by the United States of South Vietnam's émigré martyrs—and, by extension, their champion Diem—was viewed by millions of Americans as an unchristian breach of faith, a Judas kiss.

Notes

1. Bernard Fall, *Hell in a Very Small Place: The Siege of Dien Bien Phu* (New York: Vintage Books, 1968), 412; Dwight D. Eisenhower, *Mandate for Change, 1953–1956* (Garden City N.Y.: Doubleday, 1963), 351.

2. Ann Whitman File, Dulles-Herter Series: Dulles to Eisenhower, 6 February 1954: Box 2, Dwight D. Eisenhower Library, Abilene, Kansas [hereafter EL].

3. Ann Whitman File, Dulles-Herter Series: Dulles to Eisenhower, 19 February 1954: Box 2, EL.

4. Bao Dai cited in David L. Anderson, *Trapped by Success: The Eisenhower Administration and Vietnam, 1953–1961* (New York: Columbia University Press, 1991), 54.

5. Diem cited in Edward Miller, "Vision, Power, and Agency: The Ascent of Ngo Dinh Diem, 1945–54," *Journal of Southeast Asian Studies* 35 (October 2004): 454.

6. LaChambre cited in Cameron to Dulles, 5 June 1954, file 751G.00/6-554, RG 59; DeJean cited in the Chargé at Saigon to the Department of State, 13 June 1954, *FRUS, 1952–1954* (Washington, D.C.: Government Printing Office, 1982), 13:1685; Ely cited in the Chargé at Saigon to the Department of State, 15 June 1954, *FRUS, 1952–1954*, 13:1697; Mendès-France cited in the Ambassador in France to the Department of State, 20 June 1954, *FRUS, 1952–1954*, 13:1725–1727.

7. Eisenhower, *Mandate for Change*, 272.

8. Dong cited in Phillip B. Davidson, *Vietnam at War: The History, 1946–1975* (Novato, Calif.: Presidio, 1988), 289.

9. "Statement by Prime Minister Ngo Dinh Diem of the National Government, Regarding the Geneva Agreements, 22 July 1954," in *The Problem of the Reunification of Viet-Nam* (Saigon: Ministry of Information, 1958), 29; White House Office, NSC Staff Papers, 1948–1961, OCB Central File Series: Dulles to Dillon, 2 August 1954: Box 38, EL.

10. Edward G. Lansdale, *In the Midst of Wars: An American's Mission to Southeast Asia* (New York: Harper & Row, 1972), 157; Diem cited in Miller, "Vision, Power, and Agency," 457.

11. Robert F. Randle, *Geneva 1954: The Settlement of the Indochinese War* (Princeton, N.J.: Princeton University Press, 1969), 572.

12. "Bug-Out in the Delta," *Life*, 12 July 1954, 13.

13. "Bishops Bare Red Record of Viet Violence," *Monitor*, 24 December 1954; "Viet Minh Violence Angers U.S. Bishops," *Catholic Herald Citizen*, 27 November 1954; "Today's Persecution Worst in History," *Our Sunday Visitor*, Fort Wayne Diocesan Edition, 20 March 1955; "Let Our People Go!" *Advocate*, 3 December 1954; Eileen Egan, *For Whom There Is No Room: Scenes from the Refugee World* (New York: Paulist Press, 1995), 318.

14. James T. Fisher, *Dr. America: The Lives of Thomas A. Dooley, 1927–1961* (Amherst: University of Massachusetts Press, 1997), 34–35.

15. Lederer cited in Fisher, *Dr. America*, 70.

16. "Books: Briefly Noted," *New Yorker*, 5 May 1956; "Samaritan in Vietnam," *America's Book-Log*, June 1956; "Sermon in the East," *Hollywood Citizen-News*, 16 April 1956; Barbara Shaughnessy, "Dr. Dooley of Viet Nam," *Extension*, August 1956, 10; Paul Nathan, "Rights and Permissions," *Publisher's Weekly*, 10 March 1956.

17. Diem to Dooley, 25 June 1956, "Lectures I" Scrapbook, Thomas A. Dooley Collection, Pius XII Library, St. Louis University [hereafter Dooley Collection].

18. Thomas Dooley, *Deliver Us from Evil: The Story of Viet Nam's Flight to Freedom* (New York: Farrar, Straus, & Giroux, 1956), 158–159, 181, 33, 147.

19. Dooley, *Deliver Us from Evil*, 175–176, 204.

20. Dooley, *Deliver Us from Evil*, 177–178, 182.

21. USIA report cited in Eric Thomas Chester, *Covert Network: Progressives, the International Rescue Committee, and the CIA* (Armonk N.Y.: Sharp, 1995), 163; Lederer cited in Diana Shaw, "The Temptation of Tom Dooley," *Los Angeles Times Magazine*, 15 December 1991, 43–46, 50.

22. Graham cited in Martin Marty, *Modern American Religion*, vol. 3, *Under God, Indivisible, 1941–1960* (Chicago: University of Chicago Press, 1960), 135.

23. James T. Fisher, *The Catholic Counterculture in America, 1933–1962* (Chapel Hill: University of North Carolina Press, 1989), 174; Dooley, *Deliver Us from Evil*, 185; Dooley, "Deliver Us from Evil," *Reader's Digest*, May 1956, 164.

24. Lansdale cited in Cecil B. Currey, *Edward Lansdale: The Unquiet American* (Boston: Houghton Mifflin, 1988), 157.

25. Lansdale cited in William Conrad Gibbons, *The U.S. Government and the Vietnam War* (Princeton, N.J.: Princeton University Press, 1986), 1:265.

26. Robert Scheer, *How the United States Got Involved in Vietnam* (Santa Barbara, Calif.: Center for the Study of Democratic Institutions, 1965), 31.

27. Graham Greene, "Last Act in Indo-China," *New Republic*, 9 May 1955, 10.

~

CHAPTER THREE

"This Fellow Is Impossible"
The Collins Mission

The historian Frances FitzGerald observes that "in going into Vietnam, the United States was . . . entering a world qualitatively different from its own. . . . [T]here was no more correspondence between the two worlds than between the atmosphere of the earth and that of the sea." While overdrawn, FitzGerald's analogy points up the difficulty U.S. policymakers encountered in seeking to impose their concepts of good governance on the anarchy that prevailed in Saigon in the mid-1950s. What was an American diplomat to make of a city where the chief of police was also the leader of a gang of murderers, pimps, racketeers, and drug dealers? How could a coalition be effected between two South Vietnamese groups when one was led by a former seminarian living on high principle and the other by a pirate who fed welshers to his pet tiger? The Eisenhower administration's most consequential venture in nation-building could not have been undertaken in an environment less susceptible to Age-of-Consensus political philosophy. As FitzGerald, whose *Fire in the Lake* remains the most penetrating exploration of the cultural divide between Vietnamese and Americans, notes, "The effort of translation was too great."[1]

General J. Lawton "Lightning Joe" Collins proved more successful at translating Vietnamese politics into the language of Washington statecraft than most of his contemporaries. Indeed, Collins was the first, and for a long time the only, top-level policymaker to recognize the flaws in America's Diem experiment. As U.S. "special representative" in South Vietnam from late 1954 through mid-1955, Collins determined that Ngo Dinh Diem's government was incapable of winning broad indigenous support and would always require American aid to stay afloat. There was no possibility of a Diem-led South Vietnam becoming secure or stable enough to allow the United States to scale back its involvement in this Cold War outpost; rather, the opposite was true: as long as Diem remained in charge, escalation of the U.S. commitment to Vietnam was unavoidable. When President Dwight Eisenhower overruled Collins's recommendations that Diem be abandoned, he narrowed the range of options for future U.S. presidents attempting to cope with Vietnam. By the time the White House came to share Collins's views in 1963 and engineered the overthrow of the Diem regime, it was too late. The United States had sunk too much money and prestige into South Vietnam to permit a graceful exit, and Diem's nine-year reign of terror had obliterated moderate anticommunist alternatives to his administration. Most important, the manner in which Diem went about squelching dissent increased popular resentment of the Saigon government and made South Vietnam's countryside a fertile recruiting ground for the communists.

The "Collins mission," as it was referred to at the time, represented the last chance for Washington to detach itself from a losing proposition. Eisenhower's refusal to heed his special representative's advice made the cataclysm that followed, if not inevitable, at least more difficult to escape. "[T]he decision to back Diem," Secretary of State John Foster Dulles cabled Collins in April 1955, had "gone to the point of no return. . . . [E]ither he had to succeed or the whole business would be a failure." Collins's attempt to pull his country back from that point of no return was one of the pivotal episodes in America's longest war.[2]

When Collins arrived in Saigon in November 1954, the Diem experiment could not have been in greater peril. Diem's was a government in name only. Emperor Bao Dai had little confidence in the new premier and gave him only lukewarm support. This pleased French prime minister Pierre Mendès-France, who found Diem's Francophobia alarming at a time when France was attempting to retain influence in its former Indochinese colonies. Mendès-France informed Dulles that he believed other South Vietnamese politicians had "much better records than Diem" and that the United States would "be forced to consider [the] replacement [of] Diem . . . within [a] few months." French generals and diplomats unanimously expressed their belief that Diem would fail.[3]

Clearly, Diem could not count on much assistance from Paris. This was a problem because the French Expeditionary Corps (FEC) was the most powerful military force south of the 17th parallel, and an indispensable tool in maintaining order. Worse, Diem's own military, the Vietnamese National Army (VNA), was essentially under French command, headed by officers chosen and trained by the French. The VNA chief of staff, General Nguyen Van Hinh, was a French citizen who had graduated from the French Air Academy, served with French colonial forces in Algeria, and married a French woman. Not coincidentally, Hinh loathed Diem and repeatedly disobeyed him.

With no army to enforce his rule, Diem had little hope of giving South Vietnam a strong, unified government. The ordinance with which Bao Dai conferred civil and military powers on Diem meant nothing in the countryside, where control was exercised by various dueling parties. The Cao Dai religious sect reigned over the northwestern Mekong Delta. A syncretic faith that wove together Taoism, Buddhism, Confucianism, and Christianity, Cao Daism had over two million followers. Pham Cong Tac, the Cao Dai pope, commanded an armed force of twenty-five thousand troops. The Hoa Hao, a sect that practiced a species of reformed Buddhism, claimed around one million adherents. Its army of several thousand men controlled the region southwest of Saigon. Thirty-odd Montagnard tribes occupied the Central Highlands, where they had lived for centuries as a distinct cultural group, rejecting Vietnamese political authority. France permitted these factions substantial autonomy when Vietnam was part of the French empire, and they were unlikely to surrender time-honored prerogatives just because a new premier had taken up residence in the Norodom Palace. And then there were the communists. Although the Viet Minh had signed the Geneva Accords and moved thousands of their troops out of the south, they left behind a network of cadres to harass the Diem government through acts of sabotage and assassination. Some experts estimated that the Viet Minh dominated as much as one-third of South Vietnam, including most of the border with Cambodia.

If Diem's lack of influence in the provinces was distressing, conditions in Saigon were cause for despair. The South Vietnamese premier could not even control his own capital city, which was in the grip of the Binh Xuyen, Vietnam's preeminent criminal organization. Named after a village south of Saigon, the Binh Xuyen consisted of approximately forty thousand heavily armed thugs. Their leader was Le Van "Bay" Vien, a figure of gargantuan corruption who presided over an empire of vice without parallel in Asia. Among his many establishments were the Hall of Mirrors, the world's largest brothel; Le Grande Monde, a gambling complex that occupied several city blocks; and an opium factory that refined a product for distribution through-out Indochina. The compound from which Vien directed the Binh Xuyen's operations seemed stage-managed to scandalize Western observers: it was sur-rounded by an alligator-filled moat; pythons slithered around the columns on the front porch; a leopard stood guard outside the bedroom door; and a Siberian tigress lived in a nearby cage. Vien's bodyguards frequently had to clean bits of clothing and human bones out of the cage after their boss exacted retribution from those who failed to make protection payments.

In a characteristically self-serving maneuver, Bao Dai transferred control of the Sureté—the national police—to the Binh Xuyen in mid-1954. The emperor received forty-four million piasters (about $1.25 million) from Vien in exchange for this transaction, but, as the American embassy complained, he also created a situation in Saigon analogous to the "city of Chicago plac-ing its police force in [the] hands of [the] Al Capone gang during [the] latter's heyday." After sealing his bargain with the emperor, Vien levied a take on commercial traffic in and out of Saigon and continued to run his gambling casinos, houses of prostitution, and drug factories without fear of legal repri-sal. Diem seemed powerless to combat him. CIA Station Chief William Colby recalled that the premier "only controlled the space of his [own] pal-ace grounds."[4]

Diem nearly lost even that authority less than three months after the Geneva Conference adjourned. In August 1954, Chief of Staff Hinh began a series of public attacks against Diem, proclaiming that South Vietnam needed a "strong and popular" leader like himself and bragging about the coup he was arranging. Hinh's coup attempt might have succeeded if not for Colonel Edward Lansdale, whose assignment in late 1954 was to coordinate a propaganda campaign north of the 17th parallel. While he and his team of CIA operatives wreaked some havoc in Ho Chi Minh's republic, the colonel found his services more urgently required in the south. Recognizing the threat to Diem's leadership posed by Hinh, Lansdale persuaded Philippine president Ramón Magsaysay to offer the chief of staff's officers an all-expenses-paid tour of Manila's nightclubs. Most of Hinh's henchmen were flown to the Philippines on the eve of insurrection, and the general called off the coup.[5]

In addition to Lansdale, Diem had one other American partisan whose assistance proved crucial during the closing months of 1954. Senator Mike Mansfield, Congress's foremost authority on Asia, made two decisive contri-butions to the Diem experiment in that time. First, he joined Dulles in Manila to help establish the Southeast Asia Treaty Organization (SEATO), a collective defense alliance including the United States, Great Britain, France, Australia, New Zealand, the Philippines, Thailand, and Pakistan. Dulles wanted, in his words, to erect a "'no trespassing' sign" that warned the Soviets and Chinese not to expand their influence in the Western Pacific, and SEATO met that symbolic requirement. Militarily, the pact lacked teeth. Unlike the North Atlantic Treaty Organization (NATO), SEATO did not require a response from all members if one were attacked; each nation merely pledged to "consult" in the event of aggression and "act to meet the common danger in accordance with its constitutional processes." Despite such timid language, Dulles worried about obtaining the constitutionally required two-thirds vote for ratification of the treaty in the Senate. He therefore decided to sweeten the pill by inviting two senators—the Republican Alexander Stephens and the Democrat Mansfield—to accompany him at the Manila Conference.[6]

Dulles's strategy worked. Even though any "Southeast Asia Treaty" that did not include India, Burma, and Indonesia—each of which preferred an unaligned status in 1954—was hardly worthy of the name, the Senate ratified SEATO by a vote of eighty-two to one. Dulles had wanted to include South Vietnam, Laos, and Cambodia as treaty members, but Paris objected on the grounds that the Geneva Accords neutralized Indochina and barred its states from joining military alliances. The Americans found a way around this by attaching a protocol to the SEATO agreement that extended its provisions to those areas, projecting what Dulles called an "umbrella of protection" over them. Cambodia and Laos repudiated the protocol, but Diem accepted informal membership in SEATO. A decade later, the protocol would furnish a justification for American military intervention to save South Vietnam.[7]

Of more immediate consequence was Mansfield's "Report on Indochina," delivered to the Senate Foreign Relations Committee after the SEATO treaty was finalized. Mansfield visited Saigon on his way to and from the Manila Conference, and the experience convinced him it was either Diem or defeat for America's grand design in Indochina. When Mansfield addressed his fellow legislators in mid-October 1954, he bound Washington much more tightly to its Diem experiment. He depicted Saigon as an Indochinese Gomorrah, "seeth[ing] with intrigue and counter-intrigue," controlled by "gangsters, pirates, and extortionists." In Mansfield's view, only Diem offered any hope of establishing a regime deserving of U.S. support. Given that the "alternatives to Diem" were "not promising," the senator argued, Washington's course was clear: "In the event that the Diem government falls, . . . I believe that the United States should consider an immediate suspension of all aid to Vietnam." Diem had one hundred thousand copies of the report printed up and distributed within days of Mansfield's appearance before the committee. Although the Eisenhower administration never formally endorsed it, Mansfield's recommendation was widely construed as American policy.[8]

Mansfield's support was an invaluable asset, but it did little in the short run to improve conditions in Saigon, where political storm clouds continued to gather. Nine members of Diem's government resigned during Hinh's abortive bid for power, and Bao Dai recommended that Diem resign as well. Hinh still commanded the VNA and had not abandoned his plans to unseat Diem. The Binh Xuyen still controlled the police. The French encouraged Diem's rivals in their intrigues against him. Diem, by his own reckoning, had only one battalion on whose loyalty he could depend. Foreign correspondents predicted daily that the Diem regime would fall and that all of Vietnam would come under communist rule.

Eisenhower, a believer in the maxim that long faces do not win wars, complained to Dulles that he was "weary" of the tenor of panic in reports from South Vietnam. Dulles suggested that Eisenhower send a high-ranking general to serve as Washington's "special representative" in Saigon—someone "in whom the president . . . would have full confidence." Eisenhower approved of the idea, and remarked that J. Lawton Collins was "the best qualified U.S. Army officer" he could think of. Collins had served with distinction in both the Pacific and European theaters of World War II, and his postwar résumé included stints as army chief of staff and U.S. representative on the NATO Military Committee and Standing Group. He had considerable experience in Asia; indeed, he had even visited Vietnam in 1951, which made him virtually unique among American soldier-statesmen. Lightning Joe, the president assured Dulles, possessed "outstanding qualifications" for this assignment.[9]

When Dulles gave Collins his marching orders, he informed the general that the "chance of success" of his mission was "only one in ten," but that the "importance of checking the spread of communism" made the effort necessary. Eisenhower's directive to his special representative gave Collins carte blanche "to direct, utilize, and control all the agencies and resources of the United States Government" in South Vietnam. The president stressed that the "immediate . . . requirement" facing America was to "assist in stabilizing

Newly installed South Vietnamese Prime Minster Diem and General Paul Ely watch the French tricolor slowly descend the flag staff and the red-striped yellow flag of South Vietnam go up to mark the end of French rule in Indochina, c. 1954.

and strengthening the legal government of Vietnam under the premiership of Ngo Dinh Diem."[10]

Within a week of receiving his assignment, Collins was in South Vietnam, proclaiming at his first press conference: "I am here to give every possible aid to the government of Ngo Dinh Diem and to his government only." Collins brought a reputation for toughness that stood in pleasing contrast to what many Washington policymakers perceived as irresolution on the part of previous ambassadors. Collins's nickname "Lightning Joe" had been acquired as a consequence of his decisive leadership during World War II, and the administration anticipated that a jolt of that lightning would be just the thing to resuscitate America's fortunes in Southeast Asia.[11]

Eisenhower and Dulles were accordingly surprised by the tenor of Collins's "first general impressions and recommendations." "Diem is a small, shy, diffident man with almost no personal magnetism," Collins noted. "I am by no means certain [that] he has [the] inherent capacity to manage [the] country during this critical period." Collins went on to address what he considered the two outstanding difficulties facing South Vietnam's government. First, and most important, the cabinet had to be broadened: Diem was juggling the duties of minister of the interior and minister of defense, in addition to his job as premier. This was an impossible burden. Second, the VNA lacked skilled officers. It had been part of France's colonial policy to reserve positions of military command either for Frenchmen or for Vietnamese who acquired French citizenship. Consequently, Collins warned, "if [the French] Expeditionary Corps were withdrawn prematurely, [the] results could be disastrous." All of the weaponry Washington could muster would not help South Vietnam defend itself until it cultivated some native leadership.[12]

This was a candid distillation of Collins's first days in South Vietnam. The mission did not get off to an auspicious start. General Ely had decided long before Collins's arrival that Diem would have to be replaced, and he was not reticent about so informing the special representative. He told Collins that Diem was "a losing game" and bluntly asserted, "at [the] present time there is no government in Vietnam." Collins's first meeting with Diem was an exercise in frustration, as the premier subjected Collins to a two-hour jeremiad about the "insubordinate attitude of General Hinh," protesting that "Hinh was utterly untrustworthy . . . and that [the] only solution was his departure from Vietnam." Collins had no luck focusing Diem's attention on such pressing matters as cabinet reorganization, disbursement of U.S. funds to the North Vietnamese refugees, and American training and supply of the

VNA. As he would learn over the coming months, it was impossible to divert the premier once he fixed on a subject.[13]

Collins bowed to Diem's demands and urged Hinh to leave South Vietnam, although he advised Dulles that "means should be found to save Hinh's face." The chief of staff was granted a two-week grace period to make his departure look like a voluntary relocation. On 19 November, Hinh handed over control of the VNA to General Nguyen Van Vy and left for Paris. He went on to enjoy a successful career as an officer in the French Air Force. Diem had won the feud, but had done little to persuade Collins that he represented the best political talent in Saigon.[14]

With the crisis in civil-military relations resolved, Collins began collaborating with Ely on a seven-point program to improve South Vietnam's prospects for independence. Point one dealt with reforming the VNA: the two generals recommended a reduction of manpower strength from 170,000 to 77,000 by mid-1955, with half the remaining troops to be deployed against a possible invasion from the north and the remainder used to provide internal security. In its most striking departure from French policy, the new plan mandated that South Vietnamese officers command the entire VNA. Other points included refugee resettlement, economic adjustments, establishment of a national assembly as a step toward representative government, and provisions for psychological warfare.

While Diem's pro-Catholic bias disposed him favorably toward any program that gave more assistance to the refugees from the north, most of the Collins-Ely program did not sit well with him. First of all, Diem was concerned about the Binh Xuyen, Hoa Hao, and Cao Dai soldiers who had been integrated into the VNA and were drawing their paychecks from the government. Diem intended to break the power of the sects, but until his own base was more secure he saw no profit in antagonizing sect leaders by firing thousands of their troops. Collins eventually compromised by allowing the VNA to retain ninety thousand soldiers rather than the proposed seventy-seven thousand. Still, his annoyance showed in his cables back to Washington. He did not want Diem to get the impression that, as he put it, "we are just going to give him a bunch of money and let him go ahead and spend it any way he wants."[15]

More worrisome, from Collins's perspective, was Diem's hoarding of power. "None of his subordinates is delegated sufficient authority to work," Collins complained. "Diem wishes to do everything himself." Despite the premier's industriousness—he spent as much as twenty hours a day dealing with government affairs—this could not help but result in a sluggish administration, especially since Diem seemed unable to recognize the difference between doing business and being busy. He would sit up half the night deliberating whether or not to reassign a civil servant or approve a passport application while a cyclone of intrigue whirled around him. No matter how frantically Collins pleaded with him to focus on the big picture, Diem could not tear himself away from minor matters to attend to major ones. Collins determined that his most urgent task was to persuade Diem to broaden his cabinet by appointing men with administrative experience.[16]

Such men did exist in South Vietnam. Chief among them was Phan Huy Quat, whom Collins considered the ablest politician he encountered. Quat was eager to serve in the administration, preferably in his former capacity as defense minister, and Collins recommended that Diem appoint him to that post. Diem resisted the suggestion, protesting that Quat would be intolerable to the Hoa Hao, Cao Dai, and Binh Xuyen. During his tenure in the defense ministry, Quat had attempted to curb the sects' military autonomy and thereby earned their mistrust. Collins responded that Diem himself was endeavoring to co-opt the sect armies into the VNA, and that he and Quat should therefore be natural allies. After some dithering, Diem agreed to abide by Collins's wishes, but then reversed himself on the grounds that sect opposition to Quat would make it impossible for him to function effectively as a cabinet member.

Collins found this rationale preposterous. The real reason for Diem's decision to deny Quat the ministry, he informed Washington, was "fear of Quat as [a] potential successor." If Quat became defense minister, Collins argued, he might acquire "greater stature in [the] public eye," which would render him "more eligible for [a] higher post" if it were "found necessary [to] replace Diem." As far as Collins was concerned, such replacement was overdue. Diem's choice "not to appoint Quat defense minister," he declared, "is [the] final development that convinces me that Diem does not have [the] capacity to unify [the] divided factions in Vietnam, and that unless some such action is taken, . . . this country will be lost to communism." Collins recommended that the United States "[s]upport [the] establishment of another government" and identified Quat as the Vietnamese best qualified to head it.[17]

This was not what Washington wanted to hear. Dulles responded the day before Christmas with a dressing-down, insisting that while the pace of government consolidation "may not please us," Collins should remember that "major changes" in Asia came "more slowly than in [the] West." The secretary concluded that "[u]nder present circumstances, . . . we have no choice but to continue our . . . support of Diem. There [is] no other suitable leader known to us."[18]

Dulles's message marked the beginning of an anomalous stage of the Collins mission during which the special representative tailored his conduct to conform to a reconceptualization of his assignment. Collins had assumed that the mandate he received from Eisenhower gave him discretion to recommend a replacement for Diem if he determined that another politician might prove more effective. While Collins knew that such a demarche would not be received with open arms by Washington, he believed its issuance fell within the purview of his mission. Dulles's response to the call for Diem's ouster, however, made clear that Collins did not have a wide enough berth to advocate abandonment of the Diem experiment.

Although Collins never persuaded Diem to adopt a more decentralized system of government, he could report a few signs of progress as the new year, 1955, began. The Saigon regime enjoyed economic independence from the French Union's franc zone as of 1 January, when South Vietnam became the direct beneficiary of American aid. This meant that Diem, for the first time, controlled the purse strings of the VNA, which resulted in greater army loyalty to the government. Some American policymakers concluded that since Diem no longer had to worry about a VNA insurrection, he might "feel secure enough to delegate more responsibility to his ministers and carry out meaningful reforms." Collins, while noting that Diem's leverage over VNA funds could backfire if he used this newfound power to precipitate a clash with his rivals, nonetheless concluded that "prospects are brighter" in Saigon.[19]

Collins's mood of forced buoyancy carried over into Dulles's first visit to South Vietnam in February. The secretary privately assured Diem that Washington had "a great stake" in him and announced at a press conference, "today I do not know of any responsible quarter which has any doubts about backing Diem as the head of this government." This was an outrageous assertion; apart from the French officials in Saigon and Paris who had been urging Diem's removal, Dulles was aware that Collins harbored considerable doubts about Diem's political viability. Yet Dulles portrayed the Diem experiment as a success to the assembled correspondents, and Collins, standing at Dulles's side, held his tongue.[20]

Dulles's visit seems to have been interpreted by Diem as a guarantee of U.S. support against all adversaries. Shortly after the secretary's departure,

Diem set in motion the chain of events that would culminate weeks later in the Battle for Saigon. Disdaining Collins's advice, he moved to narrow, not expand, the range of factions wielding administrative power. He refused to renew the Binh Xuyen's license for their gambling enterprises and announced that the French policy of subsidizing the Cao Dai and Hoa Hao as anti–Viet Minh allies would be terminated. In response, Binh Xuyen leader Bay Vien hosted a meeting of sect leaders and told them that if the Binh Xuyen, Hoa Hao, and Cao Dai could unite long enough for a joint political act, they could demand and receive the ministries in Diem's cabinet necessary to control the fiscal and human resources of the country. If Diem refused to accept their demands, a united sect front would have sufficient strength to topple the government. Cao Dai and Hoa Hao leaders, fed up with Diem, assented, and the "United Front of All Nationalist Forces" called a press conference at which Cao Dai pope Pham Cong Tac inveighed against Diem's "dictatorship."[21]

The United Front represented a formidable challenge. Ely suggested to Collins that Diem make whatever fence-mending gesture was necessary to defuse the situation. "[The] worst tactic for Diem to adopt," Ely insisted, "would be to turn his back on Bay Vien." Diem seemed bent on doing just that. In reply to Tac's diatribe, Diem tripled his palace guard and deployed VNA troops around Cholon. On 21 March, the United Front issued an ultimatum, insisting that Diem "undertake *within five days* [a] complete re-organization of the cabinet and its replacement by a new cabinet acceptable to the United Front National Forces." Sect leaders did not state what they would do if Diem failed to comply with their demands, but Vien had never been loath to resort to bloodshed when threats failed. Collins counseled Diem to open negotiations with the United Front. Diem refused to budge. The Binh Xuyen positioned mortars around the palace. Vien, it seemed, was spoiling for a fight.[22]

The same could not be said for members of Diem's cabinet. Foreign Minister Tran Van Do resigned in anticipation of the regime's defeat by the sects. Nguyen Van Thoai, Diem's own cousin, caused a sensation by announcing his withdrawal from the government while serving on the South Vietnamese delegation at the Bandung Conference of Non-aligned Nations. Collins took the occasion of these defections to again urge Diem to take Quat into his cabinet. He noted that Diem had previously objected to making Quat defense minister because of potential "troubles with the sects," but that he could hardly have "any more troubles with the sects than he has now." Diem, Collins reported, "made no reply." Instead, he took to the airwaves. "To sow or maintain dissension is contrary to our aspirations," Diem broadcast over Saigon radio, "and nobody is entitled to do so." There would be no softening of the government's position.[23]

A typical head of state, operating without any popular mandate and subject to the whims of an absentee emperor and a superpower sponsor, would have been relieved when the United Front's five-day deadline passed without incident, and would have redoubled his efforts to avoid such confrontations in the future. Diem, however, was not typical. Believing that he had gone eyeball-to-eyeball with Vien and forced him to blink, Diem determined to break the Binh Xuyen's power once and for all. He summoned his remaining cabinet ministers and informed them that he had decided to revoke Bao Dai's grant of police powers to the Binh Xuyen; he would dismiss Vien's hand-picked police chief and replace him with someone loyal to the government. Defense Minister Ho Thong Minh advised Diem to postpone any action until his plan had been approved by the cabinet. When Diem refused, Minh resigned and went to Collins's headquarters to report his defection.

Collins could not condone Diem provoking the Binh Xuyen, especially since the premier had not bothered to consult with his American advisors before installing his own man as police chief. The special representative's concern turned to fury when Ely informed him that Diem had ordered the VNA to seize the headquarters of the Saigon police, a heavily fortified building in one of the more densely populated areas of the city. Ely persuaded Diem to suspend his order, but not before advance units of the VNA occupied the periphery of the headquarters while the Binh Xuyen remained in the HQ compound. South Vietnam had come to the brink of civil war as a consequence of a policy that Diem had initiated without informing the U.S. president's special representative.

This was too much for Collins. In a stormy meeting with Diem—the memorandum of which seems to have been dictated in a voice still choked with fury—Collins threw down the gauntlet. "I told Diem that in my judgment if his orders had been carried out there would have been severe fighting within [the] city," Collins reported. When Diem tried to blame Ely for obstructing a VNA triumph, Collins shot back that Ely had had no choice, that if the VNA had been permitted to move against the Binh Xuyen "warfare could have been expected to break out . . . and would have resulted in far greater losses than gains." Collins demanded that Diem employ "political means . . . without fighting" to resolve the crisis, and then issued his own ultimatum: "I said that if he continued his present course we would be under heavy pressure to support a change in government." Collins commanded

Diem to "consult with Ely and me before taking any additional critical steps whatever." Diem sullenly responded that "he would think over [the] situation."[24]

He did not have much time to think. That midnight, 29–30 March, explosions rocked Saigon. In response to Diem's removal of the police chief, Vien ordered an assault on VNA headquarters by two hundred Binh Xuyen troops. For three-and-a-half hours into the morning of 30 March, the VNA and Binh Xuyen clashed. The hostilities were inconclusive, but they exacted a heavy toll. The VNA suffered six killed and thirty-four wounded, the Binh Xuyen ten killed and twenty wounded. The bodies of innocent bystanders littered the sidewalk.

If Dulles's reprimand on Christmas Eve 1954 signaled the onset of a second phase in the Collins mission, during which Collins tried to harmonize the administration's commitments to both Diem and a free South Vietnam, the battle on the morning of 30 March 1955 ushered in phase three. Collins concluded that the two commitments were irreconcilable: if Diem remained premier, South Vietnam would be lost. "You and the president are entitled to my judgment," Collins wrote Dulles. "I must say now that . . . it is my considered judgment that this man lacks . . . the executive ability successfully to head a government." Collins was not ready to give up on the prospect of preserving a noncommunist state in Indochina. He felt that the economic situation was favorable, the population anticommunist, and the VNA progressing nicely under Franco-American tutelage. He was convinced, however, that unless Diem was removed from office all of these positive conditions would not be enough to keep South Vietnam from retiring behind the Iron Curtain. "I say this with great regret," wrote Collins, "but with firm conviction."[25]

The administration initially seemed inclined to take its special representative's advice. Eisenhower told Dulles that "you can't send this fellow [Collins] down there and have him work on it if his judgment is the way it is. We just have to go along with it." Dulles reluctantly concluded that "the rug is coming out from under the fellow in Southeast Asia. . . . [W]e have to cowtow [sic] to the BX [Binh Xuyen]. . . . The gangsters will have won."[26]

From Collins's perspective, the sooner Washington yanked the rug, the better. South Vietnam was sliding toward chaos. Government troops and Binh Xuyen thugs bivouacked on opposite sides of Saigon's streets, close enough to hurl insults—and the occasional grenade—at one another. French soldiers had built their own strong points throughout the city, laying miles of barbed wire and parking tanks on sidewalks and in traffic circles. Binh Xuyen gunboats, bristling with artillery, prowled the waterfront. None of these circumstances gave Collins cause for cheer, but most infelicitous was the fact that Diem's government had shrunk to a junta composed of members of the Ngo family. Collins was not optimistic about reversing this descent into Caesarism. Diem, he insisted, had to go.

Still, the stridency of Collins's cables did not translate into prompt action on the part of the administration. Dulles, for one, was in no hurry to "cowtow" to gangsters. Despite Eisenhower's disinclination to overrule the verdict of his lieutenant in Saigon, Dulles delayed responding to Collins until he had an opportunity to discuss the ambassador's conclusions with Mansfield. If recent events had caused the senator to waver in his support of Diem, it would be easier for the administration to consider Collins's demands. If, on the other hand, Mansfield refused to moderate his pro-Diem stance, then Collins would have to be reminded of the likely Senate reaction to Diem's removal. The Democrats had recaptured Congress in the midterm elections of 1954, and Dulles was trying to maintain bipartisan congressional support for the president's foreign policy. Moreover, many of Eisenhower's top-priority domestic programs were stalled in committee and at the mercy of a legislature dominated by the opposition party. It was not a good time for the White House to confront the Democrats over Indochina.

Mansfield's reaction, when presented with Collins's messages, was predictable. "The U.S. should stick to its guns in continuing to support Diem," the senator advised. "He is the only truly nationalist leader . . . who has any chance of saving Free Viet-Nam." Dulles relayed Mansfield's views to the Saigon embassy, reminding Collins that any change of premiers would be a leap in the dark; there was no guarantee that Diem's successor would manage affairs more competently. Collins responded by insisting that he understood conditions in South Vietnam better than Mansfield did, that Quat could hardly fail to be an improvement over Diem, and that Diem had to be divested of authority at the earliest possible opportunity. "If left to his own devices," Collins warned, "Diem would attack [the] Binh Xuyen . . . headquarters in [the] heart of Saigon. . . . If this is done, there will be considerable bloodshed, destruction of property, wounds will be created which will be impossible to heal, and civil war may well result."[27]

Eisenhower was troubled by the contradictory advice he was receiving about the Diem experiment. Whom should he trust: Collins or Mansfield? The former was Washington's highest-ranking official in South Vietnam and, ostensibly, its most authoritative source of intelligence, but the latter was the Senate's Indochina sage. Dulles recommended that Collins be summoned to the White House to make the case for Diem's removal in person. Eisenhower agreed, and the State Department dispatched a cable ordering the special representative home.

The morning after his plane touched down in Washington's National Airport, Collins delivered a tour de force performance before a debriefing panel consisting of representatives of the Defense Department, CIA, Treasury, Foreign Operations Administration, and the U.S. Information Agency. His point-by-point evisceration of the Diem experiment was, according to the officer who composed the minutes of the meeting, "emphatic," "vigorous," and "forceful." Diem, Collins maintained, was leading the United States to disaster in Southeast Asia. The premier had no interest in seeking a peaceful resolution to Saigon's state of emergency—on the contrary, he welcomed a shootout with the Binh Xuyen—and he was even less interested in reorganizing his government by sharing power with leading South Vietnamese politicians. Not that any of those men would agree to serve under him anyway: his policies had so discouraged patriots like Quat and former foreign minister Tran Van Do that they would only resume their government careers if Diem were out of the picture. Such disunity could not be allowed to continue, Collins argued, or South Vietnam was finished. The only way to defeat the Viet Minh was for all noncommunist elements in the country to work together, but Diem alienated precisely those men whose support he needed if his country was to survive. In short, Collins declared, "no solution in Vietnam is possible as long as Diem remains in office."[28]

Meeting with Eisenhower for lunch at the White House that same day, Collins was even more vehement. He rattled off numerous "instances wherein Diem had been persuaded at only the last moment not to do some utterly foolish thing." Most egregious, Collins claimed, was Diem's repeatedly stated intention to attack the Binh Xuyen–held police headquarters "in the heart of Saigon . . . when the streets were full of pedestrians." But this represented only one example of Diem's unsuitability for command; Collins chronicled "many other instances," venting months of frustration, before concluding that "the net of it is, . . . this fellow is impossible."[29]

Eisenhower was impressed, but he also had to consider the weight of congressional support for Diem. He advised Collins to try to sway legislators like Mansfield and Representatives Walter Judd and Edna Kelly. While Collins did his best, Congress proved more intransigent than the president. Mansfield found Lightning Joe's case against Diem flimsy, and remarked to his aide after conferring with the special representative: "Collins really doesn't know much." The Senate Foreign Relations and House Foreign Affairs Committees were unsympathetic when Collins addressed them. By coincidence, hearings on foreign aid were ongoing at the time of Collins's recall to Washington, and many in the administration worried that abandonment of Diem would make future U.S. aid to South Vietnam a target for the congressional budget axe.[30]

Yet Collins had the debating advantage of having actually been in Vietnam for almost half a year. (Mansfield, despite his reputation as an Indochina expert, had only spent six days in Vietnam in 1953 and six days in 1954.) This advantage proved crucial when Collins confronted Dulles on 23 April. As Kenneth Young of the State Department reported, a "basic shift in our approach was taken at a long luncheon meeting with the secretary. . . . [Collins] reiterated even more vigorously and firmly his view . . . that Diem must be replaced." Dulles accepted this "basic shift" in principle, but tried to hold out for interim retention of Diem "until . . . genuinely Vietnamese elements turn up another acceptable solution." Collins informed Dulles that this was an "impossible condition." The secretary laid down his arms. On 27 April, Dulles sent top-secret cables to the embassies in Paris and Saigon setting forth the steps by which Diem was to be eased from office.[31]

Six hours after the cables left Washington, Dulles received notification from Lansdale that fighting had erupted between the Binh Xuyen and the VNA. The "Battle for Saigon" was underway.

Upon receipt of Lansdale's message, Dulles cabled both Paris and Saigon, directing the embassies there to disregard the previous telegrams "until further instructions." Randolph Kidder, chargé d'affaires of the Saigon embassy, did better than that. Worried that Diem's enemies might seize on any evidence of flagging American support for the premier, he ordered Dulles's earlier telegrams burned. The secretary followed up his "blocking" cables with instructions to supply the department with as much information as possible on the fighting to enable the National Security Council (NSC) to make sound judgments about what the U.S. response should be. The NSC was scheduled to meet the following morning, 28 April, and Dulles did not want to be flying blind when he briefed his fellow policymakers.[32]

Kidder strove to keep the State Department posted, but the pace of events in Saigon had accelerated to such a dizzying speed since the first, inconclusive reports of combat that it was impossible to determine what was happening, much less assign responsibility. Fighting began around noon on 27 April and quickly escalated from small arms and mortar exchanges to include the heaviest artillery in the VNA's arsenal. By evening it had engulfed a large part of the city. No one could say for certain whether Vien's gangsters or government troops had fired the first shot, but the most plausible scenario is that Diem seized a vanishing opportunity to stave off dismissal by Washington. The timing of the military engagement was too favorable to Diem's cause to be mere coincidence. Diem probably learned of the Eisenhower administration's intention to oust him and elected to take a now-or-never gamble by engaging the Binh Xuyen.

The results were dramatic. Saigon was in frenzy by the morning of 28 April. Numerous explosions and house-to-house combat drove thousands of people into the streets. A square mile of the city became a free-fire zone. Artillery and mortars obliterated Saigon's poor districts, killing five hundred civilians and leaving twenty thousand homeless. It was difficult to discern any strategy on the part of either the government or the Binh Xuyen, as both sides relied on meat-grinder attrition to break the will of the adversary. In one of the few maneuvers that could be called tactical, the VNA tried to cut the Binh Xuyen off from reinforcements by knocking out the bridge across the canal linking Saigon and Cholon, but the rebels foiled this stratagem by throwing pontoon bridges across the canal. The conflict, it appeared, would be decided on the basis of which side was capable of absorbing and inflicting the most punishment, and neither side was deficient in those capacities. One thousand or so Binh Xuyen and VNA soldiers were killed during the first day alone.

On the morning of 28 April, Dulles telephoned Collins to inform him of the decision to suspend instructions for replacing Diem. The administration "should not act until we have further information," Dulles declared, and cited reports that the VNA "had responded pretty effectively." Washington's decision, he implied, could well turn on whether "Diem is losing control or possibly emerging as a hero." Dulles carried this theme into an NSC meeting later that morning, although Collins attended as well and thus had one more opportunity to make his case for ousting Diem before flying back to Saigon. The secretary argued that the best policy was to let events in South Vietnam run their course, to play for time and see whether "something occurs in the Saigon disorders out of which Diem will emerge as a hero." Collins vehemently dissented. He reiterated his view that "the attempt to destroy the Binh Xuyen by military action" would "produce civil war" and that a "political solution" was therefore imperative. Furthermore, he insisted, no feasible

coalition government could be formed so long as Diem played any administrative role. Politically, Collins declared, "Diem's number was up." The NSC
listened respectfully but paid no heed. Rather, they ratified Dulles's
approach. Eisenhower observed that he could "not see what else we could do
at this time."[33]

Just as the Battle for Saigon gave hope to pro-Diem figures in the administration like Dulles, so it invigorated Diem's advocates in Congress. As he had
in his 1954 report to the Senate Foreign Relations Committee, Mansfield
demanded an end to all aid to South Vietnam if Diem were overthrown.
Senator Hubert Humphrey proclaimed that "Premier Diem is an honest,
wholesome, and honorable man. He is the kind of man we ought to be supporting, rather than conspirators, gangsters, and hoodlums . . . who are diabolical, sinister, and corrupt." Through Congresswoman Edna Kelly,
members of the House Foreign Affairs Committee registered their opposition
to the administration's withdrawing support from Diem. Representative
Thomas Dodd demanded that Collins be fired and "replaced by someone
who measures up to the needs of the hour."[34]

The ardor with which the legislature rallied around Diem was surpassed
by the American press. *U.S. News and World Report* described Diem as "the
defiant, honest little premier" who was opposed by "an unholy alliance . . .
between . . . gangsters, racketeers, soldiers of fortune, and religious fanatics."
Publisher Henry Luce's weekly editorial in *Life* proclaimed: "Every son,
daughter, or even distant admirer of the American Revolution should be
overjoyed and learn to shout, if not to pronounce, 'Hurrah for Ngo Dinh
Diem!'" Diem's decision to confront the "Binh Xuyen gangsters," Luce
declared, "immensely simplifies the task of U.S. diplomacy in Saigon. That
task is, or should be, simply to back Diem to the hilt." The *New York Times*
predicted, "If Premier Ngo Dinh Diem should be overthrown by the combination of gangsters, cultists, and French colonials who have been gunning for
him, the communists will have won a significant victory."[35]

As Collins made his globe-spanning return flight to Saigon, that city continued to tear itself apart. After forty-eight hours of house-to-house combat, the
VNA began to gain the upper hand. Le Grande Monde, previously Vien's
largest gambling establishment and now serving as a Binh Xuyen citadel, was
overrun by Diem's paratroopers after defenders and attackers suffered heavy
losses. Diem's forces then stormed one of Vien's most heavily fortified strong-
holds, the Petrus Ky High School building in Cholon, and overran that as

well. By the time Collins arrived back in South Vietnam on 2 May, the battle was nearly over. The Binh Xuyen forces were broken and running for refuge. All of Vien's command posts in Saigon were reduced to rubble. Across the Arroyo Chinois in Cholon, Vien's headquarters, with its menagerie, was in ruins, his pythons, tigers, and crocodiles killed by mortar and artillery fire. Vien himself managed to escape to Paris and live out his days in moneyed obscurity. The Cao Dai pope fled to Cambodia. Most Hoa Hao leaders surrendered.

While the VNA pursued fleeing Binh Xuyen troops into the Mekong Delta and west toward the Cambodian border, throngs of people gathered

Automatic weapons fire from South Vietnamese troops pins down Binh Xuyen rebels in the Petrus Ky High School during the "Battle for Saigon," 28 April 1955.

CORBIS.

outside Diem's residence and chanted *"Da Dao Bao Dai!"* ("Down with Bao Dai!"). Dulles cabled Collins on his return to the U.S. embassy, "Events in [the] past few days have put [the] Vietnamese situation in a . . . different perspective than when you were here." Diem's triumph over the Binh Xuyen, Dulles observed, "would appear to overtake some of the principal reasons previously advanced for [the] U.S. to support Diem's removal. . . . For us at this time to participate in a scheme to remove Diem would not only be domestically impractical but highly detrimental to our prestige in Asia." In other words, despite the arguments that Collins had been drumming into Washington's ear, despite the fact that Diem had laid waste to his own capital, and despite the irrelevance of the Battle for Saigon to America's goal of containing communism in Southeast Asia, the Diem experiment would endure.[36]

The Collins mission, however, was almost over. Collins had been eager to return to his NATO assignment for some time, and the administration was happy to accommodate him in the wake of Diem's victory. The White House issued a press release announcing Collins's relief as special representative and replacement by a regular ambassador. There was no mention of Collins's difficulties with Diem.

If Collins's views had lost credibility in Washington, they echoed sentiments in Paris, where the Diem experiment, never popular, now stirred French policymakers to new heights of pique. At a foreign ministers' conference shortly after the Battle for Saigon, French premier Edgar Faure declared, "Diem is not only incapable but mad. . . . Diem is a bad choice . . . with no chance to succeed." In case Dulles, Faure's American counterpart at the conference, was inclined to dismiss this as empty rhetoric, Faure backed it up by threatening to withdraw the FEC from Vietnam if Diem were not removed. Dulles, taken aback, cabled the White House that Faure was "not bluffing." How should Washington respond to this ultimatum? Was preservation of the Diem experiment worth a rush of one hundred thousand French troops from South Vietnam, with obvious implications as to whose soldiers would succeed them?[37]

The Eisenhower administration determined that it was. Although some voices of alarm were raised, most policymakers were inclined to shoot the works. The National Security Council Planning Board issued a report claiming that withdrawal of the FEC "would clearly disengage us from the taint of colonialism. . . . [W]e should be happy to see the French leave." Dulles concurred. Although he got Faure to endorse a public statement promising continued Franco-American cooperation against the Viet Minh, the handwriting was on the wall. By spurning French demands that Diem be replaced, the Eisenhower administration absolved Paris of its responsibilities in Vietnam and demolished the illusion that the United States and France were equal partners in the enterprise to contain Southeast Asian communism. It was a true crossing of the Rubicon. Diem rubbed salt in French wounds by ordering his army to adopt American-style uniforms and the American salute, and South Vietnamese officers even held a ceremonial burning of their French-style insignia of rank. The formerly French-led VNA was renamed the Army of the Republic of Vietnam (ARVN)—or "Arvin," as American servicemen came to call it. Vietnam was well on its way to becoming an American war.[38]

Notes

1. Frances FitzGerald, *Fire in the Lake: The Vietnamese and the Americans in Vietnam* (New York: Vintage, 1972), 5–8.

2. The Secretary of State to the Special Representative in Saigon, 4 April 1955, *FRUS, 1955–1957* (Washington, D.C.: Government Printing Office, 1985), 1:196–197.

3. Mendès-France cited in Collins Papers: Dulles to Collins/Dillon, 24 November 1954: Box 25, EL.

4. The Ambassador in Saigon to the State Department, 4 July 1954, *FRUS, 1952–1954* (Washington, D.C.: Government Printing Office, 1982), 13:1460; Colby cited in Cecil B. Currey, *Edward Lansdale: The Unquiet American* (Boston: Houghton Mifflin, 1988), 152.

5. Hinh cited in Edward G. Lansdale, *In the Midst of Wars: An American's Mission to Southeast Asia* (New York: Harper & Row, 1972), 183.

6. Dulles and Southeast Asia Treaty Organization (SEATO) terms cited in David L. Anderson, *Trapped by Success: The Eisenhower Administration and Vietnam, 1953–1961* (New York: Columbia University Press, 1991), 71.

7. Dulles cited in George Kahin, *Intervention: How America Became Involved in Vietnam* (New York: Anchor Books, 1986), 71.

8. Collins Papers: Report on Indochina: A Report by Senator Mike Mansfield on a Study Mission to Vietnam, Laos, and Cambodia, 15 October 1954: Box 25, EL.

9. Dulles Papers, White House Memoranda Series: Memorandum of Conversation with the President, 30 October 1954: Box 1, EL.

10. Dulles cited in J. Lawton Collins, *Lightning Joe: An Autobiography* (Baton Rouge: Louisiana State University Press, 1979), 378.

11. Collins cited in Ellen J. Hammer, *A Death in November: America in Vietnam, 1963* (New York: Dutton, 1987), 71.

12. Collins Papers: Collins to Dulles, 13 November 1954: Box 25, EL.

13. Ely cited in Collins Papers: Collins to Dulles, 10 November 1954: Box 25, EL;

Diem cited in the Ambassador in Vietnam to the Department of State, 10 November 1954, *FRUS, 1952–1954*, 13:2229–2230.

14. Collins Papers: Collins to Dulles, 13 November 1954: Box 31, EL.

15. Collins Papers: Staff Meeting, 1 January 1955: Box 25, EL.

16. Collins Papers: Collins to Dulles, 23 November 1954: Box 25, EL.

17. Collins Papers: Collins to Dulles, 13 December 1954: Box 25, EL; Collins to Dulles, 16 December 1954: Box 25, EL.

18. Collins Papers: Dulles to Collins, 24 December 1954: Box 25, EL.

19. White House Office, NSC Staff Papers, 1948–1961, OCB Central File Series: Draft Progress Report, 19 January 1955: Box 38, EL; the Special Representative in Saigon to the Department of State, 15 January 1955, *FRUS, 1955–1957*, 1:37–40.

20. The Secretary of State to the Department of State, 1 March 1955, *FRUS, 1955–1957*, 1:101–102; Transcript Dulles Non-attributable Conference, 1 March 1955, John Foster Dulles Papers, Seeley Mudd Library, Princeton University, Princeton, New Jersey [hereafter Dulles Papers], Box 98.

21. Collins Papers: Proclamation of the Binh Xuyen, Cao Dai, and Hoa Hao Sects at the Press Conference of Pope Pham Cong Tac, 4 March 1955: Box 30, EL.

22. Ely cited in the Special Representative in Saigon to the Department of State, 10 March 1955, *FRUS, 1955–1957*, 1:116–119; Collins Papers: Voice of the Unified Front of All the Nationalist Forces in Vietnam, 21 March 1955: Box 30, EL.

23. Collins Papers: Collins to Dulles, 24 March 1955: Box 31, EL; Broadcast Statement of Premier Ngo Dinh Diem on 24 March 1955, file 751G.00/3-2455, RG 59.

24. Collins Papers: Collins to Dulles, 29 March 1955: Box 31, EL.

25. Collins Papers: Collins to Dulles, 7 April 1955: Box 26, EL.

26. Eisenhower cited in Dulles Papers, Telephone Calls Series: John Foster Dulles to Allen Dulles, 11 April 1955: Box 3, EL.

27. Mansfield cited in Young to Dulles, 8 April 1955, file 751G.00/4-855, RG 59; Collins Papers: Collins to Dulles, 10 April 1955: Box 26, EL.

28. Sebald to Dulles, 23 April 1955, file 751G.00/4-2355, RG 59.

29. White House Office, Office of the Special Assistant for National Security Affairs, Records, 1952–1961, Special Assistant Series, Chronological Subseries: Memorandum for the Record: South Vietnam—General Joe Collins's Comments, 22 April 1955: Box 1, EL.

30. Mansfield cited in Gregory Alan Olson, *Mansfield and Vietnam: A Study in Rhetorical Adaptation* (East Lansing: Michigan State University Press, 1995), 59.

31. Young to Robertson, 30 April 1955, *United States–Vietnam Relations, 1945–1971* (Washington, D.C.: Government Printing Office, 1971) [hereafter *U.S.-VN Relations*], 10:945–947.

32. Collins Papers: Dulles to Kidder/Dillon, 27 April 1955: Box 25, EL.

33. Dulles Papers, Telephone Calls Series: Dulles to Collins, 28 April 1955: Box 3, EL; Dwight D. Eisenhower, Papers as President of the United States, 1953–1961, Ann Whit-

man File, NSC Series: Memorandum of Discussion at the 246th Meeting of the National Security Council, Thursday, 28 April 1955: Box 6, EL.

34. Humphrey cited in "Conditions in South Vietnam," *Congressional Record* 101 (2 May 1955): 5288–5291; Dodd cited in "Collins's Removal as Aide Urged by Dodd," *Washington Post*, 2 May 1955.

35. "U.S. in Middle of Gang War," *U.S. News and World Report*, 13 May 1955, 39–41; Henry Luce, "Revolution in Vietnam," *Life*, 16 May 1955, 3; "Trouble in Vietnam," *New York Times*, 6 April 1955.

36. The Secretary of State to the Embassy in Vietnam, 1 May 1955, *FRUS, 1955–1957*, 1:344–345.

37. Faure cited in the Secretary of State to the Department of State, 8 May 1955, *FRUS, 1955–1957*, 1:375; the Secretary of State to the Department of State, 7 May 1955, *FRUS, 1955–1957*, 1:377.

38. Bonesteel memorandum, 9 May 1955, *U.S.-VN Relations*, 10:975.

CHAPTER FOUR

~

"Miracle Man"
Diem's Regime in Myth and Reality

The story of South Vietnam for most of the Eisenhower era was really two
stories, both of historic importance and both featuring Ngo Dinh Diem as
protagonist. First, of course, was the record of Diem's performance as South
Vietnamese leader: his policies, his methods of implementing them, their
impact on his people. Second was the manner in which Diem's leadership
was perceived in the United States. The two stories could not have differed
more completely. For citizens of South Vietnam, especially non-Catholics,
the Diem years were a time of terror, incompetence, corruption, and growing
communist strength in the countryside. In America, by contrast, Diem was
celebrated as a Miracle Man who had turned his nation into a showcase of
freedom. Although these Diem-centered narratives contradicted each other
in virtually every particular, they both contributed to the same result: the
Americanization of the war in Vietnam. Diem's inefficient and brutal reign
alienated millions of South Vietnamese from their government and
increased his nation's vulnerability to communism, while American miscon-
ceptions of what was occurring south of the 17th parallel compelled policymakers to deepen the U.S. commitment to the Diem regime. It was not until
mid-1959, when newspaper articles critical of Washington's Diem experiment prompted a congressional investigation, that the fairy tale promulgated
in the American media and the speeches of American statesmen began to
resemble the real-life horror story playing itself out in South Vietnam.

One of Diem's first acts after crushing the Binh Xuyen was to order the arrest of Ba Cut ("cut finger"), the guerrilla leader who directed most Hoa Hao forces in the Mekong Delta. Ba Cut was no communist, having led the Hoa Hao in combat against the Viet Minh since 1947. Like Diem, he was appalled when the Geneva conferees gave half of his country to Ho Chi Minh, and his principal criticism of the Diem government was that it had been "too passive" in its protest against the Geneva Accords. Ba Cut's credentials as a nationalist were as unquestionable as his anticommunism: he acquired his nickname because, as a teenager, he had cut off one of his fingers to remind him to always fight the French. He might have been considered the kind of "to-the-ender" partisan against communism and colonialism that Diem's administration needed if it were to survive.[1]

But Diem resented Ba Cut's popularity and, more so, the independent army he commanded. The premier was also insulted when Ba Cut, unlike other Hoa Hao leaders, refused to announce his allegiance to the government after the Battle for Saigon. Diem therefore sent troops of the Army of the Republic of Vietnam (ARVN) into the Delta to seize the sect chieftain. Ba Cut was captured and tried for rebellion. During the trial, he removed his shirt, showed spectators the scars he had received fighting communists, and challenged any man present to show as many. The judge, unimpressed, sentenced him to death. There were appeals for clemency from many quarters, including the CIA mission in Saigon, where Colonel Edward Lansdale felt that executing Ba Cut would antagonize the Hoa Hao and tarnish Diem's image as a humane leader. Diem paid no heed. Ba Cut was guillotined.

It ought not to have surprised anyone acquainted with Diem that this man, once in power, would become a dictator. The journalist Denis Warner notes that "the very qualities which helped Diem to survive in 1954–55 were also the qualities that brought about his own downfall." Diem's singleness of purpose, courage, and refusal to accommodate had served him well during the Battle for Saigon, not least in terms of the impression created among his partisans in the United States. "This man is going to last," the philanthropist and Diem supporter Leo Cherne noted. "This man is an almost unbreakable patriot." Diem, however, could not translate wartime unbreakability into political capital during the half-war, half-peace that prevailed in South Vietnam from 1955 until the founding of the National Liberation Front (NLF) in 1960.[2]

After besting the Binh Xuyen, Diem ought to have inaugurated a cooling-off period. Saigon was in ruins, its population terrified; a single soothing speech from the premier would have worked wonders. Many Cao Dai and

Hoa Hao, intimidated by the rout of the Binh Xuyen, would have welcomed the government's offer of an olive branch. Many fence-sitting South Vietnamese, unsure of their new leader's intentions, might have enlisted in Diem's cause had he demonstrated any inclination to let wounds heal. But Diem squandered the fruits of his momentary triumph. He could not profane his virtue by playing politics. From his perspective, he had defeated his rivals, and he had done it his way. Now the nation would be made worthy of him.

Diem swiftly moved to eliminate all opposition. He scheduled a referendum to determine who would lead South Vietnam: himself or Bao Dai. The question posed to voters was "Do the people wish to depose Bao Dai and recognize Ngo Dinh Diem as the Chief of State of Vietnam with a mission to install a democratic republic?" Some of Diem's American advisers thought that creation of a national assembly should precede any attempt to remove the emperor—so that if, as seemed inevitable, the electorate chose democracy over monarchy, there would be some alternative authority besides Diem's. The premier ignored this counsel, and his government staged the referendum on 23 October 1955.[3]

Although there was little doubt that Diem would have defeated Bao Dai in a fair election, his followers left nothing to chance. Campaigning for the emperor was prohibited. Ballot boxes were stuffed, voters intimidated, and the nation subjected to anti–Bao Dai propaganda. U.S. ambassador Frederick Reinhardt noted that large "cardboard dummies of Bao Dai all over town show him carrying bags of money on his shoulders, a pack of cards in his hands, and pix of naked women in his pocket." For good measure, the photograph of Diem on his ballots depicted him as youthful and surprisingly slim, while Bao Dai seemed bloated and hung over.[4]

To no one's surprise, Diem won the election, but his 98.2 percent of the vote raised a few eyebrows, as did the fact that he was credited with two hundred thousand more votes in Saigon than there were registered voters. Still, Bao Dai had been removed from the scene, and Diem proclaimed the birth of the Republic of South Vietnam, with himself as its first president. Five months later, he permitted elections for an assembly that would "write" a constitution he had already drafted. The results of this election were a reprise of the October 1955 referendum: U.S. Embassy officials estimated that over ninety of the 123 members chosen for the assembly were in Diem's pocket, their various party labels notwithstanding.

The constitution produced by the assembly was a curious document. Its first articles "affirm[ed]" the "'separation' of the legislative, executive, and judicial functions of government," but then backpedaled to assert that "this separation of powers does not, and cannot, mean a rigid and mechanical partition of Power." Power with a capital P belonged to Diem. "The President is vested with the leadership of the Nation," the constitution declared, and granted Diem the prerogative to "harmonize the legislative, executive, and judicial functions." Article 41 allowed Diem to issue laws by decree and change existing laws. He was moreover free to appoint or dismiss all officers in the armed forces and all civilian officials without concurrence of the legislature. Article 44 gave Diem the right to rule by emergency, and implied that he might declare an emergency whenever he wished. Article 98 delegated "[f]urther extraordinary powers to suspend temporarily certain civil liberties," such as "liberties of movement and of residence, of opinion and of the press, of meetings and of associations, of syndical liberties and the right to strike." This was hardly town-meeting democracy. Yet Diem had endowed his regime with the trappings of representative government, and the gesture pleased his American sponsors.[5]

Even the peremptory provisions of South Vietnam's constitution did not convey the extent to which the nation became, under Diem, a police state and a family dictatorship. Kinship has always played a prominent role in Vietnamese culture, and loyalty to family members was, unsurprisingly, a core value both north and south of the 17th parallel. Diem, however, took nepotism to a new extreme. Whatever authority he could bring himself to delegate, he placed in the hands of his family.

Most influential was brother Ngo Dinh Nhu, whose modest-sounding title of "political counselor" disguised his true importance. Nhu was a graduate of France's École des Chartes, a school of medieval studies, and had been employed as an archivist in the imperial library at Hue until the end of World War II. He then became involved in politics, working to whip up support for Diem among noncommunist Vietnamese during Diem's four-year exile from his homeland. The effectiveness of these promotional efforts was debatable, but Diem believed they had contributed to his installation as premier, and he turned to Nhu frequently for advice and guidance. The bond between the two men grew stronger over the course of Diem's reign, until by 1963 Nhu was virtually the only person to whom the South Vietnamese leader would listen. An intelligent and courageous man, Nhu was also devious, cruel, arrogant, and, by many accounts, an opium addict.

Nhu began to assert his authority as soon as Diem was installed at the Norodom Palace. U.S. ambassador Robert McClintock cabled Washington that the premier's brother "quite evidently" intended to serve "as an informal co-prime minister." Prior to Diem's return to South Vietnam, Nhu had

The Ngo ruling clan, 1 October 1963. U.S. embassy official John Mecklin recalled in 1965, "There probably had never before in American foreign affairs been a phenomenon comparable to our relations with the Ngo family. It was like dealing with a whole platoon of de Gaulles."
Bettman/CORBIS.

founded a political party, the Can Lao Nhan Vi Cach Mang Dang, or Revolutionary Workers' Party, to mobilize support for his older brother, and the party acquired tremendous power in the late 1950s. Eerily similar to communist organizations, the Can Lao had cadres, cells, and other features that enabled its agents to infiltrate the army, the national assembly, the police, the educational system, and the media. By 1956 Can Lao personnel controlled every facet of the administrative apparatus of South Vietnam, spying on potential traitors, pressuring government and army officials to join the party, and using torture and assassination to stifle dissent.[6]

In addition to providing Diem with his principal instrument of family rule, Nhu devised the regime's official orthodoxy, a philosophy called *Nhan Vi*, or Personalism, which Nhu claimed would enable South Vietnam to steer a path between the excesses of communism and liberal capitalism. During his studies in France, Nhu had been impressed by the philosopher Emmanuel

Mounier, who argued in his books and in the journal *Esprit* that liberalism's exaltation of the individual at the expense of the group led to exploitation and isolation, while communism, with its focus on people's material needs, ignored the spiritual dimension of their lives. Mounier advocated a middle way, a postcapitalist social order in which both individual and community could flourish; citizens of this balanced society would enjoy basic rights and civil liberties, but they would be encouraged to direct their energies toward securing the well-being of the group rather than their own selfish goals. Because Mounier believed that only such a middle path could nurture the development of the whole person, as opposed to the atomized individual or collectivized communist, he called his credo "Personalism." Mounier never worked out a political program to realize his ideals, but Nhu believed that Personalism, adapted to the conditions of postcolonial Indochina, provided the perfect guide for South Vietnam's development. Diem agreed—he liked the philosophy's compatibility with both Catholicism and Confucianism—and Personalism became his government's doctrine.

Personalism proved difficult to translate into coherent policies. Indeed, as interpreted by Diem and Nhu, it was all but incomprehensible. When the South Vietnamese president or his political counselor attempted to explain the theory to interviewers, they inevitably drew blank, if deferential, stares. John Donnell, a professor at the University of California and one of Diem's defenders, admitted that the creed was "abstruse" but insisted that it "lean[ed] heavily on . . . a conception of the dignity and value of each unique human being which originally stemmed from Christianity." Less respectful was Jean-Marie Domenach, heir to Mounier as editor of *Esprit*, who told a French journalist that Diemist Personalism was a "usurpation and travesty" of Mounier's ideas. To judge by political realities in South Vietnam during the Diem years, the philosophy did not place much value on Western-style freedoms. Dissidents were jailed, tortured, and murdered; the press, radio, and television were under government control; elections were rigged; and the legislature was a rubber-stamp body. Diem and Nhu seemed to consider Personalism a rationale for benevolent autocracy, in which the people, recognizing their leader's moral superiority, trusted his judgment, obeyed his edicts, and remembered their civic duties.[7]

Almost as influential as Nhu—and even less likable, from the perspective of most South Vietnamese—was his wife, Tran Le Xuan, better known as Madame Nhu. No member of the Ngo family made a more striking impression. Surpassingly beautiful, with lacquered fingernails, form-fitting décolleté gowns, and stiletto-heeled shoes, she attracted a great deal of press attention, although it was usually unfavorable. Her sharp tongue offended reporters, and she earned a number of derisive sobriquets: "Dragon Lady," "Queen Bee," and "Lucretia Borgia," among others. Because Diem was a bachelor, Madame Nhu became, in effect, the Republic of Vietnam's first lady. She also held a seat in the national assembly and headed the Women's Solidarity Movement, an all-female militia.

Diem's other three brothers also wielded political clout. Ngo Dinh Thuc, bishop of Vinh Long Province and later archbishop of Hue, was South Vietnam's most powerful religious leader, permitted by Diem to ask Saigon businessmen for "voluntary contributions to the Church." One proprietor complained that Thuc's requests read "like tax notices." Ngo Dinh Can was the warlord of central South Vietnam. He held no official position within Diem's administration, but his power from Pan Thiet Province north to the 17th parallel was absolute. He employed his own secret police network, determined which businesses would receive contracts, and appointed men loyal to him to all government posts in the region. He also allegedly ran a smuggling ring that distributed opium across Asia. Ngo Dinh Luyen, Diem's youngest brother, served as South Vietnam's ambassador to the United Kingdom. Other Ngo family members filled important positions: Madame Nhu's father became ambassador to the United States, her mother became South Vietnamese delegate to the UN, and her uncle became minister of foreign affairs. Dozens of Diem's nephews and cousins occupied key posts in South Vietnamese embassies, in the military, and in the civil administration. When American policymakers, exasperated by Diem's inability to trust anyone outside his family, discussed possible replacements for him in 1963, they half-jokingly listed as their top requirement for a new president: "he should be an only child."[8]

With the Binh Xuyen defeated and the religious sects subdued, the most serious threat to Ngo family rule was the communists, and Diem knew it. Shortly after the conclusion of the three-hundred-day free movement period stipulated by the Geneva Accords, Diem initiated an "Anti-Communist Denunciation Campaign" to root out Viet Minh members or sympathizers remaining in South Vietnam. Thousands of people were either jailed or detained indefinitely under house arrest. Executions were frequent. Diem escalated the campaign in January 1956 by issuing Ordinance No. 6, which removed almost all restrictions on officials combating political opponents. According to this edict, anyone considered a danger "to the defense of the state and public order" was to be thrown in jail or placed under house arrest until "order and security" had been established—however far in the future that might be. In the Delta, government-sponsored beheading and disemboweling became commonplace.[9]

Such methods were effective in reducing the number of Viet Minh in South Vietnam. Communist Party historians later wrote that the years 1955 to 1959 were "the darkest period" in their party's history, when membership in the south declined by two-thirds. Yet Diem's tactics created more enemies for his regime than they eliminated. They were so harsh and undiscriminating that many peasants and urban residents who were originally well disposed toward Diem turned against him after they or members of their families suffered torture, imprisonment, or execution. Well before the establishment of the NLF in 1960, guerrilla uprisings in the countryside were common.[10]

Although Diem's American supporters hailed him as a liberal reformer, he gave South Vietnam the most absolutist government it ever had, appointing province chiefs for the country's forty-one provinces and personally selecting administrators for its 246 districts. In order to prevent Viet Minh sympathizers from covertly controlling village governments, he abolished local village elections and appointed his own men to supervise the affairs of South Vietnam's twenty-five hundred villages and sixteen thousand hamlets. This was an unprecedented move. No unwritten political principle in Vietnam was more hallowed than the dictum: "The control of the Empire stops at the village gates." For millennia, village oligarchies had been responsible for collecting taxes, resolving disputes, and performing the functions of government. While most peasants despised the oligarchs, these traditional village councils at least *knew* the peasants, and understood how far they could be pushed before rebelling—a safeguard that did not exist under Diem's appointees.

Not content with alienating the ethnic Vietnamese, Diem turned his attention to the Montagnards. He recognized that the Montagnard Central Highlands might be of strategic importance to the Viet Minh—a potential gateway to the south—should Ho attempt an invasion. Consequently, Diem decided to resettle landless Vietnamese in the highlands and establish a Maginot Line of settlements to ward off communist infiltration. This made sense strategically, but the manner in which it was handled was tactless in the extreme. The French had administered the highlands separately and allowed the Montagnards a measure of autonomy. Diem, indifferent to the Montagnards' independence and mistrust of "lowlanders," initiated a program of population transfer whereby 210,000 Vietnamese, predominantly

Catholics, were settled in fortified villages that the Montagnards regarded as their own. As a consequence of Diem's treatment, the tribes grew receptive to Viet Minh propaganda promising them a return to autonomy in a unified, communist Vietnam.

Diem proved no more astute in his handling of the Chinese. He demanded that the three hundred thousand Chinese residents of Saigon, who were essential to the commercial life of the country, choose between becoming Vietnamese citizens and losing their rights to do business. While most Chinese complied with the government's directive rather than sacrifice their livelihoods, their initial reaction was to close the export market for rice and halt all water transport from Saigon to the Delta. The South Vietnamese economy sustained a punishing recession. Diem remained adamant; he gave the Chinese a year to register for Vietnamese nationality cards, and warned that failure to do so would result in liquidation of their businesses. The Chinese who changed their citizenship under duress did not become more loyal to the government; rather, Diem's policies succeeded in transforming a previously nonpolitical minority into a potential ally of the Viet Minh.

The most conspicuous features of the Diem regime, apart from its authoritarianism, were sanctimony and religious bigotry. Madame Nhu took the lead in the government's antivice campaign. Using her position in the national assembly and access to Diem as unofficial first lady, she managed to get a number of laws passed to enforce a stern moral code on the populace. Divorce was made almost impossible and adultery a crime. Abortion was banned, as were prostitution, blue movies, horse racing, beauty contests, boxing matches, sentimental songs, and even dancing. People were arrested for wearing loud clothing or affecting modern hairstyles. The government subsidized poster exhibits and dramatic skits to portray the evils of vice. Public bonfires of such "wicked" materials as playing cards and phonograph records occurred often.

Diem's pro-Catholic bias, already evident during Passage to Freedom, became more pronounced. He staffed his administration almost exclusively with Catholics and saw to it that Catholic villages received the bulk of U.S. aid. Catholics were de facto exempt from the corvée labor that the government obliged citizens to perform. The Catholic Church enjoyed special rights to acquire and own property. In 1959 Diem dedicated his predominantly non-Christian nation to the Virgin Mary. He outlawed "spiritualism," deliberately leaving his definition of the term vague so as to intimidate the broadest spectrum of non-Catholics. His favoritism was so flagrant that in central Vietnam thousands of people converted to Catholicism in order to

The surpassingly beautiful but poison-tongued Madame Nhu, 1 May 1956.

Time & Life Pictures. By: John Dominis. Getty Images.

avoid being uprooted and replaced by Catholic refugees from the north. The government's policies lent new urgency to the traditional Vietnamese saying, first spoken during the era of French colonialism: "Turn Catholic and have rice to eat."[11]

Although Diem's catalog of mistakes was diverse, nothing brought forth a more baneful harvest than his attempts at land reform. Most Americans stationed in South Vietnam in the mid- to late 1950s recognized that this was the issue on which the Diem experiment would succeed or fail. Vietnam was an agrarian country—agriculture supported 80 percent of the population and provided the nation's two principal exports, rice and rubber—and land ownership was concentrated to a degree unusual even for a country emerging from colonial domination. In the Mekong Delta, the most intensively farmed area of Vietnam, about 2,500 landowners, or 0.025 percent of the rural population, claimed 40 percent of the riceland. Almost the entire Delta was owned by absentee landlords and worked by tenant farmers. Although tenancy was less prevalent in central and northern Vietnam, far more Vietnamese farmers rented their land than owned it. Tenants often gave up between 50 and 70 percent of their crop in rent, and were in near-constant debt. The landlord-tenant relationship, strained under the most equitable of circumstances, was explosive in Vietnam, and any government hoping to establish a popular base clearly needed to implement a program of land redistribution.

The communists accomplished this in their zone of Vietnam by violent means: they eliminated the landlords, either by sending them to forced labor camps or killing them. About fifteen thousand North Vietnamese landlords were executed by mid-1956, and their land was parceled out among previously landless farmers. Neither Diem nor his American advisers proposed anything so drastic. Diem knew that he could not afford to make enemies among South Vietnam's landowners, who constituted the most dependably anticommunist bloc in the country. His conservative ideology, moreover, disinclined him to incite class conflict. Yet he also knew that the cardinal desire of most South Vietnamese was to acquire land, and that the government had to satisfy this yearning or lose all propaganda advantage to the communists.

Diem at first seemed prepared to move vigorously on the land-reform front. When U.S. vice president Richard Nixon visited Saigon, he found Diem bubbling over with enthusiasm about the potential for rent reduction and land transfers to "take the wind out of the communist sails." Successful land reform, Diem told Nixon, was "*the* pre-condition of meeting the threat of communism." Despite such rhetoric, Diem did not introduce any agrarian legislation until long after becoming chief of state. Because of the many challenges to his authority in the first year, he was unable to devote much attention to the conditions of tenant farmers, and even after he crushed most of his rivals he displayed little interest in land policy. Wolf Ladejinsky, an American agricultural expert who worked for the United States Operations Mission (USOM) in South Vietnam before becoming Diem's personal assistant, was frustrated by the president's indifference to what Ladejinsky called "the weak link between the national government and the farmers." In a report to the U.S. Embassy, Ladejinsky complained that "land reform problems do not appear to loom large in [Diem's] scheme of things."[12]

The first land ordinances proclaimed by the Saigon government were cautious. In January 1955 Diem declared that landlords could collect no more than 25 percent of a farmer's crop; rents could be higher if the landlord furnished supplies like fertilizer, but the days of charging half the crop in rent were over. Diem also gave tenants the right to farm abandoned or uncultivated land. These measures contained only weak mechanisms to ensure compliance with the government's orders, and many landlords ignored them. In territory still under Viet Minh domination, Diem's ordinances were unenforceable. More important, even those peasants the government could reach displayed little gratitude for the new reforms, which they interpreted as a return to the bad old days of rural exploitation and debt peonage.

The reason for the tenant farmers' unappreciativeness was simple: many of them had paid no rent at all since the outbreak of the Franco–Viet Minh War in 1946. Either wartime conditions had made collection of rent impossible in certain areas of the country or the Viet Minh had compelled landlords to abandon their holdings and flee to the safety of the cities; the communists had then confiscated the land and distributed it to the peasants before being driven back across the 17th parallel. Diem's government, in implementing rent controls and nullifying communist redistribution, antagonized thousands of farmers who now found themselves paying rent, albeit less than in prewar years, on land they considered their own. These farmers could not help but compare the Diem regime's counterrevolutionary approach to the Viet Minh's promises of "land to the tiller."

Diem also failed to nurture much goodwill among landlords, who found the new rentals too low but preferable to collecting no rent. Most went along with the government's program, relieved that Diem had affirmed their proprietary rights and given them a chance to make at least some money. Yet they were hardly enthusiastic about what Diem had done, and some defied the new rules by extorting more than the legal maximum in rent from their tenants. One American diplomat noted that the only reason landlords even pretended to observe Diem's directives was their fear that "the alternative to a government-sponsored program may be a communist one."[13]

At Ladejinsky's behest, Diem introduced a more radical reform in October 1956. Ordinance No. 57 limited individual landholdings to 115 hectares (roughly 247 acres); any land in excess of that amount was to be purchased by the government at the rate of 7,000 piasters a hectare and resold to landless farmers. Diem's admirers in the United States hailed this as a progressive piece of legislation that would appeal to both tenants and landlords; the former would get the land they craved while the latter would be justly compensated. But drawbacks in the ordinance soon became apparent. First, Diem decreed that it only applied to riceland; all other crops were exempt, which meant that about 235 million acres did not become eligible for transfer. Also, the 115-hectare limit guaranteed that extreme inequities of landholdings would persist. Similar programs in South Korea, Japan, and Formosa had established ownership ceilings at less than one-thirtieth of what Diem's government permitted. Only South Vietnam's biggest landholders were affected by the new ordinance, and even they managed to circumvent it by transferring title to some of their land to family members. In all, Ordinance No. 57 made available approximately seven hundred thousand hectares—a third of the country's tenanted land—for distribution. Of this amount, the government actually transferred only about 40 percent to new owners. Many of the recipients were outraged that they had to pay for the land; the Viet Minh had attached no such strings to their gifts.

More important than the ordinance's conservatism was the incompetent and corrupt manner in which it was put into effect. Local officials frequently lacked the initiative to carry out Diem's reforms. Ladejinsky reported after one of his trips through the countryside that "even the exceptional official tends to engage in merely verbalizing the need for the enforcement of the law." South Vietnamese vice president Nguyen Ngoc Tho and the minister of agrarian reform, Nguyen Van Thoi, oversaw the land reform program, and neither had any incentive to see it succeed. Like most officers charged with executing land transfers, these men were wealthy landlords themselves. A peasant disgusted by Thoi's inattention to duty protested to the U.S. Embassy, "he is most certainly not interested in land distribution which would divest him of much of his property." Some provincial administrators sabotaged the government's reform efforts by ignoring tenants' complaints, bribing judges in landlord-tenant disputes, and using legal stratagems to exceed the 115-hectare ceiling, such as claiming extra hectares for ancestor worship. Diem's religious prejudice compounded these problems, as he refused to transfer 370,500 acres of land owned by the Catholic Church to the government for reallocation.[14]

The results of Diem's land reforms were almost wholly negative. Only around 10 percent of the more than one million tenant households in South Vietnam acquired any new land, which they were obliged to purchase at a stiff price. Most of the nation's large estates were not broken up; by the time Diem was assassinated, one-tenth of the landholders still owned 55 percent of the riceland. Far more South Vietnamese lost land in the Diem years than gained it. If during the colonial period the landlord had been the most hated person in the Mekong Delta, he had to share that dubious honor by 1957 with representatives of Diem's government—and with Diem himself.

While Diem pursued his vision of national renewal, the American presence in his country grew. The United States Military Assistance Advisory Group (MAAG) had consisted of 342 men at the time Diem took office midway through the Geneva Conference, and the accords generated by that conference forbade the introduction of any additional foreign military forces into North or South Vietnam. No American had signed the accords, but the Eisenhower administration wanted to appear to be complying with them, and the 342-man ceiling did not seem a problem as long as the French Expeditionary Corps remained in the south. The withdrawal of French forces after the Dulles-Faure talks in May 1955, however, confronted Washington with an emergency. There were no longer enough Western advisers in South Vietnam to train Diem's army. Lieutenant General Samuel Williams, who replaced Mike O'Daniel as head of the MAAG in October 1955, requested more men. The Joint Chiefs of Staff backed Williams, informing the Defense Department that "[m]ilitary personnel restrictions for [the] MAAG . . . have become an increasingly serious handicap." The chiefs called for "a more liberal interpretation of personnel ceiling limitations."[15]

Although sympathetic to these pleas, Secretary of State John Foster Dulles vetoed any lifting of the MAAG ceiling. If Washington were to violate the Geneva Accords, he argued, it might spur counterviolations by North Vietnam's backers: the Soviets and the Communist Chinese. Was there some way to increase U.S. manpower in South Vietnam while still seeming to adhere to the accords? What about putting military men in civilian clothes? Williams and his supporters responded that this was inadequate, and that the accords had only prohibited an increase in the number of *foreign* troops; surely, Washington was justified in replacing those *French* troops who, it seemed, could not get out of Vietnam fast enough. Dulles was still unwilling to risk communist retaliation. There had to be a means of getting more Americans into South Vietnam without transgressing the accords.

Dulles himself finally came up with a solution. The French, as they withdrew from Indochina, were leaving behind immense quantities of military equipment supplied by the United States. Between $500 million and $1.2 billion worth of American tanks, aircraft, small arms, ammunition, and other supplies were left to the elements. At the central maintenance depot near Saigon, abandoned vehicles and parts covered thirty-two acres of open fields. This spectacle was infuriating to U.S. officials on the scene and tax-conscious legislators at home, but Dulles saw a silver lining. The "necessity [of] protecting . . . [these] material assets," he informed the Saigon embassy, "creates [an] extraordinary situation in respect [to] our self-imposed restraints under [the] Geneva Accords." Dulles recommended that Washington dispatch a temporary mission "for [the] purpose [of] recovering and preserving equipment now being lost due to [the] French withdrawal." There was nothing in the accords about equipment recovery, after all, and no one could object if the United States tried to save millions of dollars of its own materiel from rotting away in the tropical weather. Eisenhower liked the idea, and gave his approval to what came to be known as the Temporary Equipment Recovery Mission (TERM). The British and French governments protested that this was a transparent attempt to circumvent the rules agreed on at Geneva, but the International Control Commission charged with implementing the accords raised no objections, and the first of 350 new American troops began arriving in Saigon in mid-1956. By the end of the following year, only seven of the 350 servicemen were working full-time on equipment recovery; the rest joined MAAG personnel in training the ARVN.[16]

Diem's reaction to the rising number of Americans in South Vietnam was telling. He knew he needed U.S. support to stay in power, but he was also a Vietnamese patriot who did not like foreigners occupying his country. Moreover, he wanted to preserve the image of South Vietnam as a sovereign nation. It galled him that the Viet Minh were able to point to his American advisers as evidence of neocolonialism. No third-world leader found the label "puppet" as repugnant as Diem did, and none worked harder to prove his nationalist credentials. Often, these efforts took the form of disparaging remarks about the Americans, as when he quipped to a reporter, "If you bring in the American dog, you must accept American fleas." But his principal manner of demonstrating that he was nobody's puppet involved ignoring or defying American instructions.[17]

One of the most significant displays of Diem's independent-mindedness occurred when Washington attempted to finesse the issue of all-Vietnam elections, scheduled for 1956. Neither the Eisenhower administration nor Diem had any intention of allowing the elections to take place, but the Americans felt that Diem could make North Vietnam look like the obstacle to reunification if he insisted on conditions for ensuring fairness at the polls. When Hanoi rejected these electoral safeguards, as everyone in the White House assumed it would, then Diem could claim that the communists were blocking the elections, not him. Washington suggested that Diem announce his willingness to confer with North Vietnamese representatives to iron out terms for elections. As U.S. Embassy chargé Randolph Kidder cabled from Saigon, Diem's government "must agree [to] play the game at least in appearance."[18]

Diem had no intention of playing Washington's game. He protested that any talks with the North Vietnamese would imply that he accepted the legitimacy of the Geneva Accords and Ho Chi Minh's regime, and he did not accept either. The accords were invalid because his government had not signed them; as for North Vietnam, it was a pawn of Moscow and Beijing. Why should he submit the fate of his rule to millions of people under communist control? Diem's stubbornness was untimely for Washington because it came on the eve of an East-West summit conference where the Soviets seemed certain to insist on observance of the accords. Diem finally agreed to release a public statement affirming that his regime supported free elections, but he also underscored that South Vietnam was not a signatory to the accords and was under no obligation to abide by them.

As had been the case with the 1954 Geneva Conference on Korea and Indochina, the 1955 Geneva Summit among the leaders of the United States, Great Britain, France, and the Soviet Union proved remarkably favorable to Diem's cause. The Soviets raised the all-Vietnam election issue but did not press it, both because they wanted to ease tensions between their country and the West and because, as British foreign minister Harold Macmillan noted, Moscow did not relish drawing attention to the hypocrisy of advocating "unification based on free elections in Vietnam and resisting the same proposal in relation to Germany." The French had largely withdrawn from Vietnam by this point and were no longer concerned with Vietnamese political affairs. Great Britain was not going to risk its relationship with the United States by harping on electoral provisions for a third-world country that British policymakers considered inconsequential. North Vietnam was not represented at the summit and thus could do little to urge its superpower ally to demand compliance with the most important clause of the Geneva Accords. The deadline for nationwide elections passed with Vietnam still divided. Diem probably concluded that his uncompromising approach had been correct, and that he had been right to reject the Americans' more Machiavellian plan.[19]

Another source of friction between Washington and Saigon was the Commercial Import Program (CIP), which one historian terms "the heart of the American economic assistance effort" in South Vietnam. On paper, the CIP seemed an ingenious arrangement whereby the United States could pump huge sums of money into Diem's country, thus promoting industrialization and economic self-sufficiency, while at the same time avoiding the runaway inflation that would normally be unleashed by a rapid injection of dollars into a vulnerable economy. The mechanism was an import subsidization system. The United States gave dollars to Diem's government, which, in turn, sold them to licensed South Vietnamese importers. The importers bought the dollars with piasters at one-half the official exchange rate; they then used these bargain-rate dollars to purchase American imports. The piasters that government officials collected from selling the dollars went into a counterpart fund held by the National Bank of Vietnam, and Diem drew on this fund to pay the cost of his army, police, and civil service. His government also collected tariffs on the imports. Since U.S. dollars were not allowed to circulate freely in the South Vietnamese economy, inflation was held in check. A similar fiscal device had been employed to great effect in Western Europe with the Marshall Plan, and one U.S. economist spoke for many of his colleagues when he described the CIP as "the greatest invention since the wheel."[20]

What seemed brilliant in theory proved less so in practice. Although the availability of water skis, motorbikes, refrigerators, radios, record players, and the like delighted residents of Saigon and other South Vietnamese cities, and despite the fact that the flow of CIP funds expanded the size of the urban middle classes, there was no meaningful economic development in Diem's country. Few entrepreneurs took advantage of the CIP to import capital goods to set up factories. The licensed importers purchased more consumer and luxury items than manufacturing equipment and industrial raw materials. Corruption was rampant. Some of the counterpart funds were stolen, and government officials often demanded bribes before they would grant the lucrative import licenses. Most important, the majority of CIP assistance went to fund the ARVN rather than into any long-range projects designed to promote economic growth.

The Eisenhower administration agreed with Diem that security had to take precedence over other concerns, including political reforms and industrialization, and did not object to Diem using the CIP as a means of financing his military forces. But abuses in the program worried Washington, as did the fact that its benefits never reached into the countryside. The rural masses, who comprised 85 percent of South Vietnam's population, were untouched by the CIP—except in a negative way, since they could observe the affluence of the cities and contrast it with their own enduring poverty. Furthermore, administration officials grew frustrated by Diem's refusal, even after his regime had attained a degree of stability, to devalue the piaster and bring the CIP exchange rate into conformity with what it would be if South Vietnamese and U.S. currencies were permitted to float freely against one another. Not only did the artificially low rate of thirty-five piasters to the dollar result in American, rather than South Vietnamese, taxpayers underwriting the cost of Diem's government; it also ensured that South Vietnamese products, whenever the nation got around to generating them, would not be competitive on the world market. Diem responded that if he devalued his currency, it would cut U.S. aid to South Vietnam in half and undermine allegiance to the government among those middle- and upper-class city dwellers who supported Diem because he was able to provide them with low-cost consumer and luxury goods.

Diem's analysis was correct but short-sighted. The CIP, as established in January 1955 and maintained for two decades, may have created a façade of prosperity in the cities and purchased the loyalty of the urban middle and upper classes for Diem and his successors, but it did not advance economic self-sufficiency. Rather, it fostered increasing dependence on the United States. However shrilly Diem might insist that his nation was not a U.S. protectorate, communist charges to that effect had considerable basis in fact.

In all, the Eisenhower administration found Diem uncooperative, but it had an interest in portraying his regime in a positive light, and Washington officials made repeated pronouncements throughout the late 1950s extolling Diem's accomplishments. "President Ngo Dinh Diem stands for the highest qualities of heroism and statesmanship," declared Eisenhower in 1957.

"[T]he president of Vietnam, by his inspiring leadership, is opening up vast new areas for the peaceful progress of mankind." In a televised speech heralding Diem's victory over the Binh Xuyen, Dulles informed viewers, "I am very much impressed by Prime Minister Diem. He is a true patriot and dedicated to independence." Assistant Secretary of State for Far Eastern Affairs Walter Robertson observed in 1956, "Asia has given us in President Diem another great figure, and the entire Free World has become the richer for his example of determination and moral fortitude." The outward-seeming success of the CIP, at least in South Vietnam's cities, and other deceptively encouraging factors—such as Hanoi's decision not to attack the south after Diem blocked nationwide elections—lent credibility to such statements.[21]

In contrast to the 1960s and 1970s, Washington during the Eisenhower era did not have to worry about journalists challenging its depiction of conditions in Vietnam. There were three reasons for this. First, Vietnam was a low-priority issue in U.S. foreign policy after the 1955 Battle for Saigon. Events in West Berlin, the Formosa Strait, Japan, Hungary, and Egypt consumed more of the media's attention. Also, the 1950s were an innocent time for the American press: newsmen were inclined to trust what the administration said and report it without editorializing; the kind of investigative journalism that arose principally in response to the Vietnam War did not yet exist. Most important, however, was the fact that many of America's press lords belonged to a group called the American Friends of Vietnam (AFV) that advocated U.S. support of Diem's government.

The AFV was founded in 1955 by Joseph Buttinger, a member of the International Rescue Committee (IRC), the largest nonsectarian refugee relief organization in the world. Buttinger had been sent to Saigon in 1954 by IRC chairman Leo Cherne to investigate the possibility of the IRC contributing to Passage to Freedom. He developed a close friendship with Diem, whom he found "a man of extraordinary strength, courage, and political ability." Disturbed by Special Representative J. Lawton Collins's dissatisfaction with Diem and infuriated by anti-Diem stories in some American newspapers, Buttinger resolved to improve the premier's image in the United States. Upon returning home, Buttinger became, in his words, "a one-man lobby for Diem." He engaged publicist Harold Oram, whose Madison Avenue firm provided fund-raising services for the IRC, to "act as a public relations representative in organizing a group to be known as the 'American Friends of Vietnam.'"[22]

It would have been difficult to find a more popular cause in mid-1950s America than saving an Asian nation from communism, and the AFV attracted a large and ecumenical membership, including Democratic Senators Mike Mansfield and John F. Kennedy, Republican Senators William Knowland and Karl Mundt, liberal academics Samuel Eliot Morison and Arthur Schlesinger Jr., "celebrity saint" Tom Dooley, and even Norman Thomas, president of the American Socialist Party. Of greatest value to Diem, however, were the ministers of information: Whitelaw Reid, editor and publisher of the *New York Herald Tribune*; Malcolm Muir, publisher of *Newsweek*; Walter Annenberg, head of the *Philadelphia Inquirer*; William Randolph Hearst Jr. of the *New York Journal-American*; and, foremost among titans, Time Inc.'s Henry Luce. With such media giants in its ranks, the AFV was able to produce a tremendous amount of pro-Diem propaganda in U.S. newspapers and magazines and ensure that the drawbacks of the Diem regime received little scrutiny from the American press.

Luce proved especially useful in this regard. Founder and chief editor of *Time*, *Life*, and *Fortune* magazines, he was the twentieth century's most effective American mass communicator. No one wielded more media power. His most memorable piece of pro-Diem agitprop was a *Life* feature that hailed Diem as "The Tough Miracle Man of Vietnam." After the appearance of that article, the word "miracle" became indelibly associated with America's Diem experiment. The *American Mercury* celebrated the fifth anniversary of Diem's ascension to power with the headline "Free Vietnam: Modern Miracle"; Ernest Lindley, *Newsweek's* Washington pundit, affirmed, "Ngo Dinh Diem is living proof of what is often called a miracle"; and the *New York Herald Tribune* extolled the "Miracle-Maker from Asia—Diem of South Vietnam."[23]

Around the time that *Life* christened him a Miracle Man, Diem returned to America for the first time since his exile from Vietnam. It was a triumphal visit, coordinated primarily by the AFV. Diem flew into Washington on Eisenhower's private plane, and the U.S. president made a point of greeting his visitor in person at the airport, a courtesy that Eisenhower had extended only once before. The White House also provided an honor guard that gave Diem a twenty-one-gun salute as he emerged from the aircraft. Then Eisenhower and Diem stepped into a limousine and were driven to Blair House, where Diem would rest before addressing both Houses of Congress. A crowd of over fifty thousand people lined the reception route.

The stage was set for a barnstorming circuit that marked the height of Diem's celebrity in the United States. American journalists struggled to outdo one another in rhapsodizing about the Miracle Man's enlightened government, the humane and efficient resettlement of the Catholic refugees, the booming South Vietnamese economy, and the promising future of Southeast Asia's most vibrant democracy. Under the headline "Welcome to a Champion," the *Washington Evening Star* called Diem "a valiant and effective fighter against communism." The *Boston Globe* dubbed him "Vietnam's Man of Iron." The *Washington Post* ran a feature titled "Diem—Symbol of Free New Asia." The *New York Times* hailed Diem for "advanc[ing] the cause of freedom and democracy in Asia" and voiced the "hope that he can feel the friendly warmth of our reception as we greet a good friend." Diem was extolled as "An Asian Liberator" whose "life—all of it—is devoted to God"; "a stalwart champion of freedom"; "the authentic symbol of Vietnamese nationalism, . . . capable of fighting Ho Chi Minh to a standstill." Reporters marveled at how "this remarkable man" had brought "Western-style democracy" to a "divided and polyglot country that had to absorb nearly a million refugees." One editorial noted that Diem's "secret weapon, if any, is fearlessness."[24]

Legislators proved no less smitten, interrupting Diem's address before Congress numerous times with applause. During his four days in Washington, Diem met with Eisenhower, Dulles, and other officials to ask for more aid. Eisenhower toasted Diem at a White House dinner for demonstrating "how much moral values and the concept of human dignity could count for in the minds of men." Before Diem took his leave for New York, he and Eisenhower issued a joint communiqué that "reaffirmed close mutual friendship and support between the Republic of Viet-Nam and the United States."[25]

New York City welcomed Diem with a parade from Lower Broadway to City Hall and a speech by Mayor Robert Wagner saluting the South Vietnamese leader as "a man to whom freedom is the very breath of life." The Council on Foreign Relations, the Foreign Policy Association, and the Far East-America Council played host to Diem, as did the AFV, which arranged a dinner at the Ambassador Hotel. Fittingly, Luce chaired the dinner, and Cardinal Spellman delivered the invocation. Guests included John D. Rockefeller, Senators Mansfield and Kennedy, and Eleanor Roosevelt. "The word *friends* should be my theme for tonight," a tearful Diem pronounced to the gathering. "Looking at the newspapers since I have arrived in your country, one would think that everybody in America is now a friend of Vietnam."[26]

Moving on to Michigan, Diem received further plaudits. Governor Mennen Williams designated 15 May "Ngo Dinh Diem Day," and Diem's friends at Michigan State University gave him an honorary degree, which he accepted in front of an audience of four thousand faculty and students. From

East Lansing Diem set out for Tennessee, where he toured Tennessee Valley Authority sites and proclaimed himself "very impressed." Then it was on to Los Angeles for a banquet staged by the Los Angeles World Affairs Council. The Miracle Man's final stop was in Honolulu. After spending a few days as the guest of Admiral Felix Stump, commander-in-chief of U.S. Pacific forces, Diem returned to Saigon.[27]

The trip had been a diplomatic masterstroke in which Diem managed to avoid criticism of the human rights abuses in South Vietnam and put the world on notice that he was backed by the United States. He could not have orchestrated a more successful visit. The only discordant note had been struck beyond range of his hearing, in the basement of the auditorium where he received MSU's honorary degree. There, as faculty members donned their academic regalia, Herbert Weisinger of the English department complained to a colleague, "I don't see why we are here to pay tribute to that fascist."[28]

Diem enjoyed having his ego stroked, but he was wise enough to know that the miracle acclaimed by American politicians and reporters was a miracle of public relations. Resistance to his regime was growing in South Vietnam. Shortly before Diem's American tour, he had nearly been killed at a ceremony in the central highlands. A teenager had fired a submachine gun at the president, spraying bullets and wounding members of Diem's entourage, but Diem himself avoided being hit. When the would-be assassin's gun jammed, security agents overpowered him. Diem, to the astonishment of onlookers, showed no trace of panic, ascending the rostrum and delivering his speech as if nothing had happened. It was a virtuoso display of self-command, but Diem had clearly not succeeded in quelling unrest in his nation. On the contrary: attacks against him—verbal or otherwise—were becoming more brazen.

The new U.S. ambassador in South Vietnam presented Diem with another problem. Elbridge Durbrow replaced Frederick Reinhardt in March 1957 and brought a less indulgent approach to the job. While Reinhardt had tended to support whatever policies Diem carried out, Durbrow was more in the mold of J. Lawton Collins, meaning that he believed South Vietnam needed to be preserved as a noncommunist bridgehead but was unconvinced that Diem was the best candidate to accomplish that task. Months after his arrival in Saigon, Durbrow concluded that Diem was too focused on military issues. Economic and political conditions, the ambassador cabled Washington, were responsible for the insurgency in South Vietnam. Diem needed to implement a land reform program, allow greater freedom of speech and of the press, bring some opposition figures into his cabinet, and, most important, get rid of brother Nhu, who was not only a bad influence on Diem but was also detested throughout the country.

Diem found Durbrow's recommendations unacceptable. Military needs had to take priority over matters like land reform, he insisted. Before his government could permit expanded civil liberties or offer increased economic assistance to the peasants, it had to defeat the communist guerrillas. Diem had taken to calling those insurgents "Viet Cong" (VC)—a contraction of the Vietnamese expression for "Vietnamese communist"—because he knew that "Viet Minh" was synonymous with patriotism in the minds of many of his countrymen. Five months after Diem's visit to the United States, the VC rocked Saigon by setting off three explosions in one day: the first in an American barracks, the second in an army bus, and the third at the United States Information Services library. From Diem's perspective, this was hardly a time for him to liberalize his political control. There was a war on.

Fortunately for Diem, MAAG commander Sam Williams sided with him against Durbrow. Williams viewed the conflict in Vietnam in military terms and had little patience for the ambassador's calls for Diem to nurture democracy in a combat zone. Durbrow, Williams wrote to a friend, was "better suited to be the senior salesman in a good ladies' shoe store than to be representing the U.S. in an Asian country." Williams and Durbrow grew to despise one another. A member of the embassy staff in Saigon remembered "frequent shouting matches" between the two men, and one of Williams's deputies admitted that "[r]elations with the ambassador were about as poor as they could be."[29]

While Durbrow and Williams sparred over Vietnam policy, the U.S. Congress gave a shock to both the embassy and the MAAG—and, above all, to Diem. Eisenhower had prepared an ambitious 1957 foreign-aid package and put all of his persuasive powers into the effort to get it passed. He insisted to budget-conscious congressmen that foreign aid represented America's "best investment" and volunteered to sacrifice his own salary "to meet the pressing need of adequate funds for foreign aid." Yet the legislature slashed the administration's foreign-aid program by almost one-third. Much of the money had been earmarked for the developing world. Now nations like Formosa, South Korea, and South Vietnam would have to make do with fewer American dollars. This was upsetting to Diem because opposition to his government mounted in 1957; he believed he needed more U.S. aid, not less, and he warned Durbrow that he would cancel even those minor political and economic reforms the regime had planned before cutting funds for the army. Durbrow communicated Diem's concerns to Washington, adding his own request that aid to South Vietnam not be reduced. Dulles responded that there was nothing the White House could do; the United States had global obligations, resources were limited, and Congress was demanding retrenchment in foreign aid.[30]

More disturbing to Diem was a scandal that erupted in the summer of 1959 when Albert Colegrove, a reporter for the Scripps-Howard chain, was posted to South Vietnam to report on America's campaign to preserve a bastion of freedom at the gates of the red empire. Colegrove wrote six articles under the common heading "Our Hidden Scandal in Vietnam" that appeared in eighteen newspapers, the combined circulation of which approached three million. The subheadings of the articles left nothing to the imagination: "We Aren't Building Much Democracy in Vietnam," "Fiasco in Vietnam," "Officials Deny Vietnam Fiasco," and so on. Colegrove told of millions of dollars in U.S. assistance squandered on projects that were inappropriate to conditions in Southeast Asia and sprinkled his articles with anecdotes that, taken together, seemed to prove that Diem was running a dictatorship. Colegrove claimed to have encountered a man who had been thrown in a concentration camp because someone saw him shaking his fist in the direction of Diem's palace. Another man had met the same fate because he told an anti-Diem joke. The regime's camps, Colegrove asserted, held children as young as two.

The House Foreign Affairs Committee and Senate Foreign Relations Committee launched investigations into the veracity of Colegrove's claims. Once again, as had been the case during the Battle for Saigon, Diem's power base in Congress proved invaluable, for the subcommittees established to hold hearings were chaired by Representative Clement Zablocki and Senator Mike Mansfield, both Diem supporters. With such advocates supervising the proceedings, Diem's image was never in danger, but the scandal infuriated him anyway. As far as Diem was concerned, Colegrove's exposé furnished his enemies with ammunition and might lead to further reductions in U.S. aid.

Ultimately, the House and Senate subcommittees exonerated Diem and condemned Colegrove, whom Zablocki accused of practicing "irresponsible journalism." Senator J. William Fulbright, who later became a far-seeing skeptic with regard to American policy in Vietnam, concluded that he was "not impressed" with the quality of Colegrove's reporting. A chastened Colegrove was reduced to pleading before Zablocki's committee that he had not meant to insult Diem, who had indeed "accomplished a miracle" in

South Vietnam. Despite this victory for the Diem experiment, Congress followed up its hearings with inspection visits to Saigon that Diem found humiliating. They reminded him of French colonial practices, and he felt obliged to inform visiting legislators that "my government, like that of the United States, is sovereign and does not permit any interference in our internal affairs."[31]

The hearings prompted by Colegrove's articles constituted the only congressional probe into Vietnam policy during the Eisenhower era. By the time Fulbright chaired his own hearings seven years later, Diem would be dead and U.S. troop levels in Vietnam would be nearing their peak. In 1959, however, the American military mission in Diem's country still numbered only seven hundred men, and the American press and public paid little attention to events unfolding in a former French colony on the southeastern margin of the Eurasian land mass. Americans were unaware, as was Diem, that a few months before Colegrove published his articles, the Communist Party Central Committee of North Vietnam adopted a resolution endorsing the use of force to overthrow the Diem regime. Former Viet Minh guerrillas who had moved north after the Geneva Conference began returning south, many by way of a supply corridor through Laos that would evolve into the Ho Chi Minh Trail. The Central Committee stressed that its struggle against Diem was to remain primarily political, and the guerrillas reinfiltrating South Vietnam had to travel for the most part on foot; therefore, neither Washington nor Saigon detected a change in Hanoi's strategy for months. But the Vietnamese civil war had entered a new phase, one that would make a mockery of Diem's "miracle" and confront the United States with the choice of either abandoning its Cold War outpost in Southeast Asia or finding another Vietnamese leader to stem the communist flood.

Notes

1. Ba Cut cited in Denis Warner, *The Last Confucian* (New York: Macmillan, 1963), 105.

2. Warner, *Last Confucian*, 107; Cherne cited in Joseph G. Morgan, *Vietnam Lobby: The American Friends of Vietnam, 1955–1975* (Chapel Hill: University of North Carolina Press, 1997), 22.

3. Plebiscite point at issue cited in David L. Anderson, *Trapped by Success: The Eisenhower Administration and Vietnam, 1953–1961* (New York: Columbia University Press, 1991), 128.

4. Reinhardt to Dulles, 21 October 1955, file 751G.00/10-2155, RG 59.

5. The Constitution of the Republic of Vietnam, 26 October 1956, Douglas Pike Col-

lection, Vietnam Archive, Texas Tech University, Lubbock, Texas [hereafter Pike Collection], Unit IV—Republic of Vietnam, Box 13.

6. The Ambassador in Cambodia to the Department of State, 29 June 1954, *FRUS, 1952–1954* (Washington, D.C.: Government Printing Office, 1982), 13:1762.

7. John Donnell, "Personalism in Vietnam" in *Problems of Freedom: South Vietnam since Independence*, ed. Wesley Fishel (New York: Free Press of Glencoe, 1961), 59; Domenach cited in Philip E. Catton, *Diem's Final Failure: Prelude to America's War in Vietnam* (Lawrence: University Press of Kansas, 2002), 47.

8. Thuc opponent cited in William Brownell, "The Vietnam Lobby: The Americans Who Lobbied for a Free and Independent South Vietnam in the 1940s and 1950s" (PhD diss., Columbia University, 1993), 135–136; policymakers cited in David Halberstam, *The Making of a Quagmire* (New York: Random House, 1965), 50.

9. Diem cited in George Kahin, *Intervention: How America Became Involved in Vietnam* (New York: Anchor Books, 1986), 96–97.

10. Communist Party historians cited in James R. Arnold, *The First Domino: Eisenhower, the Military, and America's Intervention in Vietnam* (New York: Morrow, 1991), 336.

11. Aphorism cited in Piero Gheddo, *The Cross and the Bo-Tree: Catholics and Buddhists in Vietnam* (New York: Sheed and Ward, 1970), 146–151.

12. Diem cited in Catton, *Diem's Final Failure*, 52–53; Wolf Ladejinsky, Memorandum of Conversation with President Ngo Dinh Diem, 1 June 1955, reprinted in *Agrarian Reform as Unfinished Business: The Selected Papers of Wolf Ladejinsky*, ed. Lewis Walinsky (New York: Oxford University Press, 1977), 239–243.

13. Diplomat cited in John D. Montgomery, *The Politics of Foreign Aid: The American Experience in Southeast Asia* (New York: Praeger, 1962), 125.

14. Ladejinsky, "South Vietnam Revisited" reprinted in *Agrarian Reform as Unfinished Business*, 244; peasant cited in Montgomery, *Politics of Foreign Aid*, 126.

15. Memorandum from the Joint Chiefs of Staff to the Secretary of Defense, 9 December 1955, *FRUS, 1955–1957* (Washington, D.C.: Government Printing Office, 1985), 1:598.

16. The Secretary of State to the Embassy in Vietnam, 9 February 1956, *FRUS, 1955–1957*, 1:640.

17. Diem cited in James Fisher, "'A World Made Safe for Diversity': The Vietnam Lobby and the Politics of Pluralism, 1945–1963" in *Cold War Constructions: The Political Culture of United States Imperialism, 1945–1966*, ed. Christian Appy (Amherst: University of Massachusetts Press, 2000), 229.

18. The Chargé in South Vietnam to the Department of State, 3 March 1955, *FRUS, 1955–1957*, 1:105.

19. Macmillan cited in Robert D. Schulzinger, *A Time for War: The United States and Vietnam, 1941–1975* (New York: Oxford University Press, 1997), 89.

20. Kahin, *Intervention*, 85; economist cited in George Herring, *America's Longest War: The United States and Vietnam, 1945–1975*, 2nd ed. (New York: McGraw-Hill, 1986), 65.

21. Eisenhower Telegram, Transcript of Dinner in Honor of His Excellency Ngo Dinh

Diem, 13 April 1957, American Friends of Vietnam Papers, Vietnam Archive, Texas Tech University, Lubbock, Texas [hereafter AFV Papers], Box 11; Address by John Foster Dulles, 8 May 1955, Dulles Papers, Box 98; Address by the Assistant Secretary of State for Far Eastern Affairs, Washington, 1 June 1956, *The Pentagon Papers*, Gravel Edition (Boston: Beacon, 1971), 1:610–611.

22. Buttinger: Memorandum on Indochina, 22 December 1954, Joseph Buttinger Papers, Harvard-Yenching Library, Harvard University, Cambridge, Massachusetts [hereafter Buttinger Papers]; Joseph Buttinger, *Vietnam: The Unforgettable Tragedy* (New York: Horizon Press, 1977), 69; Buttinger to Oram, 22 April 1954, Buttinger Papers.

23. John Osborne, "The Tough Miracle Man of Vietnam," *Life*, 13 May 1957, 149–158; John W. O'Daniel, "Free Vietnam: Modern Miracle," *American Mercury*, March 1959, 146–151; Ernest Lindley, "A Friend Named Diem," *Newsweek*, 20 May 1957, 40; Philip Cook, "Miracle Maker from Asia—Diem of South Vietnam," *New York Herald Tribune*, 9 May 1957.

24. "Welcome to a Champion," *Washington Evening Star*, 8 May 1957; "Vietnam's Man of Iron," *Boston Globe*, 6 May 1957; Chalmers M. Roberts, "Diem—Symbol of Free New Asia," *Washington Post and Times Herald*, 8 May 1957; "Welcome, President Diem," *New York Times*, 8 May 1957; "An Asian Liberator," *New York Times*, 10 May 1957; "Mr. Diem in Washington," *Christian Science Monitor*, 10 May 1957; Ernest K. Lindley, "A Friend Named Diem," *Newsweek*, 20 May 1957, 40; "Visitor from Viet Nam," *Washington Post*, 8 May 1957; "A Welcome Visitor," *Washington News*, 7 May 1957.

25. Ann Whitman File, International Meeting Series: Toast by President Eisenhower to President Diem, 9 May 1957: Box 2, EL; White House Central Files, Confidential File, 1953–1961, Subject Series: Joint Communiqué, 12 May 1957: Box 73, EL.

26. Wagner cited in Robert Alden, "City Accords Diem a Warm Welcome," *New York Times*, 14 May 1957; Diem Address, Transcript of Dinner in Honor of His Excellency Ngo Dinh Diem, 13 April 1957, AFV Papers, Box 11.

27. Diem cited in *News from Viet-Nam*, Press and Information Office, Embassy of the Republic of Viet-Nam, 31 May 1957, Buttinger Papers.

28. Weisinger cited in John Ernst, *Forging a Fateful Alliance: Michigan State University and the Vietnam War* (East Lansing: Michigan State University Press, 1998), xiii.

29. Williams cited in Anderson, *Trapped by Success*, 185–186; embassy officer and deputy cited in Ronald H. Spector, *Advice and Support: The Early Years of the U.S. Army in Vietnam, 1941–1960* (New York: Free Press, 1985), 276.

30. Eisenhower cited in Stephen Ambrose, *Eisenhower*, vol. 2, *The President* (New York: Simon & Schuster, 1984), 380–381.

31. Statement by Clement J. Zablocki, Chairman, Subcommittee on the Far East and the Pacific, 14 August 1959, Leo Cherne Papers, Mugar Library, Boston University, Boston, Massachusetts [hereafter Cherne Papers], Box 17; Fulbright cited in O'Daniel Statement on Recent Charges against the American Aid Program in Free Vietnam, 24 August 1959, Cherne Papers; Colegrove cited in Morgan, *Vietnam Lobby*, 59; Diem cited in Montgomery, *Politics of Foreign Aid*, 233.

~

CHAPTER FIVE

"Truth Shall Burst Forth in Irresistible Waves of Hatred"

Cracks in the Façade

J. Lawton Collins cannot have been pleased when President Dwight Eisenhower ordered him to return to South Vietnam in the winter of 1958. Eisenhower, troubled by congressional complaints that the United States placed too much emphasis on military aid to developing nations, assigned Collins to a committee charged with conducting a "non-partisan analysis" of American military assistance programs. William Draper, a former general, chaired the committee, and Dillon Anderson, who had previously served as Eisenhower's national security adviser, headed a subcommittee on Southeast Asia. The president appointed Collins as Anderson's military adviser. Collins's recent stint as U.S. special representative in South Vietnam made him a logical choice for the position, but he had a combative relationship with South Vietnamese president Ngo Dinh Diem and, in fact, considered his failure to persuade Washington to depose Diem the greatest disappointment of his life. He was hardly eager to revisit the site of such frustration.[1]

Diem was similarly disinclined to allow the general to return to South Vietnam. Still smarting over Collins's negative assessment of his prospects in 1954–1955, Diem refused to meet with the U.S. delegation unless Collins was removed from it. A diplomatic blowup seemed imminent until a staff member of the Anderson Subcommittee devised a solution: Diem would permit Collins to question him if Ngo Dinh Nhu and Madame Nhu eavesdropped from behind a silk screen, invisible to the visiting Americans. One historian notes that "the scene conjured up an image of the Nhus as literally the power behind the throne." It also demonstrated the clannishness that had characterized Diem's government from the beginning and that grew deeper as years passed.[2]

The Anderson Subcommittee was not in South Vietnam long enough to conduct a detailed assessment of the effectiveness of U.S. military assistance, but they did get some sense of how important Diem believed the Army of the Republic of Vietnam (ARVN) was to the survival of his regime. When Anderson suggested that Washington might reduce funding for the ARVN, Diem objected, insisting that such a move would have a devastating effect on morale in the anticommunist nations of Southeast Asia. Cambodia, after all, had just recognized the People's Republic of China, and Viet Cong activity in South Vietnam was increasing. This was no time to cut corners with respect to military aid. Collins found that argument unpersuasive and questioned the need for Diem to maintain an army of 150,000 men. Equipping, training, and paying that many troops was absorbing all of the regime's resources, Collins noted; by cutting the number of men in arms, Diem could free up capital to develop South Vietnam's economic infrastructure, ease the condition of the rural peasantry, and begin to move his nation along the route to self-sufficiency.

Diem had not heeded such advice when other Americans offered it, and he was even less likely to be swayed when the source was Collins, a man he abominated. He listened politely but remained convinced that he understood the nature of the communist threat better than his superpower patrons. Rather than slashing the number of troops, he argued, conditions warranted that he "raise [the] force level to 170,000." Apart from Collins, no member of the Anderson Subcommittee challenged Diem on this score. Collins further rankled his host by bringing up a subject that had been a recurring theme of the 1954–1955 Collins mission to South Vietnam: Diem's "refusal to permit the development of a 'loyal opposition.'" Here U.S. ambassador Elbridge Durbrow intervened on Diem's behalf, reminding Collins that "in a country like Viet-Nam with no democratic traditions," it was not "in the interests of the free world to insist upon trying to put into effect all the trimmings of democracy."[3]

The group left South Vietnam having made no impression on its president. When the Draper Committee published its report in August 1959, it endorsed the Eisenhower administration's policies in Southeast Asia; indeed, it singled out the "effectiveness of the Vietnamese armed forces" for special praise. Collins's concerns were noted, and the Anderson Subcommittee called for reforms in South Vietnam's exchange rates, but the overall tone of the report was optimistic. Given the other issues preoccupying Eisenhower at this time—Fidel Castro's ascent to power in Cuba, Soviet demands that NATO forces vacate West Berlin, Secretary of State John Foster Dulles's recent death—the president cannot have found conditions in South Vietnam cause for alarm, at least insofar as those conditions were portrayed by Anderson and his consultants.[4]

James Arnold, one of the most perceptive students of U.S.-Vietnamese relations in the 1950s, argues that "[t]he Draper Committee was the last chance during the Eisenhower administration for a major change in Vietnam policy. Of all the committee members who went to Vietnam, only Collins saw this opportunity." Once again, Collins found himself swimming against the tide, as Washington followed its fixed course in Vietnam through Eisenhower's last day as president. The Diem experiment, launched with uncertainty in 1954, preserved with difficulty in the spring of 1955, and hailed as a miracle of nation-building for the remainder of the decade, became John F. Kennedy's responsibility in January 1961. When Eisenhower left office, Diem had been America's strongman for six years, and each passing day increased the investment of U.S. Cold War credibility in his government. Yet despite billions of dollars in aid and hundreds of American advisers, Diem's political base remained narrow and South Vietnam's economy languished. Moreover, the Diem regime received a number of shocks in 1960 that laid bare its fragility and made the word "miracle" seem suddenly and absurdly inappropriate to describe what the Eisenhower administration had created in the southern half of Vietnam.[5]

The first bombshell to shake the foundations of Diem's rule came in response to the August 1959 elections for the national assembly. As in 1956, the elections were a sham. Newspapers were not permitted to publish the names of independent candidates or reveal anything about those candidates' political positions. The Public Meetings Law prevented candidates from speaking to groups of more than five people. Many candidates were disqualified for preposterous reasons: because they gave too many speeches, because their posters were too big or too small, because the posters were outlined in red, and in one instance because a vandal drew a mustache on the candidate's billboard picture. In the provinces, government officials threatened candidates with arrest if they did not withdraw from the elections; anyone brave enough to call this bluff was tried for conspiracy with the VC, a charge that could bring

Diem at his desk, at the height of his authority, February 1958.
Bettman/CORBIS.

the death penalty. For good measure, ARVN soldiers went into some districts during the afternoon siesta and stuffed ballot boxes.

In deference to his sponsors in Washington, however, Diem permitted the best-known critic of his administration, Dr. Phan Quang Dan, to run for a seat in the assembly. The results were an embarrassment for the government. Despite Diem's sending eight thousand ARVN troops in plainclothes to vote against Dan, the Saigon physician defeated his opponent by a six-to-one margin. When the new assembly convened, Dan attempted to take his seat, but police arrested him on charges of fraud.

Sickened by the rigging of the elections, a group of eighteen South Vietnamese politicians convened at the Caravelle Hotel in Saigon and coauthored a letter to the president demanding reforms. On 26 April 1960, the soon-to-be-famous "Caravelle Group" made the letter public at a press conference. Journalists from many nations, including the United States, heard a list of grievances that implied that conditions in South Vietnam were worse than when Diem assumed office. "Continuous arrests fill the jails and prisons to the rafters," read the "Manifesto of the Eighteen." "[P]ublic opinion and the press are reduced to silence." The manifesto noted that despite South Vietnam's being a "rich and fertile country" with "a colossal foreign-aid program," the economy was in shambles. South Vietnam's armed forces were in similar shape. Even though "American aid . . . has equipped it with modern materiel," the manifesto declared, the army was hobbled by "distrust, jealousy, [and] rancor" because Diem's "criterion for promotion" was "blind submission" instead of ability. The civil bureaucracy likewise suffered from "[f]avoritism based on family connections," with the result that the "administrative machinery" was "completely paralyzed."

Tellingly, the Caravelle Group did not call on Diem to resign. Their tone toward him was respectful, and they apologized for presenting such "disagreeable criticism." Nonetheless, they warned the president if he did not make some changes, "truth shall burst forth in irresistible waves of hatred on the part of a people subjected for a long time to terrible suffering." One of the signers of the manifesto was Phan Huy Quat, whom Collins had championed as an alternative to Diem in the spring of 1955. For a time, Secretary of State John Foster Dulles had accepted this counsel and sanctioned a Quat premiership, but he had reversed his verdict when Diem triumphed over the Binh Xuyen. While Quat had not held office for years by 1960, he remained among the most prominent politicians in South Vietnam, and most of his Caravelle comrades had also been cabinet ministers or upper-echelon officials. One signer was even Madame Nhu's uncle. This was no run-of-the-mill political tract, a point underscored when the New York Times ran a front-page story on the manifesto and its demands.[6]

The press in South Vietnam, however, did not publish the manifesto or even mention it. Diem never publicly acknowledged its existence—although, according to an American journalist stationed in Saigon, his "first reaction" upon learning of it was to have the signers "sent to political re-education camps." He ultimately decided that the wisest strategy was to ignore the Caravelle Group, and the South Vietnamese media, either government-controlled or intimidated into silence, followed suit. Any hopes that the manifesto would inspire a political movement to challenge Diem were dashed.[7]

While Diem could pretend that neither Phan Quang Dan nor the Caravelle Group mattered and that his own popularity remained undiminished, members of the Eisenhower administration were finally beginning to express reservations about their Diem experiment. In a National Security Council (NSC) meeting held two weeks after the issuance of the Caravelle manifesto, Eisenhower declared that he was concerned about recent reports from Saigon. Representatives of the State Department and CIA advised the president that Diem had withdrawn into a circle of family advisers and was "not in direct touch with the people." If he did not reverse this trend, they suggested, he might meet the same fate as South Korean leader Syngman Rhee, who had just been forced from office by public protest. These were striking words, but they were not translated into any change in policy. Instead, Eisenhower concluded the discussion of Vietnam by exhorting the State Department, Defense Department, and CIA to "consult together" in finding some way to keep Diem in power. By 1960 Diem and his problems had receded from the forefront of Eisenhower's awareness. The same NSC meeting at which the president voiced his unease about Diem was almost entirely taken up with another crisis: the USSR's shooting down of an American U-2 spy plane on a surveillance mission over Soviet airspace. Eisenhower and Soviet premier Nikita Khrushchev were scheduled to meet in Paris the following week, and no one could be certain what effect the U-2 affair would have on the summit conference. There was little time to focus on a petition from eighteen out-of-office Saigon politicians.[8]

Thus preoccupied, the Eisenhower administration hewed to its policy of "sink or swim" as Diem's antidemocratic measures caused opposition to his regime to grow. South Vietnam's peasants, either out of terror or sympathy, joined the ranks of the VC in greater numbers, and the insurgency in the countryside spread. More and more districts and villages came under communist control. In some areas, roads were hung for miles with VC banners. The level of communist-inspired violence escalated to the point where it was no longer safe to travel without escort in parts of the country.

Shortly after a razor-close election determined that John F. Kennedy would succeed Eisenhower as U.S. president, the Diem experiment absorbed another blow. This time, Diem was fortunate to survive. On 11 November 1960 at 3:00 A.M., five ARVN paratroop battalions launched a rebellion, seizing the military headquarters in Saigon, the radio station, and the main airport at Tan Son Nhut. By six o'clock, the rebels had surrounded the Norodom Palace. They were led by two of the finest officers in the country: Colonel Nguyen Chanh Thi, who had fought on Diem's side against the Binh Xuyen and who presently commanded a parachute regiment, and Lieutenant Colonel Vuong Van Dong, a veteran of the Franco–Viet Minh War who had trained at Fort Leavenworth, Kansas. Thi's gallantry during the 1955 Battle for Saigon had so impressed Diem that the president often referred to Thi thereafter as "my son." As for Dong, American military advisers considered him a brilliant tactician who, at age twenty-eight, had the brightest future of any soldier in South Vietnam. That an attack that nearly toppled Diem came not from the VC or the North Vietnamese but from the elite of his own army testified to the extent of antigovernment sentiment by late 1960.[9]

Frustrated by Diem's authoritarianism and convinced that he was not prosecuting the war against the VC correctly, Thi and Dong had concluded that subtle methods of persuasion were a waste of time; the president needed to be bludgeoned into mending his ways. The two colonels and the other military men involved in the uprising were motivated by patriotism rather than political ambition. Indeed, their actions revealed an almost childlike naïveté: they neglected to take steps essential for bringing off a coup, such as setting up roadblocks around Saigon or taking over the communications network. They did not even seek Diem's removal. Dong later revealed to Western journalists that, like the signers of the Caravelle manifesto, he and Thi were willing to allow the president to stay in office provided he instituted reforms. Above all, the rebel leaders wanted Nhu and his wife out of the government, although they disagreed about whether to kill the hated couple or deport them.

The paratroopers' first assault on the palace met with surprising resistance. Nothing stood between Thi's and Dong's forces and Diem but thirty palace guards, but those guards proved capable of repulsing the initial thrust and killing seven rebels who attempted to scale the fence surrounding the palace grounds. Thi and Dong then cordoned off the palace to ensure that Diem could not escape. Saigon Radio announced that a "Revolutionary Council" was in charge of South Vietnam's government. As dawn broke over the city, civilians began massing outside the palace gates, shouting encouragement to the rebels and waving banners demanding the overthrow of the Diem regime. Many ARVN troops based in Saigon and its suburb of Cholon rallied to the insurgents. Nguyen Thai Binh, a South Vietnamese politician driven into exile by Diem, recalls, "By 9:00 A.M., Diem was lost. Any other than he would have capitulated."[10]

But Diem did not capitulate. He and Nhu retreated to the palace cellar, which had recently been renovated into a bunker, and used a radio transmitter to send out distress signals to army units in the countryside. Meanwhile, the rebels hesitated. Some, like Dong, felt the moment was ripe to overrun the palace and take Diem prisoner. Thi, however, worried that the president might be killed in the confusion. Despite his frustration with Diem, Thi could not conceive of South Vietnam being led by anyone else. Better to wait, he counseled. Through an intermediary, the rebels relayed their demands to Diem, and Dong contacted Durbrow to ask for American help. The ambassador must have been tempted, but he turned the colonel down. Durbrow did, however, urge Diem to negotiate with Thi and Dong. Pham Quang Dan, fresh off his victory and subsequent disqualification in the 1959 elections, emerged as the rebels' spokesman, holding a press conference to explain why the revolt had taken place. He gave assembled journalists a detailed account of the Diem regime's mismanagement of the anticommunist effort and refusal to broaden its political base, and insisted that the rebels had been driven to act as a last resort.

Diem declared his willingness to listen to the insurgents' demands. An indefatigable talker, he drew out the parley while his rescuers raced toward Saigon. Colonel Tran Thien Khiem, head of the Fifth Military Region in the Mekong Delta and a friend of Diem's brother Ngo Dinh Thuc, had received Diem's radio messages and assembled a relief mission that included one of the ARVN's largest tank units. Colonel Nguyen Van Thieu, infantry commander at Bien Hoa, likewise responded to Diem's summons. As Khiem's tanks rolled north and Thieu's men marched south, Diem stalled. He and Dong haggled all afternoon and into the night, with the president appearing remarkably accommodating. While he would not sack Nhu, he did agree to dismiss his cabinet and form a government acceptable to the Revolutionary Council. He also promised to implement a range of reforms: free elections, an end to press censorship, less government control over the economy, and so on. In the early morning hours of 12 November, Diem taped a speech detailing his concessions, and dissident soldiers rushed to play it over Saigon Radio.

Just as Diem's soothing words were being broadcast, two infantry divisions loyal to the regime backed by tanks approached the palace grounds. Sensing a shift in the balance of power, many of the Saigon units that had sided with the rebels the day before now declared their loyalty to Diem and turned their guns on their former comrades. A battle ensued. The paratroopers, outnumbered, fought valiantly but were obliged to fall back to defensive positions around their barracks a half mile away. About four hundred people were killed, including many civilians who had assembled to cheer the rebels on. Thi, Dong, and the other insurgent officers fled to the airport and managed to escape by plane to Cambodia, where they received asylum. Dan met a crueler fate. One of the first orders Diem issued after reestablishing command was for Dan's arrest. The doctor was seized, imprisoned, and tortured. Even though Dan was the only member of the Caravelle Group implicated in the rebellion, Diem had most of the rest jailed as well.

Diem also reneged on his promises of reform, claiming, with some justification, that they had been made under duress. Many South Vietnamese were disappointed anyway. There was plenty of ill will to go around in the wake of the failed uprising. Diem was furious at Durbrow for what he perceived as lack of U.S. support, and Nhu went so far as to accuse the ambassador of collaboration with the rebels. Durbrow protested that he had been "100% in support of Diem." Diem's friend Edward Lansdale, now working a desk job at the Pentagon, ridiculed such claims and insisted that Durbrow be recalled. The new commander of the Military Assistance Advisory Group (MAAG), Lieutenant General Lionel McGarr, shared Lansdale's views. The rift between America's diplomatic and military representatives in South Vietnam grew wider. More important was the burgeoning mistrust between Diem and his military. The paratroopers had been considered the most loyal force in the ARVN, and yet they had nearly driven Diem from office. For Diem, the lesson of the rebellion was that he needed to increase his control over the military—and if that meant an intensification of the policy of promoting men based on loyalty rather than skill, so be it.[11]

The final wound sustained by the Diem regime in 1960 was barely perceptible at first, but it proved deadlier than the others combined. On 20 December, the National Front for the Liberation of South Vietnam, better known as the National Liberation Front (NLF), was formed at Xom Giua, near the Vietnam-Cambodia border. This organization grew out of a decision taken three months earlier at the Third Party Congress of the Communist Party in North Vietnam. After six years of trying to unify the country primarily through political means, the party repudiated much of its opposition to all-out war against "the U.S. imperialists and the Ngo Dinh Diem clique." Secretary General Le Duan persuaded delegates to the congress that an increase in the level of armed violence was essential if the communists were to succeed in deposing Diem and expelling the Americans. Hanoi also needed a new political group in the south that could operate much as the Viet Minh had during the early years of Franco–Viet Minh conflict: that is, a communist-front organization that muted its ideology and was therefore attractive to nationalists of all political persuasions who had grown to hate Diem. Such a "united bloc of workers, peasants, and soldiers," Le Duan argued, would "bring into being a broad united national front" that would liberate the south and, after a transitional period, negotiate with Hanoi for reunification. The party issued a directive to its southern cadres to form a coalition along these lines.[12]

The sixty delegates who gathered in response to the September party congress decree represented many political, ethnic, and religious groups: communists, socialists, intellectuals, university students, independent professionals, Montagnards, Khmer, Chinese, Cao Dai, Hoa Hao, and even some Catholics. The NLF organizers adopted a platform that stressed patriotic rather than communist objectives. Point one was a pledge to "overthrow the disguised colonial regime of the U.S. imperialists and the dictatorial Ngo Dinh Diem administration." Other points were scarcely revolutionary: more civil liberties, redistribution of land, reduction of rents, higher wages, amnesty for political prisoners, elimination of the American presence in Vietnam, and, most important, "reunification of the fatherland."[13]

No South Vietnamese to the left of Madame Nhu could argue with this program. Therein lay its effectiveness: the NLF was not overtly communist. Most NLF leaders were not members of the Communist Party. The organization's first chairman was a Saigon lawyer with only moderate left-wing political credentials. North Vietnamese politicians could claim, with apparent candor, that there was no link between the NLF and party leadership in the north, that the NLF was an indigenous organization composed of southern nationalists who had banded together in opposition to Diem. Therefore, according to Hanoi, the crescendoing turmoil in South Vietnam after 1960 was a consequence of civil war—not invasion from the north, as the Americans insisted. Most Vietnam War historians dismiss this argument. They contend that the North Vietnamese politburo controlled the rebellion in the south and that the NLF's real, if unadvertised, leadership was communist. While it is true that profound differences existed between northern and southern communists and that difficulties in communication along Vietnam's three thousand miles of often rugged terrain gave NLF members in the south a degree of autonomy, the NLF was still tied to Hanoi, which called it into being and provided its organizational structure and direction.

Yet Diem played as important a role as Hanoi in spawning the insurrection in South Vietnam. He failed to introduce reforms that might have mobilized the population behind him, and his policies outraged millions of South Vietnamese. While the NLF was formed in response to a dictate from the Communist Party in the north, it would not have been as effective in enlisting southern support had Diem's heavy hand not created widespread pressure for armed action. If the spark came from Hanoi, Diem furnished the tinder.

John F. Kennedy may have had some inkling of the hornet's nest he was about to inherit when, on the day before his inauguration, he met with Eisenhower and members of the outgoing cabinet for a final briefing. Although Eisenhower spoke at length about conditions in Southeast Asia, he barely mentioned Vietnam, focusing instead on Laos, where the U.S.-backed government seemed on the verge of being overthrown by the communist Pathet Lao. Nonetheless, much of what Eisenhower said was equally applicable to the disintegrating situation in Diem's country. Laos, Eisenhower insisted, was "the key to the entire area of Southeast Asia." If the United States "permitted Laos to fall, then we would have to write off all the area." With the domino theory still serving as his Rosetta stone, Eisenhower argued that a communist triumph in Laos would bring on the communization of "South Vietnam, Cambodia, Thailand, and Burma." Should diplomatic attempts to preserve a noncommunist government in Laos prove "fruitless, then the United States must intervene"—unilaterally, if necessary. With that, Eisenhower turned over control of U.S. foreign policy.[14]

Diem had to be pleased that American voters chose Kennedy instead of Richard Nixon to be the nation's thirty-fifth president. Not only was Kennedy a fellow Catholic, but he was also a member of the American Friends of Vietnam (AFV), the group founded in 1955 to promote Diem's cause in the United States. Kennedy had described Diem's government as "our offspring" at an AFV-sponsored conference in 1956 and had regularly called for more aid to South Vietnam. Like Eisenhower, Kennedy was a staunch cold warrior, but he was less budget-conscious, which was a good sign from Diem's perspective. With JFK in the White House, Diem seemed likely to receive the stepped-up military assistance he had been requesting for years. Although Kennedy accepted Eisenhower's domino theory, he promised to be more vigorous than the Republicans in propping up the dominoes; indeed, Kennedy's prescription for waging Cold War—"flexible response," as opposed to Eisenhower's strategy of "massive retaliation"—was designed to check communist advances in the third world, where, Kennedy pointed out, American threats of nuclear reprisal had no credibility. The United States, Kennedy argued, needed to match the communists at any level of conflict and in various modes of combat—including guerrilla wars, such as the one in Vietnam.[15]

Diem needed all the help he could get in 1961. His most recent initiative to contain VC influence in the countryside had backfired horribly. The "agroville" campaign, based on a British program in Malaya, proposed to relocate peasants into heavily defended villages where they would be immune to communist indoctrination. Diem's government planned to construct eighty agrovilles, each designed for four hundred families and offering schools, hospitals, markets, and other amenities. As conceived, the agrovilles would deprive the VC of new recruits and raise the standard of living for the average South Vietnamese peasant, who would now have access to educational, health, and sanitary services that had previously been available only to city dwellers. It seemed a foolproof scheme to stimulate peasant support for Diem.

Yet it proved unworkable. Diem's insistence that the peasants build the agrovilles themselves—in forced labor gangs, no less, and without compensation—did nothing to improve his reputation in rural South Vietnam, but even more counterproductive was the fact that peasants grouped into agrovilles had to abandon their ancestral lands. In a culture like Vietnam's, where people were deeply attached to home and village, such uprooting was traumatic, and many South Vietnamese resisted it. Even those peasants who agreed to be resettled were disappointed by the agrovilles, which looked more like concentration camps than privileged communities and which rarely provided the comforts of urban life promised by the Saigon government. The agroville campaign spawned still greater dissatisfaction with Diem and gave the communists an inviting target for their propaganda. Shortly before Kennedy took office, Diem suspended the agroville campaign, but the damage had been done. He was more unpopular than ever, and opposition to his regime mounted. During the first half of 1961, VC guerrillas assassinated over five hundred local officials and civilians, kidnapped over one thousand more, and killed almost fifteen hundred ARVN personnel.

Diem responded the way he always had: with repression. He pushed a bill through the National Assembly that prohibited all unauthorized public meetings; even weddings and funerals could not be held without government approval. The ARVN and agents of the Can Lao Party carried out more killings and arrests. Military courts traveled from district to district with mobile guillotines, targeting anyone who "commits or intends to commit crimes . . . infringing upon the security of the state." Those accused of actual or "intended" offenses were given twenty-four hours to assemble a legal defense and denied the right to examine evidence or call witnesses. There was no provision for appeal. The results were predictable: swift conviction and execution. As always, Diem's actions aroused popular hostility. The authors of the *Pentagon Papers* note that by 1961, "it had become clear in both Saigon and Washington that the . . . operative question was not whether the Diem government as it was then moving could defeat the insurgents, but whether it could save itself."[16]

Kennedy made two crucial moves in May 1961 with respect to America's Diem experiment. First was his choice of ambassador to succeed Durbrow. There was no shortage of candidates for the post: Lansdale was eager to be appointed, and Kenneth Young, head of the State Department's Division of Philippine and Southeast Asian Affairs, likewise indicated his willingness to serve; even Attorney General Robert Kennedy seemed interested in leaving the Justice Department for the Saigon embassy. But the president decided to go with Frederick Nolting, a North Atlantic Treaty Organization diplomat with a reputation for conflict avoidance. Nolting's concern with propriety was so extreme that he once asked a TV interviewer to replace a portrait of Thomas Jefferson on the wall behind him with one of George Washington because the latter Founding Father was "less controversial." This was precisely the sort of envoy Kennedy wanted for his shift in Vietnam policy: threats were henceforth to be replaced by friendly persuasion. According to Nolting's deputy in Saigon, William Trueheart, the ambassador's instructions from Kennedy were to "Get along." None of America's ambassadors to South Vietnam developed a closer relationship with Diem than this tall, soft-spoken Virginian who had a great deal of experience in Europe but never set foot in Asia before Kennedy made him Durbrow's replacement.[17]

On the same day that Nolting took over for Durbrow, 10 May 1961, Kennedy's second gesture to win Diem's confidence got underway. Vice President Lyndon Johnson arrived in Saigon for what was officially termed a fact-finding mission but which was actually a three-day pep talk to boost South Vietnamese morale. LBJ engaged in the kind of whirlwind campaigning that had made him one of the most successful American politicians of the twentieth century. Along with attending the requisite dinners, press conferences, and meetings, he got out in the streets and "pressed the flesh" with hundreds of Saigonese. He also traveled into the countryside by bullock cart to drum up support for Diem, and the peasants seemed to like him, even if their traditional manner of greeting a visitor—bowing with palms together—did not translate well into the barnstorming etiquette of a Texas New Dealer. "Who the hell are they praying to?" LBJ asked a Secret Service agent.[18]

More substantively, Johnson bore a letter from Kennedy for Diem that offered to increase American participation in the war against the VC. JFK noted that his administration had approved a "20,000 increase of your regular forces" and assured Diem that Washington was "prepared to consider . . . the case for a further increase in the strength of your forces beyond the 170,000 limit now contemplated." In other words, U.S. support was unconditional; the restrictions of the Eisenhower years no longer applied. America was in Vietnam to win, and whatever Diem needed to save his country from communism would be provided. Johnson asked Diem if he wanted American combat troops sent to South Vietnam, an offer Diem declined on the grounds that it would give the communists a propaganda windfall. Only in the event of an all-out invasion from the north would Diem consent to such infringement on South Vietnamese sovereignty. Still, he could not help but be flattered by Kennedy's solicitousness.[19]

Papers given to Johnson on the eve of his departure for Saigon instructed him to "get across to President Diem our confidence in him as a man of great stature." The vice president more than fulfilled this duty. LBJ praised Diem at every occasion, likening him to George Washington, Andrew Jackson, Woodrow Wilson, and Franklin D. Roosevelt. At a farewell banquet, Johnson hailed Diem as the "Winston Churchill of Southeast Asia." When Stanley Karnow, who was covering events in Vietnam for the *Saturday Evening Post*, asked Johnson if such encomiums were sincere, the vice president smirked, made certain his response would be off the record, and confessed, "Shit, man, he's the only boy we got out there."[20]

That remark summarized Johnson's report to Kennedy, in which he concluded that the "existing government in Saigon is the only realistic alternative to Viet Minh control." Johnson admitted that there was "a significant level of disaffection with the government," especially in rural areas, and that "the ordinary people" were "starved for leadership with understanding and warmth." Nonetheless, Johnson argued, "there is little promise that effective leadership will emerge from the non-communist opposition to Ngo Dinh Diem." LBJ therefore recommended a program of heightened military and economic aid to the Diem regime. Kennedy agreed, and sent a "Special Financial Group" headed by Stanford University's Dr. Eugene Staley to Saigon to work out a plan for determining the nature of American assistance. Staley's report, like Johnson's, could not have been more to Diem's liking. While the professor made some vague proposals about economic and political reforms, his only specific recommendations involved military matters. "Security requirements must, for the present, be given first priority," Staley insisted. He advocated an increase in the ARVN from the just-agreed-on ceiling of 170,000 to an all-time high of 200,000, and also called for better arms and equipment to be supplied by the United States. Most important, from Diem's perspective, was the fact that Staley endorsed a policy that the Saigon government had recently adopted to provide greater protection to the civilian population: the strategic hamlet program.[21]

The origins of this program are obscure, although a scholar of the Diem years notes that it "developed as an outgrowth of local experiments in several provinces." Apparently, a number of South Vietnamese hamlets, mostly Catholic, managed to organize themselves independently for defense against VC infiltration by building watchtowers, training militias, scheduling emergency drills, and otherwise assuming the burdens of self-preservation that most citizens expected the government to shoulder. Diem found such initiative inspiring and believed it could be extended to the whole of the countryside with a bit of prodding from Saigon. In his view, strategic hamlets suggested a remedy for the defect in the agroville program: that is, that farmers, forcibly displaced from their land, were more likely to turn against the leader who relocated them than rally round him. Strategic hamlets, as envisioned by Diem, would build on existing communities instead of creating new ones. The government would assist peasants in placing fortifications around South Vietnam's sixteen thousand hamlets; the ARVN would protect the hamlets until they had time to develop their own self-defense units; the peasantry, secure against communist terror, would be won over to the government cause by land reform, better schools, improved medical facilities, and other economic and social programs; and the VC, with no villages in which to conceal themselves, would be obliged to come out into the open and fight, whereupon the ARVN would slaughter them. Given the importance of this program, Diem placed it in the hands of his most trusted confidante, brother Nhu.[22]

Diem did not inform Washington before launching the strategic hamlet program, a characteristic display of independence that irritated U.S. policymakers, but by and large the Kennedy administration was optimistic about the Saigon regime's project. Secretary of Defense Robert McNamara called strategic hamlets "the backbone of President Diem's program for countering subversion." The program also received the approbation of Sir Robert Thompson, a British counterinsurgency expert who went to South Vietnam at Kennedy's request to advise American officials on how to deal with the

VC. Drawing on his experience as a colonial administrator in Malaya, Thompson argued that the threat posed by communist guerrillas was more political than military, and that the "search and destroy" sweeps of the countryside carried out by the ARVN solved nothing; what the South Vietnamese government needed to implement, Thompson contended, was something along the lines of the strategic hamlet program, which not only promised to kill guerrillas but also to provide the peasantry with physical security and economic incentives for supporting their government. According to Thompson and other counterinsurgency enthusiasts, the strategic hamlet program would enable Diem to capture that critical variable in any revolutionary struggle: the "hearts and minds" of the people.[23]

As with the agroville campaign, Diem's new enterprise shattered on the rocks of Vietnamese reality. Even Thompson admitted that some peasants would have to be relocated for the strategic hamlet program to work, although he estimated that only about 5 percent of the rural population would undergo this hardship. Ultimately, a higher percentage were herded into fortified locations, often at gunpoint, with all of the attendant vexation one might expect from people who had formed intense loyalties to their home territories over generations. The structure of a Vietnamese hamlet did not fit Diem's conceit: while the hamlet tended to have a cluster of huts at its center, it also encompassed outlying huts, some located as much as a mile from the main cluster; those huts had to be dismantled and reassembled within a defensible perimeter. Often, entire villages had to be moved if Diem determined that they were in an especially remote location or susceptible to guerrilla attack. The government pledged to compensate those peasants who had to tear down their houses and rebuild them, but no payment or provision of social services could make up for the severing of ancestral ties. Besides, few of the government's promised reforms materialized. This was not for lack of funding: Washington provided millions of dollars for the institution of social services, but corrupt officials pocketed much of the money, and, more important, Diem seemed less concerned with the peasants' needs or problems than with consolidating his rule in South Vietnam. Thompson, initially one of the strategic hamlet program's fiercest advocates, was compelled to disavow it by 1963.

Strategic hamlets did have some advantages over agrovilles. They were smaller, as a rule, and many of their inhabitants did not have to abandon homesites. Even the peasants who were resettled usually did not have to move as far from familiar fields and markets as had been the case with the government's earlier attempts at social engineering. Nonetheless, the peasants hated the strategic hamlets, and for the same reasons they had hated the agrovilles. Because Diem believed his people needed to participate in the establishment of the hamlets to acquire a feeling of collective investment in their success, peasants were dragooned into working without pay, usually during the harvest time when they could least afford to neglect their crops. They dug moats around the hamlets, filling them with bamboo spears and planks with nails sticking out; they strung miles of barbed wire; they set up flood-lights and built walls to keep out the VC. Once completed, the hamlets were virtual prisons. Every resident was issued an identity card that he or she had to be prepared to show to a guard at any time. On the door frame of each hut was posted a list of all legitimate occupants. Every morning, before leaving to work in the fields, the hamlet dwellers had to submit to a search to ensure that they were not carrying supplies for the communists. Every night, after the curfew bell sounded, they had to be back behind the fortifications of the hamlet; if they remained outside, the night patrol was apt to shoot them. It was hardly surprising that peasants proved receptive to the VC promise: "When the Diem regime falls, . . . you will be able to go home again."[24]

The VC had little difficulty disseminating such propaganda, for the strategic hamlets failed to prevent communist infiltration. In fact, one of Nhu's assistants in administering the strategic hamlet program was a communist operative, Pham Ngoc Thao, who won Nhu's confidence and then proceeded to do everything in his power to ensure that the program would convert peasants into VC sympathizers. Thao pushed construction of the hamlets at the fastest possible speed and with no regard for locale. Hamlets were often erected in slap-bang fashion in areas with a large VC presence; the result was either that many VC were among those issued identification cards as "safe" villagers or that the hamlets were overrun by communist insurgents as soon as ARVN forces withdrew. Thao also encouraged hamlet superintendents to be brutal in punishing misbehavior, which alienated the people.

The Kennedy administration, however, continued to craft policy in the belief that what Diem required was encouragement, not criticism. Washington's primary initiative at the start of 1962 was the aptly named "Project Beefup," an enlargement of the American role in Vietnam characterized by more U.S. equipment and advisers. Hundreds of naval patrol boats, helicopter gunships, armored personnel carriers, transport planes, and trucks began pouring into the country. The increase in military personnel was the steepest yet, from thirty-two hundred to nine thousand. To oversee this expanded effort, Kennedy created a new joint service headquarters—the Military Assistance Command in Vietnam (MACV)—under the leadership of a four-

star general, Paul Harkins. Technically, the MACV and the MAAG comple-
mented one another, with the former directing the activities of U.S. army
support units and the latter advising the ARVN, but Harkins soon established himself as the preeminent American military authority in Vietnam
and the MAAG faded into the background.

Harkins believed in the power of positive thinking. "I am an optimist," he
declared upon arriving in Saigon, "and I am not going to allow my staff to
be pessimistic." His staff learned fast. The intelligence reports churned out
by the MACV were consistently upbeat. Harkins labeled them "Headway
Reports," and they teemed with heartening statistics about the number of
strategic hamlets constructed, VC killed, and zones of countryside brought
under government control. When McNamara visited South Vietnam in May
1962, Harkins assured him that the war would be "over by Christmas." Nolting never went that far, but his reports were also bullish. Six months after
McNamara's visit, the ambassador declared, "The most determined pessimist
must now concede that the tide is turning against the communists."[25]

Such statements did not arise so much from dishonesty as from the
bureaucratic imperative to report progress to superiors and, more significantly, from the fact that both the MACV and the embassy were getting
their information from Diem's government, which had an interest in making
sure that the political and strategic situation in South Vietnam appeared to
be improving. Diem made career advancement in the ARVN a function of
successful efficiency reports, and his civil appointees were likewise rewarded
for inflating or fabricating statistics to mislead the Americans. The result was
that the war portrayed in daily media briefings by the MACV and in the
elaborate graphs, charts, and color-coded maps sent back to Washington
bore little resemblance to the one actually being waged against the NLF.

There was another stream of information emanating from South Vietnam,
however, and it did not accord with the optimistic pronouncements of Nolting, Harkins, and others. In general, the Saigon press corps proved less gull-
ible than the embassy and the MACV, which made correspondents
unpopular with both Diem and his American backers. It was Diem's misfor-
tune, and the good fortune of millions of magazine and newspaper readers,
that South Vietnam in the early 1960s attracted the greatest assemblage of
American journalistic talent of the postwar era. Not all reportage from Saigon was of equal quality, and many correspondents continued to cling to the
threadbare Miracle Man myth, but on the whole U.S. journalists were more

willing to call official accounts of Diem's success into question than had been the case in the 1950s.

This caused Diem no end of annoyance, since he assumed that Washington controlled American reporters as tightly as the Saigon government controlled South Vietnamese reporters. He could never grasp the concept of an independent press, and his frustration with American policymakers' inability to make "their" journalists behave was a recurrent theme of his diatribes to Nolting. Homer Bigart of the *New York Times* was an especially weighty millstone around Diem's neck. Bigart spent six months in South Vietnam in 1961–1962 and wrote numerous articles critical of how the war against the communist rebels was being prosecuted. He was appalled by the lack of aggression displayed by ARVN troops, noting in his account of one firefight that the soldiers would not even pursue the VC after driving them from the field; instead, Bigart observed, South Vietnam's finest settled down for lunch. Bigart considered the strategic hamlet program a joke and repeatedly challenged embassy claims about the loyalties of the peasants. Even more provocative was Bigart's coining of an expression that would become synonymous with the Diem experiment. In a letter to a fellow reporter in early 1962, Bigart revealed, "I am composing a song, to be sung to the tune of 'I'm an Old Cowhand,' that runs:

> *We must sink or swim*
> *With Ngo Dinh Diem*
> *We will hear no phoo*
> *About Madame Nhu.*
> *Yippee-i-aye, i-aye, etc.*

A week later, the phrase "Sink or Swim with Ngo Dinh Diem" appeared in Bigart's article on the front page of the *Times*.[26]

Diem, outraged, insisted that Bigart leave his country. For good measure, Diem also ordered the expulsion of François Sully, a *Newsweek* reporter whose accounts of increases in VC strength and declining support for the Saigon government were so alarming that *Newsweek* had been banned in South Vietnam. Diem's actions put Nolting in a difficult position. He agreed that Bigart and Sully had behaved irresponsibly but argued that expelling correspondents from two major American publications would have adverse effects on public opinion in the United States. Diem eventually decided to allow Sully to remain until his visa expired and accepted Nolting's reassurances that Bigart would soon be leaving. But Diem demanded to know why

Washington would allow American reporters to write such slanderous stories. Nolting attempted to explain the American right of freedom of speech, with little success. Madame Nhu spoke for her brother-in-law when she told a group of reporters that South Vietnam had no use for "your crazy freedoms."[27]

Bigart left Saigon in June 1962, to Diem's relief, but his replacement, twenty-seven-year-old David Halberstam, was even less inclined to trust official reports that the tide of battle was flowing against the VC. Halberstam established himself as the brashest of a group of young correspondents who would become the scourge of the Diem regime before the year was out. Other reporters—notably thirty-two-year-old Malcolm Browne, twenty-six-year-old Neil Sheehan, and twenty-seven-year-old Peter Arnett—questioned and sometimes ridiculed the statistics supplied by the MACV and the embassy to back claims of progress. They called attention to corruption and incompetence in the South Vietnamese government. Halberstam filed stories describing VC military gains that, in Nolting's view, verged on treason. "[S]uch stories," the ambassador cabled Washington, provided "excellent grist" for the "Commie mill." Kennedy was so displeased by Halberstam's reporting that he tried, unsuccessfully, to pressure the publisher of the *Times* to transfer the journalist to another country.[28]

This was a new breed of reporter, very much of the sixties generation, and as unwelcome to Diem and the U.S. army brass as they were to older, more conservative correspondents stationed in Saigon. Marguerite Higgins of the *New York Herald Tribune* dismissed Halberstam, Sheehan, Arnett, and Browne as "arrogant upstarts." She formed a friendship with Madame Nhu, spread defamatory rumors about Halberstam in Washington and Saigon, and published a six-part series titled "Vietnam—Fact and Fiction" that contradicted everything Halberstam and his fellow "upstarts" had written. Henry Luce followed Higgins's lead and enlisted the might of his media empire in the campaign to preserve the Diem experiment. Luce's *Time* magazine blasted anti-Diem correspondents for "helping to compound the very confusion that [they] should be untangling for [their] readers back home." Joseph Alsop, one of the most influential columnists of the twentieth century, went farthest in excoriating what he called the young Saigon correspondents' "egregious crusade" against an allied government which, whatever its faults, was better than anything the communists were offering.[29]

Clearly, Diem had his advocates in the American media. There is a flawed narrative of the later Diem era that contends that the South Vietnamese regime—and, with it, America's Vietnam policy—was sabotaged by hostile correspondents who would stop at nothing to bring Diem down and who turned the American public and government against him. It is true that Halberstam and other like-minded reporters could be scathing in their accounts of how the war was being mishandled and their criticism of Diem for failing to undertake political liberalization and social reform. But their stories were counterbalanced by the reports of heavyweights like Higgins and Alsop, who reached just as large an audience and whose editorial line was viewed more favorably by Washington. Still, there is no question that the wall of optimism constructed by the MACV and the embassy had been partially breached by 1962, and that Americans were getting a more complex picture of events in South Vietnam than they had received during the early years of Diem's reign.

That picture became grimmer on the morning of 27 February 1962, when two pilots of the South Vietnamese air force flew over the Norodom Palace and dropped bombs and napalm in an attempt to assassinate Diem. Fortunately for the president, he had risen early that morning and was reading in his office when the first bomb fell on the verandah. He raced to the fortified cellar where he had sat out much of the 1960 coup attempt. For thirty-five minutes, the planes bombed and strafed the palace, destroying one wing of Diem's quarters and setting much of the building ablaze. Antiaircraft guns shot down one pilot, and the other escaped to Cambodia. The pilots had hoped that their attack would inspire an uprising against the government, but the army and air force remained loyal. While the bombing resulted in thirty-four casualties, Diem did not sustain so much as a scratch.

Kennedy sent Diem a message of support, expressing "admiration for the calm and courageous manner in which you faced this destructive and vicious act." Nolting determined that the attack had been the result of "two . . . isolated cases" and did not indicate widespread dissatisfaction with the Diem government. Yet this narrow escape hardly inclined Diem to be more tolerant of political opposition or media criticism. He shut down newspapers and ordered the arrest of dozens of men he considered untrustworthy. Ultimately, Diem became so preoccupied with ferreting out domestic adversaries that he had little time for fighting the VC.[30]

In his first postassassination attempt meeting with Diem, Nolting found the president in a foul mood, certain that the media was responsible for his troubles. As proof, Diem noted that one of the rebel pilots had been persuaded to take part in the attack because the other showed him "derogatory articles in the press." Such coverage, Diem insisted, had convinced the pilot that "the Americans were supporting the revolution." His temper rising,

Diem declared that "some journalists" were portraying the bombing as "a warning" to him, when in fact "it should be a warning to them—an indication of the danger of their irresponsibility." Joseph Mendenhall, counselor for political affairs at the Saigon embassy, tersely summarized eight years of the Diem experiment when he wrote in the margin next to the president's tirade: "Never learns."[31]

Notes

1. Eisenhower cited in footnote 2, *FRUS, 1958–1960* (Washington: Government Printing Office, 1986), 1:138.

2. David L. Anderson, *Trapped by Success: The Eisenhower Administration and Vietnam, 1953–1961* (New York: Columbia University Press, 1991), 178.

3. The Ambassador in Vietnam to the Assistant Secretary of State for Far Eastern Affairs, 16 February 1959, *FRUS, 1958–1960*, 139–143.

4. Draper Committee cited in James R. Arnold, *The First Domino: Eisenhower, the Military, and America's Intervention in Vietnam* (New York: Morrow, 1991), 348.

5. Arnold, *First Domino*, 348.

6. "Manifesto of the Eighteen, 26 April 1960," *Vietnam: Anthology and Guide to a Television History*, ed. Steven Cohen (New York: Knopf, 1983), 66–71.

7. Stanley Karnow, "Diem Defeats His Own Best Troops," reprinted in *Reporting Vietnam, Part I: American Journalism, 1959–1969* (New York: Library of America, 1998), 11.

8. Memorandum of Discussion at the 444th Meeting of the National Security Council, 9 May 1960, *FRUS, 1958–1960*, 1:446–447.

9. Diem cited in Karnow, "Diem Defeats His Own Best Troops," 12.

10. Saigon Radio cited in George Kahin, *Intervention: How America Became Involved in Vietnam* (New York: Anchor Books, 1986), 124; Nguyen Thai Binh, *Vietnam: The Problem and a Solution* (Paris: Vietnam Democratic Party, 1962), 78.

11. Durbrow cited in Editorial Note, *FRUS, 1958–1960*, 1:663.

12. Le Duan cited in Edward Doyle and others, *The Vietnam Experience*, vol. 2, *Passing the Torch* (Boston: Boston Publishing, 1983), 168–169.

13. NLF founding document cited in Truong Nhu Tang and others, *A Viet Cong Memoir* (New York: Harcourt Brace Jovanovich, 1985), 319–328.

14. Memorandum of Conference on 19 January 1961 between President Eisenhower and President-Elect Kennedy, *The Pentagon Papers*, Gravel Edition (Boston: Beacon, 1971), 2:635–637.

15. Kennedy cited in Richard Reeves, *President Kennedy: Profile of Power* (New York: Simon & Schuster, 1993), 36.

16. "The Legal Underpinnings of Government Terror in South Vietnam: Law 10/59" in *Vietnam and America*, ed. Marvin E. Gettleman, Jane Franklin, Marilyn B. Young, and H. Bruce Franklin (New York: Grove, 1995), 156–159; *Pentagon Papers*, Gravel Edition, 2:134.

17. Nolting cited in Stanley Karnow, *Vietnam: A History* (New York: Viking, 1983), 263; Trueheart cited in William Prochnau, *Once upon a Distant War: David Halberstam, Neil Sheehan, Peter Arnett—Young War Correspondents and Their Early Vietnam Battles* (New York: Vintage, 1995), 170.

18. Johnson cited in James Olson and Randy Roberts, *Where the Domino Fell: America and Vietnam, 1945–1990*, 1st ed. (New York: St. Martin's, 1996), 84.

19. National Security Files, Countries—Vietnam: Kennedy to Diem, 8 May 1961: Box 193, JFKL.

20. A Program of Action to Prevent Communist Domination of South Vietnam, 1 May 1961, *FRUS, 1961–1963* (Washington, D.C.: Government Printing Office, 1991), 1:100; Johnson cited in Roger Hilsman, *To Move a Nation: The Politics of Foreign Policy in the Administration of John F. Kennedy* (Garden City, N.Y.: Doubleday, 1967), 420; David Halberstam, *The Best and the Brightest* (New York: Random House, 1969), 135.

21. Report by the Vice President, undated, *FRUS, 1961–1963*, 1:152–157; Joint Action Program Proposed by the Vietnam-U.S. Special Financial Groups, 25 July 1961, *U.S.-VN Relations*, 11:182–228.

22. Philip E. Catton, *Diem's Final Failure: Prelude to America's War in Vietnam* (Lawrence: University Press of Kansas, 2002), 91.

23. McNamara cited in Kahin, *Intervention*, 140.

24. Viet Cong propaganda cited in Olson and Roberts, *Where the Domino Fell*, 96.

25. Harkins cited in A. J. Langguth, *Our Vietnam: The War, 1954–1975* (New York: Simon & Schuster, 2000), 163; Prochnau, *Once upon a Distant War*, 166; Nolting cited in Prochnau, *Once upon a Distant War*, 194.

26. Bigart cited in Prochnau, *Once upon a Distant War*, 48–49.

27. Madame Nhu cited in Prochnau, *Once upon a Distant War*, 180.

28. National Security Files, Countries—Vietnam: Nolting to Rusk, 13 November 1961: Box 195, JFKL.

29. Higgins cited in Prochnau, *Once upon a Distant War*, 344; "Foreign Correspondents: The View from Saigon," *Time*, 20 September 1963, 62; Joseph Alsop, "The Crusaders," *New York Herald Tribune*, 23 September 1963.

30. President's Office Files, Countries—Vietnam: Kennedy to Diem, 27 February 1961: Box 128A, JFKL; Memorandum for the Record, 1 March 1962, *FRUS, 1961–1963*, 2:189.

31. Memorandum for the Record, 1 March 1962, *FRUS, 1961–1963*, 2:193.

CHAPTER SIX

~

"A Scenario of Torture,
Persecution, and Worse"

The Diem Experiment in Decline

When, as often happened, John F. Kennedy was vexed by contradictory reports about America's Diem experiment, his response was to send a fact-finding mission to South Vietnam. These missions were short but intensive, involving tours of the battlefront, a trip to one or two strategic hamlets, and briefings by generals, intelligence service leaders, diplomats, and sometimes even South Vietnamese president Ngo Dinh Diem himself. Almost without exception, the missions served to confirm the prejudices of those policymakers charged by Kennedy with evaluating the progress of the war against the Viet Cong.

For example, JFK dispatched two of the most hyperactive "hawks" in his administration—Joint Chiefs of Staff Chairman Maxwell Taylor and Deputy Special Assistant for National Security Affairs Walt Rostow—to Saigon in late 1961, and the result was a hawkish report: Taylor and Rostow declared that the VC insurgency was part of a global offensive directed by Moscow and Beijing; they recommended an increase in military aid, a greater number of advisers, and the deployment of eight thousand U.S. troops who would ostensibly be in the Mekong Delta to "assist in the . . . reconstruction effort" after a flood but whose real purpose would be to fight guerrillas. While Kennedy did not accept the troop proposal, he otherwise went along with the Taylor-Rostow report, upgrading the U.S. Military Assistance Advisory Group (MAAG) to the U.S. Military Assistance Command in Vietnam (MACV) and increasing the number of U.S. advisers to nine thousand by

the end of 1962. The Taylor-Rostow report played a major role in the escalation of U.S. support for South Vietnam, although the two men would have
written more or less the same assessment had they stayed in Washington and
saved the American taxpayers the burden of financing a twenty-four-thou-
sand-mile trip.[1]

In contrast to the united front presented by Taylor and Rostow, career
diplomat Joseph Mendenhall and General Victor Krulak came back from
their four-day fact-finding mission with irreconcilable evaluations of how the
Diem experiment was faring. Krulak, a hawk and an optimist, had met with
MACV commander General Paul Harkins and other South Vietnamese and
American army officers; his report was positive, even ebullient, as he
recounted impressive gains by the Army of the Republic of Vietnam
(ARVN) against the communist insurgents and discounted any claims that
there was a political crisis in Saigon. Maybe some South Vietnamese disliked
Diem's brother Ngo Dinh Nhu, Krulak contended, but Diem himself
remained popular. When Kennedy asked if the United States could win in
Vietnam with Diem, Krulak affirmed, "Can do!" Mendenhall, however, had
concentrated on South Vietnam's urban areas, where he interviewed lower-
echelon embassy officials, journalists, and the Vietnamese friends he had
made during his three years of service in Saigon under Ambassador Elbridge
Durbrow. Already pessimistic about Diem's prospects, Mendenhall was
shocked by what he discovered. South Vietnam, he said, was "living under a
reign of terror." Morale was terrible. Many people in the capital and in the
coastal cities of Hue and Danang were stating that they preferred a VC victory to continuing with Diem. Dissatisfaction with the Diem regime was so
universal that a collapse of civil government loomed. If Washington wanted
to salvage this situation, Mendenhall insisted, Diem had to be deposed. After
Krulak and Mendenhall presented their reports, a nonplussed Kennedy
asked, "Did you two gentlemen visit the same country?"[2]

One man who Kennedy trusted to give him a realistic appraisal of the
Diem experiment was Senator Mike Mansfield. Not only was Mansfield Congress's expert on Asia; he and Kennedy also had a long working relationship.
They had arrived in the Senate at the same time, two Catholics of Irish
descent, both progressive Democrats in the conservative Eisenhower years,
both cold warriors who despised the xenophobia of the McCarthyites, and—
most important—both members of the American Friends of Vietnam
(AFV), with an immense stake in preserving South Vietnam from communism. When JFK assumed the presidency, he saw to it that Mansfield became
Senate Democratic leader and regularly solicited his advice on foreign pol-

icy. In October 1962 Kennedy asked Mansfield to head a fact-finding delegation from the Foreign Relations Committee to "visit selected areas of major
significance to U.S. policy," including South Vietnam.[3]

Mansfield had not visited that land since 1955, although he had corres-
ponded with Diem and praised him in speeches. He had been disturbed, however, by what he had read in the newspapers about Diem's remoteness from
his people and the inability of ARVN forces to contain the VC insurgency.
When he arrived in Saigon on 29 November—accompanied by Senators
Claiborne Pell, Caleb Boggs, and Benjamin Smith—he began to seek out
those American journalists whom the embassy, MACV, and the Diem regime
held in such contempt. Ambassador Frederick Nolting managed to steer the
senator away from such troublemakers at first; instead, the Mansfield delegation was obliged to sit through a briefing by Nolting, Harkins, and others in
which the ambassador assured the group that Diem's government controlled
between 50 and 70 percent of South Vietnam's population and that the president's hold on power was undiminished. Harkins, for his part, forecast complete victory over the communists by the end of 1963, which struck
Mansfield as preposterous.

The briefing veered from its blithesome track when Pell asked Nolting: "If
there were an election in Vietnam today, how would Diem come out?" Nolting referred the query to William Trueheart, chargé d'affaires at the embassy,
who, after casting a worried look at Mansfield, responded, "Well, . . . I'm not
sure that half the people know who Diem is." Nolting quickly contradicted
his subordinate, pointing out that Diem's picture was everywhere in South
Vietnam and that the majority of peasants *did* know who their president was.
But Mansfield seized on Trueheart's statement and asked a number of questions that probed the chinks in the embassy's optimistic portrayal. If he never
succeeded in shaking Harkins or Nolting out of their convictions that Diem
was a popular ruler and the VC were on the run, he raised doubts in the
minds of the other visiting senators and corroborated his own fears.[4]

More significant than the briefing at the embassy was Mansfield's meeting
with Diem, a surreal scene in the president's office that saw Diem speak non-
stop for two hours about Vietnamese history, his efforts to establish a stable
government, and Hanoi's attempts to subvert his regime. Diem seemed
unaware that Mansfield had followed events in Vietnam for a decade and, in
fact, had played an active part in many of the developments the president
recounted. At a subsequent dinner hosted by Diem for the delegation, Mansfield found it impossible to get a word in, as Diem continued his exposition,
self-absorbed, oblivious to his listeners.

This only made Mansfield more determined to speak with those journalists who were ruffling so many feathers. He arranged a meeting the following day with David Halberstam of the *New York Times*, Neil Sheehan of United Press International, and Peter Arnett and Malcolm Browne of the Associated Press. The conversation lasted five hours, as the correspondents, thrilled to encounter a policymaker willing to hear their side of the story, told Mansfield all of the shortfalls and falsehoods they had discovered in the Saigon government's reports by going into the field to see for themselves how matters stood. The ARVN was *not* defeating the VC, they insisted, and Diem's leadership was an obstacle rather than an asset in the counterinsurgency effort. MACV and the embassy were either deluded or dishonest, but in any case they were presenting an inaccurate picture that misled the American people.

The next day, as the Mansfield delegation gathered at Tan Son Nhut Airport and prepared for departure, an embassy official handed Mansfield a statement to read that congratulated the Diem government for "progress toward victory." The senator refused to read the statement. Instead, he commended Diem for his integrity but omitted any mention of military success or continued American aid. He also approached Trueheart, shook his hand, and said, "I think you're right"—that is, about Diem's lack of support. It was a tremendous public-relations blow for Diem. "Mr. President, I'm awfully sorry," Nolting told Diem after the delegation flew out of Saigon. "I don't know what it was, but those were rather discouraging remarks."[5]

It would get worse after Mansfield returned to Washington. His delegation took months to prepare its public report, but the senator provided Kennedy with a confidential one almost as soon as his plane touched down. Mansfield warned the president that the United States was being drawn "inexorably into some variation of the unenviable position in Vietnam which was formerly occupied by the French." He advised Kennedy to make a difficult but necessary choice and retreat from America's involvement in Southeast Asia. A diplomatic settlement that neutralized South Vietnam and allowed the United States to "lighten our commitments" was the most realistic goal for the administration to pursue. Yes, such an arrangement might result in a communist takeover of all Vietnam, but Mansfield urged the president to consider whether the national interest really required preserving a noncommunist stronghold on the Asian mainland, especially if it could only be preserved through full-scale war.[6]

Mansfield's report stunned Kennedy, who summoned the Senate majority leader to his vacation home in Palm Beach. When Mansfield greeted the president at poolside, Kennedy snapped, "Let's talk alone," and took his visitor for a cruise on his yacht. For hours, Kennedy grilled Mansfield about Vietnam, and by the end of the questioning, the president's face was red. "Do you expect me to take this at face value?" he demanded. "You asked me to go out there," Mansfield reminded him. After the two men said their icy goodbyes, Kennedy took his aide Kenneth O'Donnell aside and admitted, "I got angry with Mike for disagreeing with our policy, . . . and I got angry with myself because I found myself agreeing with him." That oft-cited remark ought not to be misinterpreted: JFK certainly did not agree with Mansfield's assertion that a U.S. position of power on mainland Asia was inessential to national security, but he began to question, as no president had since 1955, whether Washington's commitment to a noncommunist South Vietnam was inseparable from its support of Diem.[7]

Diem never knew about Mansfield's private report to Kennedy. He did, however, read the report prepared by the Mansfield committee for Congress, and that was distressing enough. "It would be a disservice to my country not to voice a deep concern over the trend of events in Vietnam," Mansfield declared. Despite the fact that officials like Nolting and Harkins were "optimistic over the prospects for success," Mansfield argued that "experience" did not warrant "drawing the kind of optimistic conclusions . . . which have been drawn." It was true that the number of VC casualties had gone up in recent months, but so had the estimated total of communist guerrillas in the countryside. The Diem regime had failed to nourish any self-sustaining growth that might lead to South Vietnam's economic independence. It had also failed to develop an army capable of fighting the VC without ever-increasing amounts of U.S. aid and supervision. Diem's prestige among the peasantry, never strong, seemed to be deteriorating. In sum, the Diem experiment was a washout. To continue the present policy, Mansfield concluded, would "involve an expenditure in American lives and resources on a scale which would bear little relationship to the interests of the United States."[8]

Nolting recognized the Mansfield report as a deathblow. This was not some third-string reporter writing disagreeable articles; this was the Senate majority leader, a friend of President Kennedy, and Congress's authority on Asia calling for an abandonment of the Diem experiment. "Mansfield's report wounded President Diem deeply," Nolting recalled. "I personally thought Mansfield's report did a great disservice to . . . our cause." Nolting declined to underscore the irony of the situation as he portrayed it: If Mansfield had been indispensable in saving Diem during the mid-1950s, his 1963 report was, in Nolting's words, "the first nail in Diem's coffin."[9]

～

Nolting was actually a month or so off in his chronology. The VC drove the first nail into Diem's coffin on 2 January 1963 at a village called Ap Bac, thirty-five miles southwest of Saigon. For weeks, ARVN intelligence reports had noted the presence of a heavy concentration of communist troops in that area, which seemed to indicate that the enemy was preparing to engage the South Vietnamese army in a set-piece battle. American military officials were delighted at the prospect; they had often bragged that the guerrillas could be defeated "if they would stand and fight." Now the MACV got its wish. Lieutenant Colonel John Paul Vann, senior adviser to the ARVN Seventh Division in the northern Mekong Delta, prepared a seemingly can't-miss three-pronged attack: over three thousand ARVN soldiers, supported by American-operated helicopter gunships, M-113 armored personnel carriers, fighter bombers, and other high-tech equipment, would advance on the approximately 320 rebel troops from the north, south, and west; the rice fields to the east were deliberately left unguarded so that when the VC attempted to escape in that direction, aircraft and artillery fire could mow them down. It was, Vann believed, a golden opportunity to boost the ARVN's stock among South Vietnam's rural population and demonstrate that the momentum of the war was in Diem's hands.

As with much of America's nation-building effort in Vietnam, what sounded good in theory proved unworkable in practice. The problem was the ARVN, whose officers were incompetent and whose troops were unwilling to fight. Colonel Bui Dinh Dam, commander of the Seventh Division, gave away the element of surprise when he delayed launching the attack for a day on the grounds that American chopper pilots needed more time to sleep off their New Year's Eve hangovers. The guerrillas learned what was coming and prepared defensive positions behind tall trees, grass, and shrubs, with a clear view of the surrounding territory. When ARVN soldiers finally advanced on Ap Bac, they did so with agonizing slowness, in piecemeal fashion, and the VC picked them off with ease.

More impressively, the guerrillas, who had previously fled whenever American helicopters and personnel carriers appeared, now stood their ground and proved that these machines of war were not invincible. Fourteen of the fifteen helicopters that took part in the Battle of Ap Bac were hit by VC gunfire; five went down, and the others were disabled. The ten-ton personnel carriers, thirteen of which were deployed in the battle, could not overrun the VC defenses. Indeed, Captain Ly Tong Ba, the ARVN officer in charge of the M-113 armored unit, refused to move, claiming that his heavy vehicles could not travel through the network of canals, paddy fields, and bogs leading to Ap Bac. Vann, flying overhead in a spotter plane, demanded that Ba advance, to which the captain replied, "I don't take orders from Americans." Only after Vann threatened to have Ba shot did the M-113s start rolling, *very* slowly, toward the entrenched enemy line. Four hours later, they arrived—not abreast of each other, as planned, but separately, which enabled the VC to concentrate their fire on individual carriers for maximum effectiveness. Fourteen ARVN gunners were killed. The rest crouched inside their hatches, unable to see the guerrillas, firing their 50-caliber machine guns aimlessly into the sky. One VC squad leader leapt out of his foxhole and tossed a grenade into an M-113. Soon other guerrillas emulated his example, and the armored unit began to retreat. The ARVN regular troops cowered behind the downed helicopters or burrowed into the mud of the paddies. They ignored orders to counterattack and even refused to return fire. Eventually, Colonel Dam, at the behest of his civilian superiors in Saigon, broke off the engagement.[10]

As night fell, the VC slipped out of Ap Bac. Their losses were estimated at about eighteen. The ARVN suffered sixty-one killed and over one hundred wounded. Vann, beside himself with rage, did not mince words when a journalist asked him how the battle had gone. "A miserable fucking performance, just like it always is," he spat. He was even more disgusted when the MACV tried to portray Ap Bac as a victory because government troops had "taken the objective," meaning Ap Bac itself. It was true that the enemy had abandoned the field, but only because the VC were less interested in holding territory than in discrediting the ARVN and Diem in the eyes of South Vietnam's citizenry. In this regard, they succeeded brilliantly. By mid-1963, most villages in the northern Delta region either supported the VC or assumed a neutral stance.[11]

Ironically, the day after ARVN forces were mauled at Ap Bac, Diem threw himself a party. It was his sixty-second birthday, and Saigon's elite gathered at Gia Long Palace to pay tribute to the president. (The Ngos had relocated to Gia Long in February 1962 after pilots bombed the Norodom Palace, the ruling family's official home.) Diem surprised many by appearing in mandarin robes rather than his customary white sharkskin attire; he looked more than ever like a man out of his time. Still, the toasts were effusive. One guest raved that Diem was "born to be a leader." Another prated that the president's "genius" was "outweighed only by his virtue." Private assessments in Washington and Saigon were more grounded in reality. A report for President Kennedy prepared by Michael Forrestal of the National Security Council described South Vietnam as a "dictatorship" and bemoaned Diem's "tendencies of arbitrariness, failure to delegate, and general pettiness." At a dinner held in Nolting's residence, ARVN Generals Tran Van Don and Tran Thien Khiem told the ambassador that a coup might be necessary to save their country from communism. Diem, they insisted, was "no good." Nolting, indignant, replied, "The United States is not going to get into this question of a coup d'etat." But the Kennedy administration would soon get into precisely that question.[12]

～

Mansfield delivered his gloomy report to the Senate in early March 1963, on the heels of the debacle at Ap Bac. It was a jolting one-two combination. Diem's government was clearly in trouble, but few could have predicted the rapidity of its collapse. After all, Diem had survived more crises than almost any Asian statesman of his generation: after being sentenced to death by the communists in 1950, nearly toppled by the Binh Xuyen in 1955, shot at by a would-be assassin in 1957, held captive by his best troops in 1960, and bombed in his home in 1962, he was still alive, still chief of state. Given the storms he had weathered, the event that precipitated the self-destruction of the Diem experiment seems, in retrospect, trivial.

It all started with an argument about flags. On 7 May 1963, Buddhists in the old imperial capital of Hue joined in festivities commemorating the 2,527th birthday of the Buddha. Many homes and pagodas were hung with Buddhist flags, and the deputy province chief in charge of security, a Catholic major named Dang Xi, chose this inopportune moment to invoke a law banning the display of religious flags without government permission. Diem had proclaimed this law in the mid-1950s as part of his campaign to curb the power of the sects; since he wanted to forge a unified country out of the patchwork of independent satrapies that was South Vietnam's countryside, he decreed that only the national flag could be flown in public. But the law had rarely been enforced, and Hue's Buddhists pointed out that just the week before, their city had been festooned with papal flags celebrating the twenty-fifth anniversary of Diem's brother, Ngo Dinh Thuc, as archbishop. No one had ordered *those* flags taken down. Why put the decree into effect now? Major Xi was unsympathetic. Police pulled down the Buddhist banners.

The following day, 8 May, thousands of Buddhists gathered in front of the Hue radio station to protest the flag ban. The chief bonze of central Vietnam, Thich Tri Quang, prepared to deliver an address over loudspeakers.

Bonzes and Buddhist laymen called on the station director to broadcast the speech, but he claimed that he could not do so because Tri Quang's words had not been approved by the government censor. When the crowd grew restive, the director called Major Xi, who arrived with a company of men and armored cars. Xi ordered the protestors to disperse. They did not comply, or at least not quickly enough to suit the major, and Xi told his troops to fire. The soldiers shot directly into the crowd and hurled at least fifteen grenades. The result was a bloodbath: nine people were killed and fourteen wounded. Two of the dead were children. They had been crushed beneath the tracks of the armored vehicles.

Diem responded to this tragedy with shocking insensitivity. He blamed the affair on the VC, claiming that a communist agent had thrown a grenade into the crowd, sparking a melee, and that the nine victims had been trampled to death as people fled the scene. Xi, an official statement announced, had acted properly. There was no need for any disciplinary action. Unfortunately for Diem, bystanders had taken home movies of the demonstration, and the films showed government troops firing into the crowd. Diem refused to be swayed by this evidence, stuck to his story, and ordered the nine bodies buried without autopsy. This stimulated further protests. In a demonstration in Hue on 10 May, Tri Quang proclaimed a five-point "manifesto of the monks" that demanded freedom to fly the Buddhist flag, legal equality between Buddhists and Catholics, indemnification for the families of the victims of the massacre, punishment for the officials responsible, and an end to arbitrary arrests. Major Xi himself told the assembled Buddhists that Diem should compensate the families of the wounded and the dead.

Diem would do no such thing. From his perspective, payment to the families would be a sign of weakness. He did agree to meet with a Buddhist delegation, but this only aggravated matters, as he spent the meeting lecturing the bonzes. He insisted that what had happened in Hue on 8 May had nothing to do with religion; some of the victims, after all, had been "non-Buddhists." Furthermore, the order prohibiting the display of religious flags applied to all religions, not just Buddhism; there was nothing discriminatory about it. He could not end arbitrary arrests, he said, because this would aid the VC. Finally, South Vietnam's constitution guaranteed freedom of worship. He knew this because he *was* the constitution. What more did the Buddhists want? Diem called his guests "damn fools" for demanding a right they already enjoyed. Remarkably, a government communiqué detailing the encounter included Diem's expression "damn fools."[13]

This was not good public relations, either in Washington's view or in the opinion of Diem's brother Ngo Dinh Can, who controlled Hue and the central provinces and who recognized that Diem had taken a minor incident and turned it into a potential disaster. There was a difference, Can argued, between restricting Buddhist rights to own property and running over Buddhist children with tanks. Whether Diem liked it or not, the majority of his fellow South Vietnamese were Buddhists. He needed at least their passive acquiescence, if not their support, to stay in power. Can had two representatives of Hue in the National Assembly inform the president that he must conciliate the Buddhists. Make an appearance at a prominent pagoda, Can advised his brother. Pay reparations. Issue a statement acknowledging that government troops had erred. At the moment, Can observed, Diem's standing in Hue was so low that if he were to return to the city where he was born, "not even a cat" would turn out to welcome him. Diem laughed when he received this message, remarking, "My brother has lost his courage."[14]

During these early days of what came to be known as "the Buddhist crisis," Kennedy and his advisers had little time to concentrate on conditions in South Vietnam. A civil rights battle was unfolding at home—principally in Birmingham, Alabama—and Kennedy was obliged to deal with protests against his own government rather than Diem's. Photographs and television footage of high-pressure hoses blasting African-American children, police-trained dogs attacking demonstrators, and the Reverend Martin Luther King Jr. stewing in a jail cell inflamed passions in the United States and required Kennedy to devote most of his waking hours to managing the situation. When Forrestal brought him a report of the Buddhist demonstrations in Hue, Kennedy looked at his aide uncomprehendingly and asked, "Who are these people?"[15]

"These people" were becoming difficult to ignore. Although Nolting insisted that the charges of religious discrimination were overblown, he was a diplomat and understood the importance of appearances. Diem's public posture, whatever his motivations, gave the impression of callousness. After days of coaxing, Nolting got Diem to compensate the families of the victims in Hue. The amount paid—500,000 piasters, or about $7,000—was ungenerous, but at least Diem had made a gesture of conciliation. Diem also agreed to dismiss Xi and the Hue province chief. His publicly stated reason for doing so, however, was that these officials had failed to maintain order in the city, not that they had taken unnecessarily severe measures in breaking up the 8 May demonstration. Diem continued to deny that his government bore any responsibility for what occurred on that day. Yet his concessions were sufficient for Nolting, who turned over the embassy to Chargé Trueheart and left South Vietnam on 23 May for a sailing vacation in the Aegean.

Less than a week after Nolting's departure, the head of the Buddhist hierarchy in Vietnam, Thich Tinh Khiet, called for a two-day fast to protest the Diem regime's policies. One thousand monks and nuns obeyed, and hundreds of Buddhists gathered outside the National Assembly Building in Saigon, carrying banners that demanded government compliance with their five demands. On 3 June the Buddhist crisis turned violent, as government troops attacked demonstrators in Hue. Diem had forbidden public demonstrations in that city, but a throng of fifteen hundred defied the ban and assembled at Ben Ngu Bridge to march to Hue's main religious building, the Tu Dam Pagoda. Six times ARVN troops used tear gas and attack dogs to scatter the demonstrators, but the crowd reassembled again and again, screaming taunts and obscenities. Finally, the soldiers poured brownish-red liquid on the heads of praying Buddhists, sixty-seven of whom had to be hospitalized for respiratory ailments and burns. By midnight, Diem had put Hue under martial law, imposing a dusk-to-dawn curfew.

Matters were spinning out of control. Xa Loi, the premier pagoda in Saigon, became a center of dissident activity, where bonzes held press conferences denouncing Diem, mimeographed antigovernment pamphlets, and organized mass meetings. They proved skillful at using American correspondents to publicize their cause. From the beginning, they printed their protest signs and press releases in English as well as Vietnamese, and they selected one of the few English-speaking bonzes in Vietnam to be their spokesman. Diem, furious that the American press would dignify these people with a hearing, proclaimed repeatedly that there was no religious persecution in his country, that South Vietnam's Buddhists supported the government, and that the bonzes stirring up trouble were VC agents. Trueheart, less inclined to appease Diem than Nolting, demanded that the government do something to ease tensions. The State Department concurred. Diem's policies vis-à-vis the Buddhists were making the United States appear a handmaiden to dictatorship. Secretary of State Dean Rusk advised the Saigon embassy that Diem "must be made to realize [the] extent not only of [his] own stake in [an] amicable settlement with [the] Buddhists but [the] U.S. stake as well."[16]

With undisguised reluctance, Diem made a few concessions—nominal by U.S. standards, colossal by his own. He announced the appointment of an interministerial committee to deal with Buddhist grievances. He offered to meet with Buddhist leaders and try to reach some accord on their five demands. He even broadcast an address in Hue that used the word "errors" to describe the actions of government officials. Each of these moves cut Diem deeply, but he needed American aid, and with Nolting on holiday the embassy would not tolerate any temporizing.[17]

When Diem's committee met with Thich Thien Minh, representative of the General Association of Buddhists, it may have been the government's last opportunity to compose the Buddhist quarrel. At first, Diem seemed to rise to the occasion. Both sides gave ground, although Diem obliged the Buddhists to give more. In return for a Buddhist pledge to "cease all demonstrations," the government would "remove . . . all uniformed personnel from [the] vicinity of pagodas." There would, both parties agreed, be a "standfast on propaganda." The Buddhists promised to "recognize the superiority of [the] national flag" and "display it outside pagodas on official, non-religious holidays." On religious holidays, Diem henceforth would permit religious flags to be flown, provided they were accompanied by national flags. As for freedom of religion, Diem continued to insist that this was already "guaranteed by the constitution," but he vowed that the government would "undertake corrective action" if the Buddhists could "specify where [the] constitution [was] not being respected." Finally, he declared that he was "prepared to pay more" than the sum already awarded to the victims' families in Hue, but wanted it understood that this would "[involve] no acceptance of responsibility."[18]

While Diem had not satisfied the Buddhists' five demands, he had gone as far as he felt he could, and a resolution of the crisis seemed within reach. "I am keeping my fingers crossed," Trueheart cabled the State Department. Only a day after the truce terms supposedly went into effect, however, disaster struck. Government airplanes flying over Hue dropped leaflets denouncing Tri Quang and calling on Tinh Khiet to make his followers behave. This was hardly a "standfast on propaganda." Worse, Madame Nhu, through her Women's Solidarity Movement, issued a resolution to the press that same day that ran counter to the government's policy of reconciliation. Madame Nhu described Buddhist protesters as traitors "controlled by communism," and demanded that the government "expel all foreign agitators whether they wear monks' robes or not." In her most provocative statement, she cautioned Diem to "keep vigilance on . . . those inclined to take Viet Nam for [a] satellite of [a] foreign power."[19]

This obvious swipe at the United States enraged Washington. Trueheart insisted that Diem "repudiate [the] resolution," to which the president replied that Madame Nhu was free to express her opinions. He did, however, order that the resolution not be publicized in the print media or on the radio, but this directive came too late to stop the *Times of Vietnam* from citing it. Rusk was livid, cabling the embassy that "Madame Nhu's intolerant statement . . . has greatly increased [the] difficulty of [the] U.S. role as [a] supporter of [the] GVN [government of Vietnam]."[20]

That difficulty was about to become greater. On Monday, 10 June, a Buddhist spokesman informed American correspondents that "something important" would happen the following morning on the road outside the Cambodian legation. Most of the reporters disregarded the tip; the Buddhist crisis was in its second month, "old news," and they had no desire to cover another demonstration. But Malcolm Browne, Saigon bureau chief of the Associated Press, decided to check it out. The images captured by his camera would doom the Diem experiment.[21]

"[H]uman beings burn surprisingly quickly," noted David Halberstam in his report on the events of 11 June 1963. That matter-of-fact statement testified to the inadequacy of prose, even that of so gifted a stylist as Halberstam, to convey the scene that unfolded when Thich Quang Duc, a seventy-three-year-old bonze dressed in a saffron robe, sat down in the middle of one of Saigon's major boulevards and performed his final act of devotion. He had arrived shortly before 10:00 A.M. as part of a procession that began at a nearby pagoda. About 350 monks and nuns, preceded by a grey Austin sedan, marched in two phalanxes, carrying banners that denounced the Diem government and demanded that it live up to its promises. As usual, the banners were in Vietnamese and English. When the procession reached the intersection of Phan Dinh Phung Boulevard and Le Van Duyet Street, it stopped. Quang Duc emerged from the car, along with two other monks. One placed a cushion on the pavement. Another opened the trunk of the car and took out a five-gallon gasoline can. As the marchers formed a circle around him, Quang Duc seated himself on the cushion in the traditional lotus position. His comrade poured the contents of the gasoline can over Quang Duc's shaved head, while the old monk fingered a string of holy oak beads and murmured over and over, *"nam mo amita Buddha"*—or "return to eternal Buddha." Then he lit a match.[22]

His body burst into flames, and for ten minutes the inferno consumed him. The air filled with the stench of burning flesh, a sickly sweet smell that nauseated many in the crowd, including Malcolm Browne, who nonetheless retained sufficient presence of mind to keep taking pictures. For a moment, a breeze blew the flames from Quang Duc's face, and onlookers could see his

Buddhist self-immolation, 11 June 1963. Hulton Archive.
By: Keystone. Getty Images.

features contorted in agony, but he never cried out, never moved, as his skin turned black, shriveled, and fell away. Police who tried to reach him could not break through the ring of bonzes. When a fire truck arrived, monks threw themselves in front of its wheels and prevented it from getting close enough to extinguish the blaze. The spectators were mostly stunned into silence, although a few wailed and several offered up prayers. Many of the attendant monks and nuns prostrated themselves before Quang Duc's motionless, fire-blackened figure. As the flames roared, a monk repeated over and over into a microphone, first in Vietnamese and then in English, "A Buddhist priest burns himself to death. A Buddhist priest becomes a martyr."[23]

Finally, after what seemed an eternity, Quang Duc toppled forward onto the pavement, dead, and the fire subsided. A delegation of monks covered the smoking corpse with robes, picked it up, and tried to force it into a coffin, but what remained of Quang Duc's limbs would not bend to fit inside; one of his arms stuck out from the wooden box as the monks carried him to Xa Loi Pagoda. There, they placed his charred heart on display in a glass chalice.

Students unfurled banners outside the pagoda that read, in Vietnamese and English, "A Buddhist priest burns himself for our five requests." That evening, thousands of Saigon residents claimed to see Buddha's face in the sky as the sun descended. Buddha, they said, was weeping.[24]

When Quang Duc consigned his body to the fire on that fateful June day, he reduced America's Diem experiment to ashes as well. Diem would hang on to power for five more months, but his regime had entered its final stages. After Browne's photographs spread across the world wire services and leapt off the front page of newspapers everywhere, no amount of pleading could retrieve Diem's reputation. John F. Kennedy first saw the image of Quang Duc's self-immolation while talking to his brother Robert on the phone. The attorney general was giving his views on the chaos in Alabama when suddenly JFK exclaimed, "Jesus Christ!" The president later remarked that "no news picture in history has generated so much emotion around the world as that one."[25]

Madame Nhu made a ghastly situation worse when, in an interview for CBS television, she sneered, "What have those so-called 'Buddhist leaders' done? . . . All they have done is to barbeque a bonze." Even Americans inclined to give the Diem regime the benefit of the doubt were appalled by this statement, and by Diem's refusal to denounce it. Madame Nhu may have had a right to her own views, critics charged, but she was the president's sister-in-law, she lived in the palace, and she held a seat in the National Assembly. It was natural to assume, in the absence of a presidential disavowal, that she spoke for the government. Americans could not support a regime that expressed itself this way. Marguerite Higgins, Diem's foremost defender in the Saigon press corps, conceded that the "barbeque" statement was "barbaric." "[A]nyone capable of so insensitive and callous a remark," Higgins wrote, "surely qualified as the villainess in a scenario of torture, persecution, and worse."[26]

Washington stepped up its pressure on Diem to mollify the Buddhists. Rusk instructed Trueheart to tell Diem that he "must fully and unequivocally meet Buddhist demands." Trueheart lost no time in delivering the State Department's message. Diem sulkily agreed to comply. His interministerial committee met again with a delegation of Buddhists, and this time the government gave way further. Diem promised clemency for "all those who are involved in the movement"; anyone who had demonstrated against his regime would receive a pardon, and need not fear retribution. Religious activities that had previously required governmental permission could now take place at any time without interference by the authorities. While Diem still refused to admit guilt for the killings of 8 May, he promised to sponsor an "investigation to determine . . . punishment for those government officials responsible"—an acknowledgment that the regime bore some culpability.[27]

This agreement, presented to the press on 16 June, was commonly known as the joint communiqué, and seemed to contain the elements of a settlement. Tinh Khiet, who negotiated the communiqué on behalf of the General Association of Buddhists, sent a letter of thanks to Diem and exhorted Buddhists throughout South Vietnam to work with the government to ensure implementation of the agreement. He expressed his "conviction that the joint communiqué will inaugurate a new era and that . . . no erroneous action from whatever quarter will occur again." He also declared that the movement that had begun on 8 May in Hue was over.[28]

Yet rioting broke out in Saigon the next day, and police put it down brutally, using fire hoses, tear gas, clubs, and gunfire. One demonstrator was killed and dozens injured. Despite Diem's promises of clemency, many Buddhists arrested during the previous month remained in jail. The failure of the joint communiqué to survive twenty-four hours discredited moderate Buddhist leaders and handed control of the movement to more radical monks who were less concerned with reforming Diem's government than overthrowing it. Their demonstrations took on a political tone, with the banners and the slogans now calling for either an entirely new regime or at least the removal of the Nhus. Buddhist rabble-rousers like Tri Quang cultivated Western correspondents even more assiduously. Aware that the media provided a channel to the United States that Diem could not censor, Tri Quang repeatedly told correspondents that no progress in the war was possible "until we get rid of Diem and Nhu."[29]

More significant than these increasingly secular demands was the fact that Quang Duc's self-immolation was not an isolated event. Other Buddhist priests and nuns followed his example, most of them younger than the monk who seized the world's attention on 11 June. Nguyen Hoan, only twenty-one, burned himself to death in the fishing port of Phan Thiet. A seventeen-year-old novice priest in Hue wrapped himself in a Buddhist flag soaked with kerosene, lit a match, and went up in flames. A Buddhist nun, also in her teens, sat down in a Catholic school playground in the village of Ninh Hoa and ignited herself. In most instances the searing images were captured on film and broadcast in the United States.

By this point, everyone in the Kennedy administration, whether they favored replacing Diem or not, had lost faith in the Saigon embassy's capacity to manage affairs. Nolting was still on vacation, unaware of the bedlam in South Vietnam, and Trueheart was pursuing the "get tough" policy urged on him by Washington; he met with Diem on a daily basis and made innumerable telephone calls and visits to lesser officials. Trueheart's hard line, while different from the kid-gloves treatment practiced by Nolting, was no more successful; if anything, it caused Diem to intensify his government's repression of the Buddhists. Kennedy decided that the State Department needed a new representative in Saigon, someone who could make Diem listen to American counsel. He initially intended to appoint Edmund Gullion, recent U.S. ambassador to the Congo, but Rusk persuaded him to offer the post to Henry Cabot Lodge instead.

Lodge was an appealing candidate for several reasons. He spoke French, which would enable him to converse directly with Diem rather than through an interpreter. As a newspaperman during the 1930s, he had visited Vietnam; hence, the country would not be entirely unfamiliar to him. He was a three-time United States senator and former ambassador to the United Nations, which would make him the most distinguished envoy Washington had sent to South Vietnam since J. Lawton Collins. Most important, Lodge was a Republican; indeed, he had lost his Massachusetts Senate seat to the Democrat Kennedy in 1952 and had been Richard Nixon's running mate in the 1960 election that JFK had won by a narrow margin. Appointing Lodge to succeed Nolting was a way for Kennedy to maintain bipartisan support for his Vietnam policy and ensure that, in the event of a VC triumph, there would be no Republican backlash against his administration. Lodge had an additional qualification for this assignment, one of which Kennedy was unaware: his uncle was a Buddhist.

Although the risk of becoming Kennedy's scapegoat for a failed policy did not appeal to Lodge, he agreed to serve. No one in the State Department informed Nolting that he was being replaced; the ambassador first heard the news while listening to a radio broadcast aboard ship in the mid-Atlantic. He irately quipped that he had been "disLodged." His distress was nothing compared to Diem's. The South Vietnamese president perceived that this change in ambassadors signaled a less tolerant approach by Washington toward his government, and he responded, characteristically, with defiance, telling an aide: "They can send ten Lodges, but I will not permit myself or my country to be humiliated."[30]

Since Lodge would need some time to prepare, Nolting was permitted to return to Saigon and make one last attempt to persuade Diem to settle the Buddhist crisis. It was a hopeless task, but the lame-duck ambassador did his best. His final month in South Vietnam featured near-constant meetings with Diem, who railed against the Buddhists, the foreign press, and the VC in equal measure while Nolting tried to explain that the American tradition of religious toleration made it impossible for Washington to condone what the regime was doing. Even if Diem had good cause for placing barbed wire around pagodas and having police beat and arrest unarmed monks and nuns, these actions were destroying his image in the United States.

Diem paid no heed. He assumed an increasingly confrontational stance toward the Buddhists throughout the summer of 1963. In early July he announced that the investigation into the Hue massacre had confirmed what he had been saying all along: the VC were responsible and the regime blameless. No one believed these claims, and they spurred further Buddhist demonstrations on the streets and agitation in the pagodas. During a demonstration at Cholon's Giac Minh Pagoda, government police kicked, punched, and clubbed hundreds of bonzes and laypeople and carted them off to jail in American trucks decorated with the "clasped hands" symbol of U.S. aid. Nolting persuaded Diem to make an appeal for calm over nationwide radio, but if the ambassador nourished any hopes that this gesture would lead to a breakthrough in the crisis, they were dashed when he heard Diem's address—a lecture that lasted less than two minutes, offered only a minor compromise on the question of flying religious flags, and announced the formation of another cosmetic commission to investigate Buddhist grievances.

Apart from this speech, Nolting had little to show for his final days in Saigon. Three more Buddhists burned themselves to death in late July and early August. Madame Nhu's public statements became more indefensible. She told a correspondent for *Life* magazine that the Buddhists were "cryptocommunists" and promised, "Once this affair is finished, . . . Buddhism will die in this country." The torch suicide of a Buddhist nun drew a shrug and a sneer: "[I]f they burn thirty women, we shall go ahead and clap our hands." Nolting left South Vietnam on 15 August, reputation in tatters, destined never again to work for the U.S. Foreign Service.[31]

Less than a week after Nolting flew out of Tan Son Nhut Airport, government forces armed with rifles, submachine guns, grenades, and tear gas canisters launched a midnight raid on pagodas throughout South Vietnam. In Saigon, squads of soldiers smashed down Xa Loi Pagoda's gates and stormed through the temple, arresting hundreds of monks and nuns. Those who resisted were stomped with boot heels and battered with rifle butts and bayonets. The gong in the pagoda's tower clanged an alarm, but it was soon drowned out by the bursts of automatic-weapons fire, the screams of people being dragged from their rooms, the crump of exploding grenades, and the crash of shattering glass. The violence in Hue was worse, as monks and nuns barricaded themselves inside Dieu De Pagoda and fought off troops and police for eight hours before the government brought in armored cars; by the time the pagoda was overrun, thirty people were dead, two hundred wounded, and ten truckloads carted off to prison. Monks and nuns put up similar resistance at Hue's Tu Dam Pagoda, with similar consequences: many Buddhists were shot or clubbed to death, a statue of Buddha was toppled, and government forces set off an explosion that leveled the building. In all, some two thousand pagodas were raided and more than fourteen hundred monks, nuns, student activists, and ordinary citizens arrested. The number killed was never confirmed, but some sources placed it as high as several hundred.

At daybreak, Diem spoke over Saigon Radio, declaring that negotiations had failed and that, for the good of the nation, he was placing South Vietnam under martial law. Until further notice, there would be a 9:00 P.M. to 5:00 A.M. curfew—troops and police had orders to shoot anyone on the streets between those hours—and public gatherings were prohibited. The army had taken over all civilian functions. Full military censorship was in effect for outgoing press cables. The country was, in short, an armed camp. There seems little doubt that Diem deliberately took these measures at a time when the U.S. embassy was leaderless. He intended to present the incoming ambassador, Lodge, with a fait accompli, a crisis that had been resolved not through compromise but force. He knew this was not the outcome Washington wanted, that Lodge would complain, that press reaction would be negative, and that the Kennedy administration might go so far as to condemn what Diem had done. But the Americans would eventually recognize that there was no alternative to the present government in Saigon. They would continue to sponsor their Diem experiment. They always did.

This time, however, Diem misjudged the degree to which he had exhausted Washington's patience. After the assault on the pagodas, Kennedy and his advisers began to talk about engineering a coup. The State Department issued a press release declaring that Diem's action represented "a direct violation" of his promise to pursue "a policy of reconciliation" and that the administration "deplore[d] repressive actions of this nature." This was as strong as diplomatic language got. Diem also underestimated the impact of the raids on public opinion in his own country. Many urban South Vietnamese, previously apolitical, defied the government's ban by holding anti-Diem rallies. Students at Saigon University boycotted classes and rioted in protest against the regime. Diem had the students arrested, the ringleaders beaten, and the university shut down. He also closed South Vietnam's other university at Hue. Then the high school students demonstrated, and Diem was compelled to arrest them; one morning, army trucks hauled more than one thousand students from the nation's finest high school to indoctrination centers. Eventually, Diem closed the high schools, too. His own foreign minister, Vu Van Mau, resigned his post, shaved his head like a Buddhist monk, and asked Diem for permission to leave the country on a religious pilgrimage. Diem threw him in jail. South Vietnam's ambassador to the United States, Tran Van Chuong, also resigned in protest, telling American reporters that Diem had "cop[ied] the tactics of totalitarian regimes." Chuong, reporters could not help but note, was Madame Nhu's father. Americans in Saigon began joking that the policy of "Sink or swim with Ngo Dinh Diem" had given way to "You cannot win with Ngo Dinh Diem."[32]

Notes

1. National Security Files, Countries—Vietnam: Report on General Taylor's Mission to South Vietnam, 3 November 1961: Box 203, JFKL.

2. Krulak, Mendenhall, and Kennedy cited in Richard Reeves, *President Kennedy: Profile of Power* (New York: Simon & Schuster, 1993), 595; President's Office File, Countries—Vietnam: Mendenhall to Hilsman, 9 September 1963: Box 128A, JFKL.

3. National Security Files, Countries—Vietnam: Kennedy to Mansfield, 16 October 1962: Box 197, JFKL.

4. Pell and Trueheart cited in Howard Jones, *Death of a Generation: How the Assassinations of Diem and JFK Prolonged the Vietnam War* (New York: Oxford University Press, 2003), 214–215.

5. Prepared statement cited in Don Oberdorfer, *Senator Mansfield* (Washington D.C.: Smithsonian Books, 2003), 191; Mansfield cited in Gregory Olson, *Mansfield and Vietnam* (East Lansing: Michigan State University Press, 1995), 109; Nolting cited in Jones, *Death of a Generation*, 216.

6. Report by the Senate Majority Leader, 18 December 1962, *FRUS, 1961–1963* (Washington, D.C.: Government Printing Office, 1991), 2:779–787.

7. Kennedy cited in Reeves, *President Kennedy*, 442; Kennedy and Mansfield cited in David Halberstam, *The Best and the Brightest* (New York: Random House, 1969), 208; Kenneth P. O'Donnell and David F. Powers, *"Johnny, We Hardly Knew Ye": Memories of John Fitzgerald Kennedy* (Boston: Little, Brown, 1970), 15.

8. National Security Files, Countries—Vietnam: "Vietnam and Southeast Asia: Report of Senator Mike Mansfield, Senator J. Caleb Boggs, Senator Claiborne Pell, and Senator Benjamin A. Smith to the Committee on Foreign Relations, United States Senate," 25 February 1963: Box 197, JFKL.

9. Frederick Nolting, *From Trust to Tragedy: The Political Memoirs of Frederick Nolting, Kennedy's Ambassador to Diem's Vietnam* (New York: Praeger, 1988), 98.

10. Ba cited in A. J. Langguth, *Our Vietnam: The War, 1954–1975* (New York: Simon & Schuster, 2000), 201.

11. Vann cited in Robert Mann, *A Grand Delusion* (New York: Basic, 2002), 278; Harkins cited in Roger Hilsman, *To Move a Nation: The Politics of Foreign Policy in the Administration of John F. Kennedy* (Garden City, N.Y.: Doubleday, 1967), 449.

12. Party guests cited in William Prochnau, *Once upon a Distant War: David Halberstam, Neil Sheehan, Peter Arnett—Young War Correspondents and Their Early Vietnam Battles* (New York: Vintage, 1995), 239; Memorandum from Michael V. Forrestal of the National Security Council Staff to the President, 25 January 1963, *FRUS, 1961–1963*, 3:49–62; Don, Khiem, and Nolting cited in Jones, *Death of a Generation*, 424.

13. Diem cited in the Embassy in Vietnam to the Department of State, 18 May 1963, *FRUS, 1961–1963*, 3:309–310; Prochnau, *Once upon a Distant War*, 305.

14. Can and Diem cited in Ellen J. Hammer, *A Death in November: America in Vietnam, 1963* (New York: Dutton, 1987), 119.

15. Kennedy cited in Reeves, *President Kennedy*, 490.

16. National Security File, Countries—Vietnam: Rusk to Trueheart, 3 June 1963: Box 197A, JFKL.

17. Diem cited in Terence Maitland and others, *The Vietnam Experience*, vol. 3, *Raising the Stakes* (Boston: Boston Publishing, 1984), 76.

18. Diem cited in National Security File, Countries—Vietnam: Trueheart to Rusk, 5 June 1963: Box 197A, JFKL.

19. The Embassy in Vietnam to the Department of State, 5 June 1963, *FRUS, 1961–1963*, 3:358; Madame Nhu cited in National Security File, Countries—Vietnam: Trueheart to Rusk, 8 June 1963: Box 197A, JFKL.

20. The Embassy in Vietnam to the Department of State, 8 June 1963, *FRUS, 1961–1963*, 3:362; National Security File, Countries—Vietnam: Rusk to Trueheart, 8 June 1963: Box 197A, JFKL.

21. Monk cited in Hilsman, *To Move a Nation*, 473.

22. David Halberstam, *The Making of a Quagmire* (New York: Random House, 1965), 211.

23. Monk cited in Maitland and others, *Raising the Stakes*, 75.

24. Banners cited in the Embassy in Vietnam to the Department of State, 11 June 1963, *FRUS, 1961–1963*, 3:375.

25. Kennedy cited in Reeves, *President Kennedy*, 517; Vietnam Memoir, Henry Cabot Lodge Papers, Massachusetts Historical Society, Boston, Massachusetts.

26. Madame Nhu cited in National Security Files, Countries—Vietnam: Trueheart to Rusk, 8 August 1963: Box 198, JFKL; Marguerite Higgins, *Our Vietnam Nightmare* (New York: Harper & Row, 1965), 59–60.

27. The Department of State to the Embassy in Vietnam, 11 June 1963, *FRUS, 1961–1963*, 3:381; communiqué cited in Editorial Note, *FRUS, 1961–1963*, 3:397–398.

28. Tinh Khiet cited in Maitland and others, *Raising the Stakes*, 77.

29. Tri Quang cited in Anthony Bouscaren, *The Last of the Mandarins: Diem of Vietnam* (Pittsburgh: Duquesne University Press, 1965), 102.

30. Nolting cited in Richard F. Newcomb, *A Pictorial History of the Vietnam War* (Garden City, N.Y.: Doubleday, 1987), 73; Diem cited in Francis X. Winters, *The Year of the Hare: America in Vietnam, January 25, 1963–February 15, 1964* (Athens: University of Georgia Press, 1997), 37.

31. Madame Nhu cited in Clyde Edwin Petit, *The Experts* (Secaucus, N.J.: Lyle Stuart, 1975), 141; Prochnau, *Once upon a Distant War*, 355.

32. Press release cited in National Security Files, Countries—Vietnam: Ball to Trueheart, 21 August 1963: Box 198A, JFKL; Chuong cited in Maitland, *Raising the Stakes*, 81; Americans cited in Newcomb, *Pictorial History of the Vietnam War*, 73.

CHAPTER SEVEN

~

"No Respectable Turning Back"
Collapse of the Diem Experiment

Shortly before Frederick Nolting yielded his post at the Saigon embassy to Henry Cabot Lodge, South Vietnamese president Ngo Dinh Diem asked the outgoing U.S. ambassador, "Does your departure mean that the American government has changed its policy?" Nolting replied, "No, Mr. President, it does not." This was disingenuous: everyone in Saigon knew that Lodge's appointment marked a watershed in U.S.–South Vietnamese relations. The fact that there was a two-week interval between Nolting's departure and Lodge's arrival spoke volumes about the Kennedy administration's toughening stance toward Diem; it was a signal to enemies of the Diem regime that Washington might welcome a coup, and it put Diem on notice that he could not make Lodge his dupe as he had Nolting. Madame Ngo Dinh Nhu recognized the gap between ambassadors for the diplomatic slight it was, exclaiming: "They are sending us a proconsul!"[1]

Lodge confirmed Madame Nhu's misgivings after he arrived in Saigon on 22 August 1963. When Diem welcomed the new ambassador at Gia Long Palace, the American did not give his host the opportunity to plunge into one of his legendary monologues. Instead, Lodge delivered his own speech. "I want you to be successful. I want to be useful to you," Lodge declared. "I don't expect you to be a 'yes man.' I realize that you must never appear . . . a puppet of the United States." Nonetheless, he insisted that Diem had to face the fact that American public opinion had turned against him. The United States, Lodge asserted, "favors religious toleration," and Diem's policies were "threatening American support of Viet-Nam." Diem had to set his house in order, and that meant dismissing his brother Ngo Dinh Nhu, silencing Madame Nhu, punishing the officials responsible for the 8 May massacre in Hue, and conciliating the Buddhists. Washington was no longer prepared to support the Diem regime unconditionally. It had to reform itself, or the $1.5 million in aid spent in South Vietnam every day would be cut.[2]

After this most undiplomatic first encounter, America's top diplomat in Saigon made no effort to negotiate with Diem. In fact, he seemed determined to avoid further contact with the president or any member of his government. When a reporter asked Lodge why he had not visited the palace in weeks, he responded, "They have not done anything I asked. They know what I want. Why should I keep asking?" Lodge could be just as stubborn as Diem, and he had the might of the world's greatest superpower backing him up. Moreover, as a prestigious public servant from the opposition party who had accepted the ambassadorship as a favor to Kennedy, Lodge retained the option of resigning his post. Should he exercise that option and dump Vietnam into the Democrats' laps, it would hardly hurt his standing among Republicans. On the other hand, as Diem recognized, the Saigon government was so unpopular in America that if it were overthrown, the coup would redound to Lodge's political benefit. Lodge, in other words, held all the advantages in this high-stakes game of chicken, and he knew it. By early September, bureaucrats in the U.S. Embassy began taunting South Vietnamese officials: "Our old mandarin can whip your old mandarin."[3]

Lodge would insist in the years following Diem's murder that he had not been sent to South Vietnam with orders to remove its chief executive. Kennedy merely wanted Diem to reform his treatment of the Buddhist majority, democratize the country, and prosecute the war against the Viet Cong more effectively. This had been Washington's agenda before Lodge replaced Nolting and, therefore, the change in ambassadors did not represent a new direction in U.S. policy. Still, there is no doubt that Lodge came to Saigon prepared to countenance Diem's deposal and, if necessary, to use American funds to expedite it.

The new ambassador therefore responded differently to overtures from Diem's enemies than his predecessor had. Whereas Nolting refused even to discuss the possibility of a coup with dissident generals, Lodge seized on every hint of rebelliousness in the Army of the Republic of Vietnam (ARVN) and sought to exploit it. Lodge determined that the ARVN presented the only alternative to Diem; South Vietnam's civil bureaucracy, he felt, had been so purged of strong personalities that any nonmilitary solution to the crisis was

Diem meets American Ambassador Henry Cabot Lodge for the first time, 1 September 1963.

Time & Life Pictures. By: Larry Burrows. Getty Images.

unrealistic. Lodge told his subordinates—notably Lucien Conein, a former CIA agent—to make contact with high-ranking South Vietnamese officers and let them know that the United States would not look unfavorably on a change in government. The ambassador wanted to find out which ARVN generals seemed capable of unseating Diem, how much support they would require, and how soon they would be prepared to move. Conein proved suited to the task of digging up this information because he was friendly with most of the generals, having fought alongside them against the Japanese in World War II.

Less than twenty-four hours after his arrival at Tan Son Nhut, Lodge received the first report from Conein about prospective insurrectionists. Conein submitted a memorandum detailing his conversation with General Tran Van Don, whom Diem had just placed in charge of the ARVN. Don revealed that Nhu had been responsible for the recent pagoda raids, and that while many South Vietnamese still respected Diem, it was essential to get rid of Nhu to prevent a communist takeover of the country. Unfortunately, Don noted, separating Diem from Nhu would be "impossible"; Diem would not permit it. If Washington wanted to eliminate Nhu, it would have to eliminate Diem as well. That same day, a report landed on Lodge's desk from Rufus Phillips, chief American adviser on the strategic hamlet program. Phillips had just conferred with Brigadier General Le Van Kim, considered by many Americans the most intelligent military man in South Vietnam, and their discussion mirrored that between Don and Conein. Kim expressed hatred for Nhu, who he claimed had turned the ARVN into his "puppet." The general confided that all of the "explosives and arms found in the pagodas" after the raids of 21 August—which the Diem regime had used to justify martial law—had been "planted" by Nhu's secret police. The Buddhists posed no threat to the government; the real problem, Kim proclaimed, was Nhu, and if the United States supported action to remove Nhu from power, the ARVN "would be able to carry it out." All that was required was a signal from Washington. Nguyen Dinh Thuan, South Vietnam's secretary of state, likewise spoke to Phillips that day, arguing that the ARVN "would turn firmly against Nhu" if it could count on the Kennedy administration's support.[4]

Lodge passed these reports along to Washington, as well as other dispatches suggesting that the Diem experiment was on the ropes. Taken together, these documents seemed to make the case for a U.S.-supported coup, but Lodge backed away from that precipice in a cable assessing his first day on the job. No coup leader had yet emerged and several military commanders were still presumed loyal to the regime. Lodge also did not have enough information to gauge the balance of power; Diem might have an edge over his rivals. Therefore, Lodge concluded, "[a]ction on our part in these circumstances would be a shot in the dark." He recommended deferring any decision on a coup, while keeping the lines of communication to the generals open and "continuing to watch [the] situation closely."[5]

That disclaimer was not enough to counteract the alarmist tone of recent messages from Saigon, especially when those messages were augmented by accounts of the Buddhist crisis in America's leading newspapers. One day after Don and Kim spilled their guts to American listeners, a front-page story in the *New York Times* proclaimed that Nhu had "taken power" in South Vietnam and depicted Madame Nhu as "exuberant" over the pagoda raids. The headline in the *Washington Post* read "POWER SHIFT TO NHU SEEN IN VIET-NAM"; an accompanying article described Diem's brother as "the real ruler of the country." The *Times* and the *Post* ran these pieces the same morning that cables summarizing Don's and Kim's anti-Nhu tirades arrived at the State Department, accompanied by other telegrams setting forth the groundswell of military and civilian support for Nhu's expulsion. It was Saturday, 24 August, and most of the top officials in the Kennedy administration were out of town or otherwise indisposed.[6]

As fate would have it, the response Lodge received from Washington was drafted by Roger Hilsman, assistant secretary of state for Far Eastern affairs, with the collaboration of roving Ambassador Averell Harriman and Michael Forrestal of the National Security Council. These were perhaps the staunchest opponents of the Diem experiment in the administration, and they took advantage of their superiors' absence to compose what one historian calls "the single most controversial cable of the Vietnam War." The "U.S. government cannot tolerate [a] situation in which power lies in Nhu's hands," the cable read. "Diem must be given [a] chance to rid himself of Nhu. . . . If, in spite of all your efforts, Diem remains obdurate and refuses, then we must face [the] possibility that Diem himself cannot be preserved." Lodge was instructed to tell "key military leaders" that the "U.S. would find it impossible to continue to support [the] GVN [government of Vietnam]" unless the Buddhist grievances were redressed and Nhu divested of power. The cable also ordered Lodge to "examine all possible alternative leadership and make detailed plans as to how we might bring about Diem's replacement if this should become necessary."[7]

The words "coup" or "overthrow" never appeared in this directive, but it was equivalent to ordering Diem's ouster, as its drafters realized. Hilsman,

Forrestal, and Harriman must have known that one of Lodge's predecessors, Elbridge Durbrow, had also demanded that Diem drop Nhu, with no success, and that Diem was even less likely to comply with this dictate now that the Buddhist crisis had driven everyone except his family into the enemy camp. The 24 August cable was, in effect, a command to terminate the Diem experiment, written, ironically, at a time when the four most important members of the administration were out of the policymaking loop: President Kennedy was spending the weekend at his Cape Cod estate; Secretary of State Dean Rusk was in New York attending a special session of the United Nations; and Secretary of Defense Robert McNamara and CIA Director John McCone were on vacation. Maxwell Taylor, Chairman of the Joint Chiefs of Staff, later called the cable an "egregious end run" by an anti-Diem faction in the government.[8]

Taylor overstated matters: both Kennedy and Rusk cleared the cable, although hastily and over the phone, and Undersecretary of State George Ball studied it carefully before giving his approval. While there is no question that this message ought to have been handled more conscientiously, the fact is that it was never rescinded. Indeed, Kennedy polled his advisers when they convened on Monday, 26 August, asking each man in turn if he stood by the cable or wanted to change it. No one voted to back off. Whatever second thoughts Kennedy and others may have had, Washington stuck with the policy established on 24 August until Diem's assassination made it obsolete.

Years later, Lodge would claim that he had been "thunderstruck" by the 24 August cable and felt the administration was moving too fast. The directive did, in fact, run counter to Lodge's advice to adopt an approach of watchful waiting. Still, the ambassador not only endorsed the shift in policy; he encouraged Washington to go further. Since "the chances of Diem's meeting our demands are virtually nil," he observed, there was no point in presenting the president with another ultimatum. That strategy had never worked; it only made Diem more stubborn. Lodge proposed that he say nothing to Diem about U.S. demands but go directly to the generals and tell them that "we [are] prepared [to] have Diem without [the] Nhus, but it is in effect up to them whether to keep him." In other words, if the generals decided that neither Diem nor Nhu could remain in power, Washington would support the removal of both men, and American aid would continue to flow to South Vietnam. The State Department replied at once: "Agree to modification proposed."[9]

Lodge did not have to worry about the State Department sanctioning a coup. The Pentagon, however, was less enthusiastic, although McNamara had agreed to sign off on the 24 August cable. Paul Harkins, commander of the Military Assistance Command in Vietnam (MACV), contended that there was no guarantee that a new government would do better than Diem and that, moreover, the coup plotters might not have a sufficient military advantage to force Diem from office. Harkins also believed it was possible to get rid of Nhu without overthrowing Diem. At least, Harkins argued, Washington should give Diem a chance to remove his brother. Lodge disagreed, insisting, "We are launched on a course from which there is no respectable turning back: The overthrow of the Diem government." There must be no "sign of American indecision," the ambassador advised, because the generals were already unsure about U.S. intentions and might get cold feet if they sensed that Washington was thinking about pulling back its go-ahead.[10]

Kennedy agreed to set the machinery for a coup in motion, but he wanted to leave himself the option of "chang[ing] course" if necessary. With the fiasco at Cuba's Bay of Pigs fresh in his memory, JFK observed, "I know from experience that failure is more destructive than an appearance of indecision." Lodge found this proviso unrealistic. "To be successful," the ambassador replied, "this operation must be an essentially Vietnamese affair with a momentum of its own. Should this happen, you might not be able to control it, i.e., the 'go signal' may be given by the generals."[11]

The generals, however, were reluctant to give that "go signal," and Lodge soon recognized that his primary task would be to light a fire under the anti-Diem forces rather than rein them in. By the end of Lodge's first week in South Vietnam, none of the generals had taken charge of the coup planning process and none seemed eager to lead an ARVN revolt. "The days come and go and nothing happens," Lodge complained to Rusk. "I am sure that the best way to handle this matter is by a truly Vietnamese movement, even if it puts me rather in the position of pushing a piece of spaghetti." All participants in this still inchoate conspiracy had reasons to resist the ambassador's pushing. First, they had yet to receive the kind of cue from Washington that would convince them that the Americans were behind a coup and would see it through to completion. Lodge had suggested to Kennedy that a cutoff in aid to Diem would furnish such a high sign, but JFK had thus far demurred. Also, the coup planners had been unable to recruit Brigadier General Ton That Dinh to their side. For a coup to succeed, Dinh had to be on board. When Diem had declared martial law, he made Dinh military governor of Saigon, and the general could call on twenty-five hundred paratroopers, fifteen hundred marines, and seven hundred military police; those forces might be sufficient to put down a rebellion. In addition, the dissident generals were anxious about John Richardson, CIA station chief in South Vietnam, who had worked with Nhu in developing the regime's intelligence capacity. What if Richardson tipped off Nhu about an impending coup? Finally, there was the lack of cohesion in the generals' own ranks. No one trusted any of the others not to divulge their plans to the government, and all knew the consequences of such a betrayal.[12]

Of all ARVN commanders, the one who appeared most capable of rallying the rest was General Duong Van Minh, who was well-liked by the troops and had a reputation as a man of action. His upper front teeth had been snapped off at the roots by Japanese interrogators during World War II, and he refused to have the teeth replaced; the gap in his smile was, for him, a testament to his physical toughness. He had proven himself in combat, notably in the 1955 Battle for Saigon, when he helped Diem crush the Binh Xuyen. Most important, for Lodge's purposes, was the fact that Minh had a grudge against Diem, who had relieved him of authority and "promoted" him to a meaningless post as military adviser. Minh suspected that Diem had considered him a rival and sought to sidetrack his career. The general required little prodding from Conein to reveal his interest in a coup.

Yet Minh was no more inclined than the other generals to become a martyr, and he informed Lodge on 31 August that he had "called off the planning." The generals, he said, "were not ready." Neither he nor his coconspirators wanted to "start anything" they could not finish. Lodge, disgusted, told Rusk that Washington had no choice but to stick with Diem a bit longer while attempting to reactivate the coup plotters. Unfortunately, he noted, his cover had probably been blown: "I believe the government suspects us of trying to engineer a coup."[13]

Lodge was correct. Nhu's cadres in the Can Lao Party had many Americans under surveillance and almost certainly found out about embassy contacts with the rebel generals by the end of August. As had been the case in 1955 during the Collins mission, Diem was determined to outmaneuver any American who sought to topple his regime. On this occasion, he went so far as to entertain the possibility of reducing his dependence on Washington by making a deal with Hanoi that would neutralize both North and South Vietnam and lead to a reconciliation between the two countries. Diem authorized Nhu to conduct back-channel negotiations with the communists, and Nhu dropped hints to European ambassadors that he was on the verge of concluding a separate peace. By mid-September, the north-south rapprochement was an open secret in Saigon.

Numerous statesmen were willing to help Diem extend peace feelers to the north, including French president Charles de Gaulle, who announced that no military solution to the Vietnam conflict was possible. There had to be a political settlement, de Gaulle declared, and France would support any treaty that resulted in Vietnam's "internal peace." De Gaulle proposed to convene a conference in Paris that would unify and neutralize France's former colony. The Kennedy administration was appalled by this proposal, but Diem, despite his anticommunist convictions, did not reject it.[14]

After de Gaulle's announcement, a bid to heal the breach between the two Vietnams was spearheaded by Roger Lalouette, France's ambassador to South Vietnam, and Ramchundur Goburdhun, the Indian chair of the International Control Committee (ICC), which had been established in 1954 to ensure compliance with the Geneva Accords. Lalouette and Goburdhun used the Polish delegate of the ICC, Mieczyslaw Maneli, as a go-between to facilitate dialogue between Hanoi and Saigon. Conditions were ideal, they felt, to broker an agreement. If Diem was finding his great-power ally overbearing, the same held true for Ho Chi Minh, who, in the words of a British diplomat stationed in Hanoi, was walking a "tightrope" between the Soviet Union and the People's Republic of China. The two communist behemoths, openly feuding, pressured Ho to take sides in their rivalry and threatened to use North Vietnam as the battlefield in a USSR-PRC war. A trade-off seemed feasible: American withdrawal south of the 17th parallel, Chinese and Soviet withdrawal north of it, and Vietnamese withdrawal from the Cold War. Prospects for such an arrangement were enhanced by the fact that North Vietnam was experiencing its worst drought in a decade. Ho had been compelled to turn to Moscow and Beijing for food, which only increased his reliance on them and left Hanoi more at the mercy of their tug-of-war. The Mekong Delta in the south—Vietnam's "rice bowl"—looked inviting to Ho and made him more inclined to want to make Vietnam one nation again.[15]

The results of Maneli's shuttle diplomacy were impressive: by the time the ARVN generals informed Lodge that their coup would have to wait, the Politburo in Hanoi had already consented, in principle, to a unified Vietnam with a federated, as opposed to a coalition, government; this would have allowed Diem to remain in command in the south. "We can come to any agreement with any Vietnamese," Prime Minister Pham Van Dong told Maneli. There was only one nonnegotiable point: "The Americans have to leave." Ho told Goburdhun that he bore no ill will against Diem, who was, he asserted, "a patriot in his way." "Shake hands with him for me if you see him," Ho said.[16]

Some historians have pointed to these statements as evidence that the

United States threw away an opportunity in 1963 to extricate itself from Vietnam with minimal loss of blood and treasure. Had Washington encouraged Saigon to accept the terms proposed by Hanoi, this argument runs, neither the communist nor noncommunist superpowers could have claimed victory, since Vietnam would have become a neutral country like India and not a "domino" that had fallen left or right. Even if a unified Vietnam eventually succumbed to communism, a peace agreement would have furnished Kennedy with a face-saving means of pulling American forces out of Southeast Asia and given the United States what Henry Kissinger would later call "a decent interval" between U.S. departure and communist takeover. In light of what happened after 1963, that alternative scenario looks appealing.

On the other hand, there are scholars whose views reflect those of U.S. policymakers at the time, including Lodge. They insist that Nhu's overtures to Hanoi were calculated to gain leverage for Diem over his American sponsors. How could Diem or Nhu have believed they had any future in a "federation" that was certain to be dominated by the more-populous north and the more-popular Ho? Diem would have been lucky to survive six months in power following a deal with Hanoi, and to secure those six months he would have had to abandon principles he had risked death to uphold for decades. Is it not more plausible to conclude that the Nhu-Maneli exchanges were a means of blackmailing the United States into reaffirming its support for the Diem experiment? Whatever the sincerity of Nhu's contacts with the communists, they did nothing to repair the rift between Washington and Saigon. Rather, they gave American officials another reason for wanting Diem out of the picture and lent urgency to Lodge's campaign to spark a coup.

On 2 September, Kennedy gave the dissident ARVN generals the signal they required when he sat for an interview with Walter Cronkite, news anchor for CBS, at the Kennedy estate in Hyannis Port. Kennedy's appearance was the highlight of CBS's first half-hour evening news program, and the president knew the interview would attract a large viewing audience. He chose his words with care. When Cronkite asked about the war in Vietnam, JFK responded, "I don't think that unless a greater effort is made by the government to win popular support that the war can be won." Cronkite posed the obvious question: "Do you think this government has time to regain the support of the people?" Kennedy's response must have drawn howls of outrage from Gia Long Palace. "I do," he said. "With changes in policy and perhaps with personnel, I think it can win. If it doesn't make those changes, I would

think that the chances of winning would not be very good." Those three words—"changes . . . with personnel"—constituted, one historian notes, "the public equivalent of the August 24 telegram." Tran Van Don, when asked years later how he had interpreted JFK's statement, replied that it seemed as though Kennedy "would support any change." At least the Cronkite interview let Diem know that Washington would tolerate no more procrastination on the question of his brother. Either Diem must rid himself of Nhu, or the Americans would rid themselves of Diem.[17]

Kennedy underscored the seriousness of this warning in late September when he sent Defense Secretary Robert McNamara and JCS Chairman Maxwell Taylor on an inspection tour of South Vietnam. Like most such missions, this resulted in its participants drawing conclusions that could have been reached without leaving Washington. McNamara and Taylor were hawks, and they praised the accomplishments of the ARVN and the MACV. On the other hand, both men had begun to have doubts about Diem, and these were reflected in their report. "The Diem-Nhu government is becoming increasingly unpopular," McNamara and Taylor observed, noting that "[f]urther repressive actions by Diem and Nhu could change the present favorable military trends." They advised taking limited sanctions "to impress upon Diem our disapproval of his political program." Specifically, they wanted to suspend funding for the Commercial Import Program (CIP), an economic aid project that, as discussed in chapter 4, provided South Vietnam with many of its commercial imports and most of the revenue for its army, and they proposed an elimination of financial support to Diem's Special Forces, six battalions of elite soldiers that operated as the president's "praetorian guard." As for a coup, Taylor and McNamara shared Kennedy's conviction that failure would be worse than indecisiveness. They were not so much opposed to helping the ARVN generals overthrow Diem as worried that the generals might not prevail. Consequently, the Taylor-McNamara report ended with the recommendation that Washington should not "encourage actively a change in government."[18]

Kennedy decided to take a wait-and-see approach. He cabled Lodge on 2 October: "No initiative should now be taken to give any covert encouragement to a coup." Yet three days later, Lodge contacted the president with stunning news. Conein had met with Minh and learned that a coup was in the offing; in fact, it was going to occur "within the very near future." Minh told Conein that he did not expect "any specific American support for an effort . . . to change the government"; all he wanted was "American assurances" that Washington would "not attempt to thwart this plan" and that there would be "a continuation of American military and economic aid" after Diem was overthrown.[19]

Wittingly or not, Minh had handed the Kennedy administration a rationale that would allow policymakers like Lodge, Hilsman, and the president himself to disclaim any responsibility for the fate of Diem and Nhu when the generals struck. Washington had not promoted a coup, they would argue; it had declined to obstruct one. There was a difference. The coup was a "Vietnamese effort," Kennedy declared less than a week after Diem's assassination. It had been "purely a Vietnamese affair," Lodge insisted eight months later. "We never participated in the planning. We never gave any advice. We had nothing whatever to do with it." Whether the speakers themselves believed these assertions is debatable; a slew of historians have rejected them. The Kennedy administration hardly pursued a hands-off course in South Vietnam during the summer and fall of 1963. From the day he arrived in Saigon, Kennedy's ambassador had approached potential insurgents, urged them on in their antiregime efforts, and concealed his own role in the conspiracy from Diem, who, it bears emphasizing, was chief of state in a nation allied with the United States.[20]

Such details did not trouble Lodge. The instant Conein presented him with Minh's "not attempt to thwart" formula, the ambassador was inclined to accept it, and his resolve only deepened when, later that same day, a bonze burned himself to death in Saigon's central marketplace. It was the first self-immolation since the pagoda raids a month earlier, and it gave the lie to Diem's assertions that the Buddhist crisis was under control. This torch suicide, the eighth overall, was especially distressing for the Kennedy administration because it was the first such spectacle to be photographed in color, which made viewing it in the pages of American magazines even more horrific.

The situation was intolerable, Lodge cabled Washington, and could not be allowed to continue. Lodge recommended that Minh be told that "the U.S. will not attempt to thwart his plans." Furthermore, Conein should "[a]ssure Minh that U.S. aid will be continued to Vietnam" after Diem was unseated. Kennedy agreed, but cautioned Lodge that no Americans should appear to be involved in the rebellion. "While we do not wish to stimulate [a] coup," the president declared, "we also do not wish to leave [the] impression that [the] United States would thwart a change of government or deny economic or military assistance to a new regime." The language was self-deluding—how could Washington remove all obstacles to a coup and at the same time not "stimulate" one?—but the green light had been flashed. Con-

ein met with Minh and conveyed Kennedy's position. Thus began, one journalist noted, "the last episode of this insane period."[21]

Given the number of legendary figures associated with the Diem experiment—Dwight Eisenhower, John Foster Dulles, J. Lawton Collins, John F.
Kennedy, and Diem himself—it is ironic that the conclusion to that experiment came to depend so heavily on a buffoon like General Ton That Dinh.
Dinh was one of Diem's favorite officers, one of the few whom the president
trusted. This may have been because Dinh owed Diem everything. When
Diem came to power in 1954, Dinh had converted to Catholicism in hopes
of advancing his career. He had been amply rewarded, rocketing past more
capable men in the ranks of the ARVN as the regime promoted him again
and again. By the time of the August pagoda raids, Dinh was the youngest
general in the army. Americans stationed in Saigon knew Dinh as a man-
about-town; he was seen at the city's finest clubs, often drunk, always in a
skintight tiger suit. For Diem, the general's libertinism was outweighed by his
loyalty. Diem's decision to make Dinh military governor of Saigon ensured
that the troops under Dinh's command would be the regime's first line of
defense in the event of a rebellion.

The ARVN generals plotting to overthrow Diem knew they needed
Dinh's help if their coup was to succeed. Washington policymakers likewise
recognized this fact. As Hilsman informed Kennedy, Dinh was "the key to
the situation. We must find out if he can be corrupted, and, if so, attempt to
get him to go against Diem." Corrupting Dinh proved easy. Despite the
favors bestowed on him by the regime, Dinh threw in his lot with the conspirators in mid-September. Tran Van Don, one of the dissident generals,
exploited Dinh's ego and weakness for alcohol to enlist him in the rebel
cause. After a weeklong drinking bout, during which Don repeatedly told
Dinh that he was a hero to whom all Vietnam was indebted, Dinh screwed
up his courage and asked Diem for one more promotion. He wanted a cabinet
post—minister of the interior, to be exact. As Don anticipated, Diem
refused, and it was a simple matter for Don to win Dinh's cooperation by
promising him the interior ministry if the coup succeeded. Changing alle-
giances troubled Dinh's conscience no more than had changing religions.[22]

With Dinh now in the revolutionary fold, anti-Diem forces in Washington and Saigon made final preparations for the putsch. Kennedy, in compliance with the Taylor-McNamara report, cut off funding for Diem's Special
Forces and postponed loans for the Saigon-Cholon Waterworks and Saigon

electric power project. The president also recalled CIA Station Chief Richardson from South Vietnam, an indication to the rebel generals that the Americans would not stand in their way. For their part, the generals kept Lodge informed of their plans, but not overly informed; while the ambassador learned which ARVN units would take part in the coup, the generals did not reveal other details for fear of leaks. Lodge found this arrangement ideal: he did not want extensive knowledge of the plot; a measure of American ignorance made claims of U.S. noninvolvement more convincing. Eventually, the generals contacted Lodge through Conein and promised to supply him with an "eyes only" operation plan forty-eight hours before the coup took place. In a later communication, Don informed Lodge that the window of opportunity had shrunk: the U.S. Embassy would now only get four hours' advance notice. Lodge assented to these terms.

Kennedy, however, did not. As October wore on, he began having second thoughts, worried that he was losing control over circumstances in Saigon. He wanted to get the coup plan earlier, and he did not like the fact that the embassy's only contact with the generals was Conein, who was known to be something of a maverick. Was not there some other, more reputable, channel who could give Lodge intelligence on the generals' scheme? The worst possible outcome, Kennedy believed, would be a failed uprising that everyone would blame on his administration. As National Security Adviser McGeorge Bundy cabled Lodge, "we would like to have [the] option of judging . . . any plan with poor prospects for success." Bundy acknowledged that this was a "large order," but emphasized that Kennedy wanted Lodge to "know of our concern."[23]

Lodge, exasperated, cabled back that it was not a large order but an impossible one. Either the generals were running the coup or they were not, and they refused to divulge more information about their plotting because they feared being betrayed. Saigon was crawling with Nhu's secret police, the ambassador pointed out; the conspirators could not be too careful. Washington should count itself lucky that it could call on a man like Conein, who, whatever his eccentricities, had managed to win the generals' trust. Lodge moreover reassured the White House that, should the coup fail, the Kennedy administration's involvement in it was "within the realm of plausible denial."[24]

The ambassador made a strong case, but his was not the only voice Kennedy heard. Policymakers were divided about whether to support Diem or his opponents. Some advanced the familiar argument that, yes, Diem was a flawed administrator, but there were no alternatives to him. Others went further, notably MACV commander Paul Harkins, who belittled the rebel generals as amateurs. "In my contacts here I have seen no one with the strength of character of Diem," Harkins cabled from Saigon. "Certainly, there are no generals qualified to take over." Besides, Harkins argued, "we have backed Diem for eight long years. To me, it seems incongruous now to get him down, kick him around, and get rid of him." Robert Kennedy, always a powerful influence on his brother, sided with Harkins, advising the president that Diem's shortcomings ought not to obscure the fact that Washington was at least *aware* of those defects; the administration knew *nothing* about the generals who proposed to take Diem's place. What guarantee did Washington have that these figures could offer South Vietnam anything better than Diem had provided?[25]

JFK, torn, observed that "[i]f we miscalculated, we could lose our entire position in Southeast Asia overnight." Kennedy was roiled by Lodge's assertion that "the coup is comparable to a stone running down hill which can't be stopped." This was a reckless way to run foreign policy, the president complained, insisting that it was not unreasonable to ask the "coup promoters" to assume "the burden of proof" and "show that they can overthrow the Diem government." Cables flew back and forth between Washington and Saigon during the final week of October, Kennedy demanding more evidence that the rebels would attain their objective, Lodge responding that he could not furnish such information and that it was too late to turn back.[26]

While this war of words raged via telegraph across the Pacific, Saigon was in ferment. Another bonze burned himself to death, choosing an especially provocative locale for his sacrifice: he lit a match to his gasoline-soaked robes in front of Saigon's main cathedral, just as the communicants emerged from mass. Nhu's agents became more brutal, arresting children as young as five for writing antigovernment slogans on walls. A student at the still-closed University of Hue was seized by Can Lao policemen and tortured for being an "American spy" because she had visited the United States Information Service library. According to some accounts, Nhu at this time was supplementing his opium use with heroin. His public statements grew increasingly irrational. In an interview with the journalist Joseph Alsop, Nhu raved, "Even if you Americans pull out, I will win the war here at the head of the great guerrilla movement which I have prepared."[27]

Madame Nhu, with her unfailing instinct for doing the wrong thing, chose to set out on a speaking tour of the United States. Apparently, she believed that she could bring off the kind of public-relations triumph Madame Chiang Kai-shek had achieved in the 1940s, when the American people, indifferent to China's plight until that time, were won over by the wife of Generalissimo Chiang and became more inclined to support a policy in favor of the Nationalist Chinese and against Japan. Kennedy was loath to grant Madame Nhu a visa, certain that her visit would embarrass his administration, but he ultimately decided that the backlash would be worse if he denied her entry. This proved a shrewd judgment. Far from whipping up support for Diem in the United States, Madame Nhu's tour made Diem's removal seem imperative if America was to retain its right to appeal to morals in the Cold War. She arrived in New York and began a circuit that included twenty-nine public appearances, ten of them televised. Every time she spoke, her trigger-happy tongue fired buckshot, and Americans recoiled. "These so-called Buddhists, they are just hooligans," she proclaimed to a college audience. She asserted that the Buddhist self-immolations were "a communist-inspired plot" and asked one correspondent, "Why is it that all of the people around President Kennedy are pink?" By the time the tour reached its end, polls indicated that Madame Nhu's approval rating in America was less than 8 percent.[28]

While Diem's brother and sister-in-law seemed determined to accelerate his regime's downfall, Diem himself adopted a different approach. After weeks of refusing to meet with Lodge, he broke the silence, inviting the ambassador and his wife to accompany him to Dalat to attend the inauguration of an atomic energy center. Lodge, perplexed, accepted the invitation, even though he expected the rebel generals to rise up against Diem at any moment. Some in the State Department thought Diem's gesture indicated that he was "moving in [the] direction we desire," which would obviate the need for a coup, but Lodge was convinced that that stone had already begun rolling downhill. He could not cancel the coup, he cabled Washington, except by betraying the plotters to Diem, and that "would make traitors of us"; no Vietnamese would ever trust America's word again.[29]

Lodge and his wife spent two days being entertained by Diem. First came an inspection tour of a strategic hamlet near Dalat, interrupted by a seven-course meal served on antique settings. When the party arrived at Diem's villa in the mountain resort, they enjoyed another extravagant meal that lasted until 1:30 in the morning. Diem then showed the Lodges to his guest house, where they spent the night on beds covered with silk quilts. The following day was the inauguration ceremony for the atomic energy laboratory, preceded by a sumptuous luncheon. Lodge had to admit in his account of the visit that "Diem was at his best. . . . He is very likeable."

All affectionate feelings vanished, however, when the discussion turned to issues plaguing U.S.–South Vietnamese relations. On this score, as always, Lodge found Diem "unbelievably stubborn." Diem would not change his position on any matter of substance. A frustrated Lodge finally asked, "Mr. President, every single specific suggestion I have made you have rejected. Isn't there some one thing you may think of that is within your capabilities to do and that would favorably impress U.S. opinion?" Diem, Lodge reported, "gave me a blank look." Lodge returned to Saigon more certain than ever that Diem had to be replaced.[30]

The coup, when it unfolded, both delighted and appalled Washington. It was over in less than a day, to the relief of Kennedy and others who worried that the rebels would only be able to manage a stalemate against forces loyal to Diem, thus plunging South Vietnam into civil war. Such fears proved unfounded. There was no nationwide conflagration, the fighting did not spread beyond Saigon, and despite concerns about the generals' professionalism, rebel troop movements were carried out with precision. Moreover, the

Diem near the end of his reign, 1 January 1962.
Time & Life Pictures. By: Howard Sochurek. Getty Images.

balance of forces turned out to be overwhelmingly in favor of the insurgents: rebels outnumbered loyalists from the start, and defections to the rebel side swelled their ranks as the coup played itself out. The rapidity of the regime's collapse testified to Diem's unpopularity and the eagerness of the South Vietnamese to be rid of him. Yet policymakers who predicted that barely a shot would be fired in Diem's defense were disappointed. While brief, the coup was violent, and it left the Kennedy administration allied with a junta whose means of ousting Diem—assassination—revolted world opinion.

As anyone who knew him could have predicted, Diem went down fighting. He gave his approval to a scheme contrived by Nhu to outflank Lodge and the ARVN rebels and restore him to Washington's good graces. Codenamed "Operation Bravo," this was a phony coup under the direction of Colonel Le Quang Tung, head of the Special Forces, and General Dinh, whom Diem still trusted. Dinh, as overall Saigon commander, was to order Tung's troops into the countryside on an ostensible raid against VC guerrillas. When the Special Forces were out of Saigon, ARVN soldiers loyal to the regime would stage a bogus "rebellion," and Diem, Nhu, and members of the palace household would "escape" to a seaside town southeast of the capital. Saigon would then be swept by mob violence, as "rioters" ransacked homes and murdered Buddhist and student leaders. Saigon Radio, seized by the "rebels," would announce the formation of a "revolutionary government" composed of Diem's enemies. This new government, citizens would learn, was committed to appeasing the communists. After a few days, Tung's Special Forces would reenter the city, put down the "rebellion," and allow Diem to return in triumph. The Americans, shamefaced, would realize that only Diem could keep order in South Vietnam, that his opponents were all communists, and that the army was loyal to him; it had, after all, quashed the rebels instead of joining them.

Nhu's project might have worked if not for the fact that Dinh had already turned traitor by the time Nhu told him about Operation Bravo. While Dinh pretended to go along with the stratagem, he conveyed its details to the rebel generals, who thus remained one step ahead of the palace. Diem and Nhu, however, were confident that their preemptive defense would con Washington into renewing its support. Operation Bravo would have the added benefit of making ARVN dissidents easy to identify: they were certain to come into the open when it appeared Diem had been overthrown, and Nhu could have them arrested and shot.

Diem's faith in Operation Bravo explained his aplomb on the morning of 1 November, when he and Lodge met for the last time. Lodge and Admiral

Harry Felt, commander in chief of U.S. Pacific forces, paid a call on Diem at 10:00 A.M. at Gia Long Palace and were treated to a typical two-hour monologue. As the visit drew to its close, Diem surprised his guests by noting that there were rumors of a coup. The Americans should not be alarmed, he said; he had everything under control. When Lodge rose to leave, Diem took him aside and said, "Please tell President Kennedy that I am a good and frank ally. . . . I take his suggestions very seriously and wish to carry them out." Lodge interpreted this as "a reference to a possible coup" and reported, "In effect, [Diem] said: Tell us what you want and we'll do it."[31]

A month, or even a week, earlier, this statement might have saved Diem. But it was too late for that now—at least from Lodge's perspective, and he had taken command of Washington's Vietnam policy. As Lodge and Felt bade Diem farewell, rebel troops were already beginning to deploy around Saigon. They took up blocking positions on the city's outskirts to prevent Diem from summoning provincial soldiers, as he had in 1960. One of General Don's aides called Conein at noon and told him to report to the headquarters of the ARVN Joint General Staff (JGS); the coup would begin in two hours.

When Conein arrived at JGS headquarters, he found Minh in command of the situation. Minh had invited many of his colleagues, insurgents and noninsurgents alike, to join him for lunch, and as they sat around the table, he announced that a coup was underway. Military police then burst into the room brandishing weapons. Minh told the assembled officers that South Vietnam would soon be ruled by a revolutionary council, and asked every man present to swear allegiance to the new government. All complied but one; he was dragged from the room and executed. Minh produced a tape recorder, read a statement listing the reasons why the coup had been necessary, and had everyone say their names for the record and affirm their support for replacing Diem. He then ordered copies of the tape made and stored in different places throughout Saigon, in case the coup failed and any of the officers tried to deny having participated in it.

Rebel military operations commenced at 1:30 P.M., when South Vietnamese marine, airborne, and army battalions poured into Saigon. The generals had wisely decided to strike in the late afternoon. Most Saigonese were taking their after-lunch siesta, and the streets were clear, enabling rebel troops to maneuver freely. They met almost no resistance, swiftly capturing the airport, police headquarters, and central post office. Radio Saigon proved a tougher nut to crack. ARVN soldiers loyal to Diem kept the rebels from taking the radio station for two hours, but the outcome of the contest was never in doubt; the coup forces were too strong. By 3:30 P.M., people listening to Radio Saigon heard Minh proclaim: "During the past nine years, we have lived under a cruel family dictatorship. . . . The army has decided to do away with the Diem regime."[32]

Diem and Nhu, secure in Gia Long Palace, were initially unconcerned when they heard the crackle of small-arms fire and the thump of mortars. They assumed that Nhu's pseudo-coup had begun. When a police officer telephoned Nhu in a panic, claiming that tanks were firing on his headquarters, Nhu calmly told him, "It's all right. I know all about it." This self-assurance disappeared, however, when the palace and its nearby presidential guard barracks came under attack. Artillery shells reduced the barracks to rubble, and fighter-bombers swooped over the palace, firing rockets. While antiaircraft guns managed to drive the planes away, this was clearly not part of Operation Bravo. Something had gone wrong. Diem tried to contact Dinh, to get him to launch a counteroffensive, but Dinh did not return the president's calls. Unable to believe that Dinh had betrayed him, Diem concluded that he must have been arrested. Attempts to reach other officers presumed loyal to the regime likewise proved fruitless. As the evening wore on, Diem received word that all key points in the city had fallen. Not only was this coup genuine; it was on the verge of succeeding.[33]

Diem remained defiant. When the rebel generals telephoned the palace demanding surrender, he refused to speak with them. Then, changing tactics, he decided to call on his talent for drawing out negotiations; perhaps, as in 1960, he could keep the coup leaders talking long enough for loyal troops to reach Saigon. He telephoned Don and invited the generals to the palace to "talk about the strengths and weaknesses of the regime." Surely they could "find a solution acceptable to both sides." Don's comrades would have none of this. Diem was stalling, they insisted, and besides, there was nothing to discuss. The government had fallen. If Diem and his brother surrendered, they would receive safe passage out of the country; anything less, and there would be an assault on the palace. Don telephoned Diem and relayed these terms, which the president rejected.[34]

It was at this stage that Diem had his final phone conversation with Lodge, who feigned unawareness of the coup but offered to do what he could to ensure the president's "physical safety." According to one account, Lodge proposed to send his own limousine to pick Diem and Nhu up at the palace and fly them out of Saigon. Diem spurned the offer. "I cannot agree to fleeing," he said, "because this is all a tempest in a teapot. . . . I know that the real troops are loyal to me." This afforded Lodge an exit from the conversation. He put down the receiver, drafted a cable for the State Department, and sat down to dinner.[35]

Shortly thereafter, the rebels called the palace again. They were giving Diem one last chance, they said. His position was hopeless. The only honorable solution was for him to surrender and spare the lives of the guardsmen protecting the palace. To lend weight to this ultimatum, each rebel general got on the phone and identified himself. Now that Diem knew who the coup leaders were, he grasped that they commanded virtually all combat units adjacent to Saigon. This was a more serious challenge than he had faced in 1960. His enemies enjoyed numerical superiority, and, more important, the Americans seemed to be supporting them. Yet Diem still refused to surrender; indeed, he made a point of hanging up on Minh in mid-conversation, which caused the ARVN general to lose face in front of his coconspirators. Furious, Minh phoned the palace again, telling Diem he had five minutes to comply with the rebels' demands. Diem responded by calling for "the immediate surrender of the coup forces." Then he hung up.[36]

The rebel generals were at an impasse. While they knew they could overwhelm any resistance they encountered from the palace, they had not anticipated having to do so. Minh and the others had assumed that Diem, his back to the wall, would capitulate rather than risk needless bloodshed. That he had never, in similar circumstances, chosen that option before ought to have given the generals pause, but they had not planned for an assault on the palace. None of them were eager to launch such a blitzkrieg, not only because of the loss of life it would entail but also because many retained respect for Diem. Even if they felt he could not continue in office, he was the only president South Vietnam had ever had, and the generals found the prospect of storming the palace and taking him prisoner distasteful. It was an American who persuaded Minh that he had no choice. Conein, in radio contact with the rebel commander from JGS headquarters, warned him that his credibility was on the line, that Diem was pursuing the same strategy that had foiled coup leaders in 1960, and that every second Minh vacillated worked to Diem's advantage. "If you hesitate," Conein declared, "you will be lost."[37]

It was not until 10:00 P.M. that the siege began. From point-blank range, machine guns and cannon pounded Gia Long's cream-colored stucco walls in a withering barrage. Demolition specialists set charges to blow the palace up. Fighter-bombers made strafing passes overhead. The palace guards fought heroically, laying down a heavy counterfire that destroyed several rebel tanks, but it was not enough, and the defensive perimeter around the palace began to crumble. When, at 4:00 A.M., it appeared that victory was moments away, Minh ordered Colonel Nguyen Van Thieu, commander of the Fifth Infantry Division, to lead the final charge.

Thieu's division first attempted to storm Gia Long, but its defenders clung to their positions and hurled the rebels back. Thieu then orchestrated a series of progressively heavier attacks, complete with mortar, tank, and artillery fire. Rebel forces pumped so many rounds into the palace that television camera crews called to the scene were able to film the battle without using floodlights; the light from the gun flashes was sufficient. At 6:00 A.M., someone waved a white flag from the first-floor window of the palace's southwest corner. A cheer went up from the rebel troops, who believed this meant surrender, and some of them advanced in the open toward the building. A burst of automatic fire cut them down. Enraged, the rebels resumed their attack, the firing increased in weight and tempo, and forty-five minutes later it really was finished, the palace overrun. Rebel soldiers helped themselves to bottles of Nhu's whiskey and waved Madame Nhu's negligees for the TV cameras.

The coup had lasted seventeen hours. Casualties were officially placed at thirty-three killed and 236 wounded. Compared to the Kennedy administration's worst-case scenarios, this was a smooth governmental transition. It was also tremendously popular. The people of South Vietnam seemed overjoyed to learn that Diem had fallen. Celebrations broke out all over Saigon, as crowds tore up Diem's portrait, offered food and liquor to the coup troops, and hailed any American they saw. The Saigonese, at least, had no illusions about U.S. complicity in the coup; more than one reveler told American journalists that if Lodge ran for president of South Vietnam, he would win by a landslide. Policymakers in Washington breathed a collective sigh of relief. All things considered, they felt, the coup had been a success.

There was only one problem. Where was Diem? Minh had intended to enter the palace in triumph, escort the fallen president to JGS headquarters, and conduct a ceremony in which Diem relinquished power. This would all be filmed for television and tape-recorded for repeated broadcasts over Saigon Radio; it would lend legitimacy to the new regime. But Diem foiled Minh's plans. When the rebels took the palace, they could not find Diem or Nhu. Indeed, Minh learned, to his horror, that the brothers had fled Gia Long hours before the final assault—perhaps as early as 8:00 P.M. the previous night—and had conducted their subsequent phone conversations with rebel leaders from a remote location that had a direct link with the palace communications system. Neither the rebel forces besieging the palace nor the presidential guards defending it had known that the prize they contended over, Diem, was gone. All of the deaths and injuries sustained in those last hours of combat had been unnecessary.

Minh may have decided at this point to have Diem killed. Or he may still have intended to send his former commander-in-chief into exile. But he was hardly in a forgiving mood as he stood amid the debris in the palace's entrance hall, forcing a smile, blinking at flashbulbs, and ordering subordinates to search all areas frequented by the Ngo family. The depth of his anger became clear when Diem contacted the generals with an offer to resign. All Diem asked for in return was "the honors due a departing president"—the same favor Minh had been disposed to grant before discovering that the Ngo brothers had left the palace. Now Minh refused and demanded that Diem disclose his location. The line went dead. Half an hour later came the unconditional surrender Minh wanted. Diem called from St. Francis Xavier Church in Cholon, accepted Minh's terms, and told the rebels where he was. He would, he said, be waiting with Nhu for representatives of the new government to pick him up.[38]

Minh convened a meeting of coup leaders at JGS headquarters. How should he respond to Diem's call? Three-quarters of the men in attendance voted to exile Diem. The rest wanted him assassinated, or at least held for trial. After a few minutes' discussion, Minh concluded that the first order of business was to get Diem and Nhu into custody, and that the council could determine their fate later. He told General Mai Huu Xuan to take an armored personnel carrier, a few jeeps, and as many men as he needed to fetch the Ngo brothers from Cholon. According to one account, Minh turned to Captain Nguyen Van Nhung, who would accompany Xuan on this mission, and raised two fingers of his right hand. It was a signal to kill Diem and Nhu.

Fittingly, the early-morning mass at St. Francis Xavier had celebrated All Souls' Day, the day of the dead, just before Diem entered the church to pray and take communion. Within an hour, the first president of South Vietnam would be murdered. At 11:00 A.M., the convoy headed by General Xuan returned to JGS headquarters bearing the corpses of Diem and Nhu. Minh appeared pleased, but most coup leaders reacted with horror when they saw the carnage on the deck of the armored car. Colonel Nguyen Van Quanh, Minh's assistant, collapsed across a table. Several officers sobbed. Even General Dinh, who had betrayed Diem after years of the president's patronage, was shaken when he saw Diem's carcass. "I couldn't sleep that night," Dinh admitted.[39]

The coup leaders' guilty consciences led them to promulgate a number of absurd official versions of how Diem and Nhu had died: that they had taken poison, that they had wrestled a gun from their captors and committed suicide with it, that they had blown themselves up with a grenade, and so on. Nobody believed such stories, and when the CIA in Saigon obtained photographs of the brothers' bodies that showed their hands tied behind their backs, the new regime had to come clean, at least to an extent. Yes, Minh declared, Diem and Nhu had been killed, although it was difficult to assign blame. No one was ever prosecuted for the murders.

Washington recognized the new Minh regime, but Diem's murder came as a jolt to President Kennedy. JFK first heard the news that Diem was dead during a meeting with advisers on Saturday, 2 November. Forrestal presented the president with a cable from Saigon claiming Diem and Nhu had committed suicide, an assertion that Kennedy, a Catholic like the Ngo brothers, recognized as false. Taylor recalled years later that Kennedy "rushed from the room with a look of shock and dismay on his face." Kennedy considered this a shabby conclusion to nine years of U.S.–South Vietnamese cooperation. Whatever Diem might have done, Kennedy declared to an adviser, "it should not have ended like this."[40]

But expressions of remorse were rare in Washington and Saigon, where officials succumbed to what McNamara called "a certain euphoria" now that Diem was gone. Lodge cabled the State Department that "prospects of victory are much improved . . . as compared to the period . . . during the Diem regime." Minh and the other rebel generals seemed committed to democratic reform: they suspended Diem's constitution, dissolved the fraudulently elected National Assembly, and put together a new cabinet made up of pro-American politicians. Even better, they were determined to prosecute the war against the VC more effectively by abolishing Diem's system of military promotion based on loyalty and accepting greater U.S. participation in the anticommunist struggle. "They're putting some young tigers in command," *Newsweek* magazine noted, "and they could make an all-out effort to finish off the Viet Cong."[41]

Such statements appeared foolish a few months hence, when the number of guerrilla incidents in the Mekong Delta rose to a record level, divisions in South Vietnam's governing junta caused the Minh regime to collapse, and Washington rushed more U.S. "advisers" to Southeast Asia to stave off catastrophe. Ultimately, over a dozen governments would rise and fall in South Vietnam, none lasting as long as America's Diem experiment, all incapable of arresting the disintegration of the country. Diem's assassination, in the final analysis, solved nothing. It did not matter *who* led the government in

Saigon. The United States could not preserve the fiction that South Vietnam was an independent nation except by increasing America's military investment until the total firepower used by U.S. forces against the North Vietnamese and VC exceeded the amount spent in all of America's previous wars combined. Even then, the United States failed in its objective and South Vietnam was conquered by those same guerrillas whom Diem could never seem to subdue.

Notes

1. Diem and Nolting cited in Ellen J. Hammer, *A Death in November: America in Vietnam, 1963* (New York: Dutton, 1987), 163; Madame Nhu cited in Anne E. Blair, *Lodge in Vietnam: A Patriot Abroad* (New Haven, Conn.: Yale University Press, 1995), 22.

2. Lodge cited in the Embassy in Vietnam to the Department of State, 26 August 1963, *FRUS, 1961–1963* (Washington, D.C.: Government Printing Office, 1991), 3:644; Blair, *Lodge in Vietnam*, 21.

3. Lodge cited in Terence Maitland and others, *The Vietnam Experience*, vol. 3, *Raising the Stakes* (Boston: Boston Publishing, 1984), 82; embassy workers cited in William Prochnau, *Once upon a Distant War: David Halberstam, Neil Sheehan, Peter Arnett—Young War Correspondents and Their Early Vietnam Battles* (New York: Vintage, 1995), 381.

4. Don cited in the Central Intelligence Agency in Saigon to the Agency, 24 August 1963, *FRUS, 1961–1963*, 3:614–620; Kim cited in the Embassy in Vietnam to the Department of State, 24 August 1963, *FRUS, 1961–1963*, 3:613–614; Thuan cited in the Embassy in Vietnam to the Department of State, 24 August 1963, *FRUS, 1961–1963*, 3:611–612.

5. The Embassy in Vietnam to the Department of State, 24 August 1963, *FRUS, 1961–1963*, 3:621.

6. Headlines cited in David Kaiser, *American Tragedy: Kennedy, Johnson, and the Origins of the Vietnam War* (Cambridge, Mass.: Belknap, 2000), 229; Richard Reeves, *President Kennedy: Profile of Power* (New York: Simon & Schuster, 1993), 560.

7. John W. Newman, *JFK and Vietnam* (New York: Warner, 1992), 346; The Department of State to the Embassy in Vietnam, 24 August 1963, *FRUS, 1961–1963*, 3:628–629.

8. Maxwell Taylor, *Swords and Plowshares* (New York: Norton, 1972), 292.

9. Lodge cited in Michael Charlton and Richard Moncrieff, *Many Reasons Why: The American Involvement in Vietnam* (New York: Hill & Wang, 1977), 95; Michael V. Forrestal of the National Security Council Staff to the President at Hyannis Port, Massachusetts, 25 August 1963, *FRUS,1961–1963*, 3:634; Message from the Acting Secretary of State to the Ambassador in Vietnam, 25 August 1963, *FRUS, 1961–1963*, 3:635.

10. The Embassy in Vietnam to the Department of State, 29 August 1963, *FRUS, 1961–1963*, 4:21–22.

11. Message from the President to the Ambassador in Vietnam, 29 August 1963, *FRUS, 1961–1963*, 4:35; Lodge cited in Footnote 2, *FRUS, 1961–1963*, 4:36.

12. Cablegram from Ambassador Lodge to Secretary Rusk, 30 August 1963, *The Pentagon Papers*, Gravel Edition (Boston: Beacon, 1971), 2:739–740.

13. Minh cited in the Commander, Military Assistance Command, Vietnam, to the Chairman of the Joint Chiefs of Staff, 31 August 1963, *FRUS, 1961–1963*, 4:64–65; the Embassy in Vietnam to the Department of State, 31 August 1963, *FRUS, 1961–1963*, 4:66.

14. De Gaulle cited in Kaiser, *American Tragedy*, 241.

15. Diplomat cited in Fredrik Logevall, *Choosing War: The Lost Chance for Peace and the Escalation of War in Vietnam* (Berkeley: University of California Press, 1999), 10.

16. Dong cited in Mieczyslaw Maneli, *War of the Vanquished* (New York: Harper & Row, 1971), 128; Ho cited in Hammer, *Death in November*, 222.

17. Interview for CBS News, 2 September 1963, *Public Papers of the Presidents: John F. Kennedy, 1963* (Washington, D.C.: Government Printing Office, 1964), 650–653; Reeves, *President Kennedy*, 587; Don cited in Charlton and Moncrieff, *Many Reasons Why*, 99.

18. National Security Files, Meetings and Memoranda: Memorandum for the President, 2 October 1963: Box 314, JFKL.

19. Kennedy cited in Stanley Karnow, *Vietnam: A History* (New York: Viking, 1983), 294; Minh cited in National Security Files, Countries—Vietnam: Lodge to Rusk, 5 October 1963: Box 204, JFKL.

20. Kennedy cited in Howard Jones, *Death of a Generation: How the Assassinations of Diem and JFK Prolonged the Vietnam War* (New York: Oxford University Press, 2003), 407; Lodge cited in Karnow, *Vietnam: A History*, 295.

21. The Embassy in Vietnam to the Department of State, 5 October 1963, *FRUS, 1961–1963*, 4:367; CIA to Lodge, 6 October 1963, *Pentagon Papers*, Gravel Edition, 2:769; John Mecklin, *Mission in Torment: An Intimate Account of the U.S. Role in Vietnam* (Garden City, N.Y.: Doubleday, 1965), 221.

22. Hilsman cited in Jones, *Death of a Generation*, 327.

23. National Security Files, Countries—Vietnam: Bundy to Lodge, 25 October 1963: Box 204, JFKL.

24. National Security Files, Countries—Vietnam: Lodge to Bundy, 25 October 1963: Box 204, JFKL.

25. Memorandum from the Commander, Military Assistance Command, Vietnam, 30 October 1963, *FRUS, 1961–1963*, 4:479–482.

26. Kennedy cited in Memorandum of a Conference with the President, White House, Washington, 29 October 1963, *FRUS, 1961–1963*, 4:472.

27. Nhu cited in Joseph Alsop, "In the Gia Long Palace," December 1963, reprinted in *Reporting Vietnam, Part I: American Journalism, 1959–1969* (New York: Library of America, 1998), 91.

28. Madame Nhu cited in Clyde Edwin Petit, *The Experts* (Secaucus, N.J.: Lyle Stuart, 1975), 151–154.

29. National Security Files, Countries—Vietnam: Rusk to Lodge, 25 October 1963: Box 204, JFKL; Lodge to Rusk, 30 October 1963: Box 204, JFKL.

30. National Security Files, Countries—Vietnam: Lodge to Rusk, 29 October 1963: Box 204, JFKL.

31. Diem cited in National Security Files, Countries—Vietnam: Lodge to Rusk, 1 November 1963: Box 201, JFKL.

32. Minh cited in National Security Files, Countries—Vietnam: Lodge to Rusk, 1 November 1963: Box 201, JFKL.

33. Nhu cited in Stanley Karnow, "The Fall of the House of Ngo Dinh," reprinted in *Reporting Vietnam, Part I: American Journalism, 1959–1969* (New York: Library of America, 1998), 102.

34. Diem cited in Karnow, *Vietnam: A History*, 322.

35. Diem and Lodge cited in Jones, *Death of a Generation*, 413.

36. Diem cited in National Security Files, Countries—Vietnam: Harkins to Taylor/Felt, 2 November 1963: Box 201, JFKL.

37. Conein cited in William Rust, *Kennedy in Vietnam* (New York: Scribner, 1985), 170.

38. Diem cited in Karnow, *Vietnam: A History*, 309.

39. Dinh cited in Karnow, "Fall of the House of Ngo Dinh," 105.

40. Taylor, *Swords and Plowshares*, 301; Kennedy cited in Newman, *JFK and Vietnam*, 415.

41. McNamara cited in William Rust, *Kennedy in Vietnam* (New York: Scribner, 1989), 179; National Security Files, Countries—Vietnam: Lodge to Rusk, 6 November 1963: JFKL, 202; *Newsweek* cited in Jones, *Death of a Generation*, 419.

CHAPTER EIGHT

Conclusion

None of America's Cold War allies did more to undermine the power and reputation of the United States than Ngo Dinh Diem. From 1954, when he became premier, to 1963, when he was assassinated, Diem ran South Vietnam as a police state while the United States bankrolled his tyranny. The administrations of Dwight Eisenhower and John F. Kennedy invested billions of dollars and incalculable moral capital in what policymakers termed the Diem experiment despite accumulating evidence that the goal of an independent, noncommunist South Vietnam under Diem's captaincy was unattainable. Diem never cultivated a base of popular support, refused to delegate authority, and favored his fellow Catholics in a nation 90 percent Buddhist. American directives to "open up" the government in Saigon to dissenting viewpoints were consistently ignored, as were requests to implement meaningful land reforms. Although the White House promoted the image of Diem as a progressive modernizer, he remained an autocrat until the day he died.

Diem's one-man rule resulted in administrative inefficiency and, more important, widespread discontent. Over time, Diem antagonized his country's army, its political talent, and the majority of its common people. He destroyed the indigenous leadership in South Vietnam's villages and replaced it with his own appointees. He mounted a repressive campaign against potential opposition in the urban areas and a merciless antisubversion program in the countryside. He ordered the execution, internment, or deportation of thousands of perceived "traitors." Such violations of human rights were not compensated by gains in political stability or security. When the Diem experiment imploded, South Vietnam was more susceptible to communist takeover than it had been a decade earlier.

America was also unalterably pledged to its defense. The nature of the

U.S. commitment to South Vietnam was different at the conclusion of the Diem experiment than at its inception. Washington had underwritten France's war against the Viet Minh for years by the time Diem assumed office, but there were only a sparse number of U.S. military advisers in Indochina at that juncture. By 1963, however, America was no longer supporting a European power in its struggle to hang onto an Asian colony. South Vietnam was, at least nominally, a sovereign state in which sixteen thousand U.S. advisory troops were stationed. It was also, according to White House pronouncements, a "vital interest" whose preservation from communism was essential to American security. The consequences of a North Vietnamese victory were far graver for Kennedy—and his successor, Lyndon Johnson—than they would have been for Eisenhower in the mid-1950s. That is why LBJ was unable to exercise the restraint Eisenhower displayed when he refused to intervene to save the French garrison at Dien Bien Phu. America's stake in South Vietnam had grown during Diem's reign, and the loss of that country to communism in the wake of his murder would, Johnson believed, constitute an unendurable blow to U.S. credibility. Therefore, when the generals who deposed Diem seemed about to succumb to Viet Cong pressure, Johnson made the fateful decision to authorize a sustained bombing of North Vietnam and the introduction of American ground forces into the south. The militarization of Washington's Southeast Asian policy—what one historian calls "the Americanization of the Vietnam War"—was complete.[1]

The fact that conditions in South Vietnam did not improve after Diem's death led some policymakers to conclude that it had been a mistake to abort the Diem experiment, that Washington should have stuck with Diem, despite his faults, because there was no more competent and popular alternative. Johnson himself called the 1963 anti-Diem officers' coup "the worst mistake we ever made," and Senator Mike Mansfield lamented in mid-1965—when the number of American troops in Vietnam verged on two hundred thousand—that "We are paying for our sins in getting rid of President Diem." It is true that Diem's administration seemed a paragon of order compared to the ephemeral regimes that followed. While the Diem experiment lasted for over nine years, Duong Van Minh was good for only three months. In 1964 alone, there were seven governments in Saigon, none of which proved more responsive to the needs of South Vietnam's people or successful in combating the VC than Diem had been.[2]

For the most part, Diem's successors shared his faults—authoritarianism, ruthlessness, remoteness, political ineptitude—while lacking his virtues: courage, patriotism, diligence, and, most significant, selflessness. When

South Vietnam's last president, Nguyen Van Thieu, fled his country before the communists overran Saigon in 1975, he flew out of Tan Son Nhut Airport on a U.S. transport plane loaded with fifteen tons of baggage, most of it bars of gold. Embassy officials could not help but recall that Diem, by contrast, never visibly profited from the aid America funneled into his regime. Even after becoming president, he lived an austere life. The South Vietnamese might not have loved Diem, but they respected him, admired his strong-willed nationalism, and acknowledged his accomplishments in getting rid of Bao Dai, subduing the Binh Xuyen, and generally beating the odds longer than anyone thought possible. None of South Vietnam's other presidents enjoyed such stature.

A few historians go so far as to argue that if the United States had continued its policy of "sink or swim with Ngo Dinh Diem," the future course of events in Vietnam might have been radically different. They claim that Washington was headed in the right direction in the late 1950s and early 1960s, and that America's failure to stand by Diem deprived the "free world" of the only leader capable of barricading the southern against the northern half of Vietnam. "The removal of Diem," notes R. B. Smith, "opened a Pandora's box of political and military rivalries, which was very soon completely beyond American control." Diem was Washington's best hope, Smith concludes, and a prolongation of the Diem experiment could have resulted in U.S. victory in the Vietnam conflict. Other scholars contend that even if the war was unwinnable, retention of Diem might have led to a less catastrophic outcome, because, as Ellen Hammer observes, Diem "would never have allowed the Americans to bring 500,000 men to fight on [his] soil."[3]

Such arguments are unpersuasive. Diem may have been the most effective president South Vietnam ever had, but he was still a dictator who did little to generate enthusiasm for his regime. During the nine years he held office, he steadily reduced his domestic support until, at the end, it barely extended outside his own family. He never came close to creating a nation that could stand on its own two feet without external support; as even his friends at Michigan State University conceded in their report on South Vietnam's progress from 1955 to 1962, Diem's country was a "permanent mendicant," dependent on American charity for its survival. Diem was never able to compete organizationally or ideologically with his communist adversaries; the VC were gaining rather than losing ground when Diem's reign came to an end. Even if Washington had sustained its Diem experiment for a few more years, the preservation of an anticommunist South Vietnam would still have required the presence of a huge American army by 1964. That the strongmen who followed Diem proved even less equal to their jobs ought hardly to inspire nostalgia for the Diem era. Still less should it fuel counterfactual speculations about whether America's war in Vietnam might have turned out better if policymakers had allowed Diem to remain in command.[4]

Rather, Diem's "accomplishment"—measured against the dismal record of subsequent revolving-door governments—only underscores the futility of what Washington sought to achieve when it intervened in a far-off land among people trying to work out their own unique destiny. Vietnam, the political scientist George Kahin stresses, was "a nation whose nationalist ferment was as strong as that of any country in the twentieth century." Neither Diem's regime nor any of the succeeding juntas and civilian cliques that Washington underwrote could take the mantle of Vietnamese leadership from Ho Chi Minh because they all owed their existence to a foreign power and were not expressions of indigenous nationalism. No matter how much money, materiel, and blood America expended, it could not win legitimacy and popular support for its client government in Saigon. Indeed, the reverse was inevitable, as North Vietnamese premier Pham Van Dong noted in an interview during the final stages of the Diem experiment. "Monsieur Diem's position is quite difficult," Dong observed. "He is unpopular, and the more unpopular he is, the more American aid he will require to stay in power. And the more American aid he receives, the more he will look like a puppet of the Americans, and the less likely he is to win popular support."[5]

Herein lay the most tragic aspect of the Diem experiment, because Diem was *not* a puppet. He was as fanatical a nationalist as Ho, every bit as willing to dedicate—and, as it turned out, to sacrifice—his life for the good of his country. He resented his dependence on the United States, strove to keep his superpower patron at arm's length, and resisted American military, political, and economic advice in order to prove his independence. As a young man, he had witnessed the worst excesses of French colonial domination of his homeland, and he had no desire to exchange one master for another. Yet Diem needed the Americans to acquire high office and to stay in power. His survival rested on his capacity to meet Washington's standards of performance. The relationship between his government and the United States was always a neocolonial one, and this tormented him, for he believed he was destined to lead a unified, sovereign Vietnam. Unlike his successors, he could not play the role of agreeable stooge, even when failure to do so cost him everything. Graham Greene was more insightful than he could have known when in 1955 he called Diem "The Patriot Ruined by the West."[6]

There are few monuments in Diem's honor in Vietnam today. One will not even find a gravestone marking his final resting place. On the morning that Diem and his brother Ngo Dinh Nhu were murdered, a relative claimed their bodies at army headquarters and took them to Saigon's St. Paul's Hospital, where a doctor issued a statement of death but declined to conduct an autopsy. Minh's government refused to reveal where the bodies were buried, and rumors persist to this day: some say the brothers are interred in a prison graveyard, others claim they lie in the municipal cemetery, and there are even some accounts of cremation. But traces of Diem's rule are rare. According to Frances FitzGerald, they became so almost as soon as Diem was gunned down, gangland style, in the back of a personnel carrier supplied by the United States. "After the [Buddhist] crisis had passed," FitzGerald observes, "the people of Saigon rarely spoke of the Diem regime again. There was nothing more to be said." Perhaps it was appropriate that so few people mourned the death of Ngo Dinh Diem. After all, his ordeal in Vietnam was over. America's was just beginning.[7]

Notes

1. Fredrik Logevall, *Choosing War: The Lost Chance for Peace and the Escalation of War in Vietnam* (Berkeley: University of California Press, 1999), xvii.

2. Johnson cited in Henry Graff, *The Tuesday Cabinet: Deliberation and Decision in Peace and War under Lyndon B. Johnson* (New York: Prentice Hall, 1970), 53; Mansfield cited in Steven Pan and Daniel Lyons, *Vietnam Crisis* (New York: East Asian Research Institute, 1966), 133.

3. R. B. Smith, *An International History of the Vietnam War* (New York: St. Martin's, 1985), 1:190; Ellen J. Hammer, *A Death in November: America in Vietnam, 1963* (New York: Dutton, 1987), 317.

4. *Final Report Covering Activities of the Michigan State University Vietnam Advisory Group for the Period 20 May 1955–30 June 1962* (Saigon, June 1962), 4.

5. George Kahin, *Intervention: How America Became Involved in Vietnam* (New York: Anchor Books, 1986), 323; Dong cited in Loren Baritz, *Backfire* (New York: Ballantine, 1985), 88.

6. Graham Greene, "The Patriot Ruined by the West," *New Republic*, 16 May 1955, 13.

7. Frances FitzGerald, *Fire in the Lake: The Vietnamese and the Americans in Vietnam* (New York: Vintage, 1972), 171.

~

Bibliographic Essay

Students seeking a scholarly biography of Ngo Dinh Diem will be disappointed. Denis Warner's *The Last Confucian* (New York: Macmillan, 1963) is a hostile, unidimensional portrait, and Anthony Bouscaren's *The Last of the Mandarins: Diem of Vietnam* (Pittsburgh: Duquesne University Press, 1965) is sheer hagiography. Both works were written decades before most government documents relating to the Diem experiment were declassified. They remain useful sources of information about Diem's early years, however, as do Robert Shaplen, *The Lost Revolution* (New York: Harper & Row, 1965); John Mecklin, *Mission in Torment* (Garden City, N.Y.: Doubleday, 1965); Bernard Fall, *The Two Viet-Nams* (New York: Praeger, 1963); Hilaire du Berrier, *Background to Betrayal* (Belmont, Mass.: Western Islands Press, 1965); and Marguerite Higgins, *Our Vietnam Nightmare* (New York: McGraw-Hill, 1965). More recent treatments of Diem's prepresidential career may be found in Neil Jamieson, *Understanding Vietnam* (Berkeley: University of California Press, 1993); Ross Marley and Clark Neher, *Patriots and Tyrants* (Lanham, Md.: Rowman and Littlefield, 1999); and Bruce McFarland Lockhart, *The End of the Vietnamese Monarchy* (New Haven, Conn.: Yale Council on Southeast Asian Studies, 1993). Edward Miller's article "Vision, Power, and Agency: The Ascent of Ngo Dinh Diem," *Journal of Southeast Asian Studies* 35 (October 2004): 433–458, is the most authoritative treatment of this period in Diem's life.

For Diem's networking in the United States, see Joseph Morgan, *The Vietnam Lobby* (Chapel Hill: University of North Carolina Press, 1997); Seth Jacobs, *America's Miracle Man in Vietnam* (Durham, N.C.: Duke University Press, 2004); Andrew Smith, *Rescuing the World* (New York: State University of New York Press, 2002); and William Brownell, "The Vietnam Lobby"

(PhD diss., Columbia University, 1993). John Ernst, *Forging a Fateful Alliance* (East Lansing: Michigan State University Press, 1998) provides an analysis of Diem's success in enlisting the support of American academics, and Robert Packenham, *Liberal America and the Third World* (Princeton, N.J.: Princeton University Press, 1973) examines why Diem supporters like Professor Wesley Fishel came to believe that their expertise was a valuable weapon in combating third-world communism.

The most comprehensive study of the 1954 Geneva Conference that divided Vietnam and spurred the Passage to Freedom exodus is Robert Randle, *Geneva 1954* (Princeton, N.J.: Princeton University Press, 1969). For a shorter review, see James Cable, *The Geneva Conference of 1954 on Indochina* (New York: Oxford University Press, 1986). Passage to Freedom is covered in detail in Richard Lindholm, ed., *Viet-Nam: The First Five Years* (East Lansing: Michigan State University Press, 1959). Other useful accounts include Louis Weisner, *Victims and Survivors* (Westport, Conn.: Greenwood, 1988); Piero Gheddo, *The Cross and Bo-Tree* (New York: Sheed and Ward, 1970); Aaron Levenstein, *Escape to Freedom* (Westport, Conn.: Greenwood, 1983); and Eileen Egan, *For Whom There Is No Room* (New York: Paulist Press, 1995). Tom Dooley, the most prominent chronicler of this mass migration, is the subject of a biography by James Fisher, *Dr. America* (Amherst: University of Massachusetts Press, 1997).

Dwight Eisenhower's Vietnam policy is analyzed in David L. Anderson, *Trapped by Success* (New York: Columbia University Press, 1991); James Arnold, *The First Domino* (New York: Morrow, 1991); and Daniel Greene, "Tug of War" (PhD diss., University of Texas at Austin, 1990). For Mike Mansfield's contribution to that policy, see Don Oberdorfer, *Senator Mansfield* (Washington, D.C.: Smithsonian Books, 2003); and Gregory Olson, *Mansfield and Vietnam* (East Lansing: Michigan State University Press, 1995). For John Foster Dulles's role, see Frederick Marks, *Power and Peace* (New York: Praeger, 1993); Townsend Hoopes, *The Devil and John Foster Dulles* (Boston: Little, Brown, 1973); and Richard Immerman, ed., *John Foster Dulles and the Diplomacy of the Cold War* (Princeton, N.J.: Princeton University Press, 1990).

The 1954–1955 Collins mission to South Vietnam received its first extended treatment in David L. Anderson, "J. Lawton Collins, John Foster Dulles, and the Eisenhower Administration's 'Point of No Return' in Vietnam," *Diplomatic History* 12 (Spring 1988): 134–148. Anderson later incorporated this article into *Trapped by Success*. Arnold's *The First Domino* and Jacobs's *America's Miracle Man in Vietnam* also offer detailed assessments. For

Collins's own narrative of his mission to Vietnam, see *Lightning Joe: An Auto-biography* (Baton Rouge: Louisiana State University Press, 1979).

The most vivid accounts of the 1955 battle for Saigon may be found in Edward Lansdale, *In the Midst of Wars* (New York: Harper & Row, 1972); Howard Simpson, *Tiger in the Barbed Wire* (New York: Brassey's, 1992); and Joseph Buttinger, *Vietnam: A Dragon Embattled* (London: Pall Mall, 1967). For Lansdale's sponsorship of Diem during the battle and afterward, see Cecil Currey, *Edward Lansdale* (Boston: Houghton Mifflin, 1988); and Jonathan Nashel, *Edward Lansdale, the Cold War, and the End of American Innocence* (Amherst: University of Massachusetts Press, 2005).

Diem's "Miracle Man" years are well covered in Ronald Spector, *Advice and Support* (New York: Free Press, 1985); Robert Scigliano, *South Vietnam: Nation under Stress* (Boston: Houghton Mifflin, 1963); and John Montgomery, *The Politics of Foreign Aid* (New York: Praeger, 1962). For an uncritical but informative account, see Wesley Fishel, ed., *Problems of Freedom: South Vietnam since Independence* (New York: Free Press of Glencoe, 1961). The best analysis of Diem's attempts to translate his political philosophy into workable programs is Philip Catton, *Diem's Final Failure* (Lawrence: University Press of Kansas, 2002). Also valuable is Edward Miller, "Confucianism and 'Confucian Learning' in South Vietnam during the Diem Years, 1954–1963," *Journal of Southeast Asian Studies*, forthcoming.

Analysis of John F. Kennedy's Vietnam policy has become a cottage industry. The best works are William Rust, *Kennedy in Vietnam* (New York: Scribner, 1985); John Newman, *JFK and Vietnam* (New York: Warner, 1992); Lawrence Freedman, *Kennedy's Wars* (New York: Oxford University Press, 2000); Fredrik Logevall, *Choosing War* (Berkeley: University of California Press, 1999); and David Kaiser, *American Tragedy* (Cambridge, Mass.: Belknap, 2000). Richard Reeves, *President Kennedy: Profile of Power* (New York: Simon & Schuster, 1993) is gossipy but exhaustively researched. The most provocative memoirs by Kennedy-era policymakers are Roger Hilsman, *To Move a Nation* (Garden City, N.Y.: Doubleday, 1967); Robert McNamara, *In Retrospect* (New York: Simon & Schuster, 1995); Frederick Nolting, *From Trust to Tragedy* (New York: Praeger, 1988); and Maxwell Taylor, *Swords and Plowshares* (New York: Norton, 1972).

William Prochnau, *Once upon a Distant War* (New York: Vintage, 1995) is a lively account of the impact of journalism on Americans' perception of events in Vietnam in the Kennedy era. A. J. Langguth, *Our Vietnam* (New York: Simon & Schuster, 2000) also focuses on the tribulations of correspondents like Homer Bigart, David Halberstam, and Neil Sheehan as they attempted to cover the Diem regime's collapse during the early 1960s. For two excellent memoir/monographs by journalists posted to South Vietnam, see David Halberstam, *The Making of a Quagmire* (New York: Random House, 1965); and Neil Sheehan, *A Bright Shining Lie* (New York: Random House, 1988).

There are so many first-rate accounts of the 1963 Buddhist crisis that one hesitates to rank them, but if pressed I would give primacy of place to Howard Jones, *Death of a Generation* (New York: Oxford University Press, 2003). Contesting for runner-up are Ellen Hammer, *A Death in November* (New York: Oxford University Press, 1987); Francis Winters, *The Year of the Hare* (Athens: University of Georgia Press, 1997); and Stanley Karnow's classic *Vietnam: A History* (New York: Viking, 1983). For Henry Cabot Lodge's contribution to Diem's downfall, see Anne Blair, *Lodge in Vietnam* (New Haven, Conn.: Yale University Press, 1995).

Index

Note: Page references in italics indicate illustrations or captions.

~

About the Author

Seth Jacobs is an associate professor in the Department of History at Boston College. His other books include *America's Miracle Man in Vietnam: Ngo Dinh Diem, Religion, Race, and U.S. Intervention in Southeast Asia* (2004). In 2002 the Society for Historians of American Foreign Relations (SHAFR) honored him with its Stuart Bernath Prize for the best article published in the field of diplomatic history, and he won SHAFR's Bernath Book Prize in 2006. He is presently working on a study of U.S.-Laotian relations during the Eisenhower and Kennedy years.